Performing Power
A New Approach for the Singer-Actor

Performing Power

A New Approach for the Singer-Actor

H. WESLEY BALK

106673

University of Minnesota Press   Minneapolis

Published by the University of Minnesota Press,
2037 University Avenue Southeast, Minneapolis MN 55414
Printed in the United States of America

Library of Congress Cataloging in Publication Data

Balk, H. Wesley.
  Performing Power.
  Bibliography: p.
  Includes index.
  1. Acting in opera.   I. Title.
MT955.B216 1986   782'.07   85-1195
ISBN 0-8166-1366-4
ISBN 0-8166-1367-2 (pbk.)

To all the Barbaras in my life —
and two in particular

my wife, who taught
me about the power of
love in performing;

my teacher, who
teaches all of us about
the power of light in
life.

Contents

Foreword
John M. Ludwig

Public opinion to the contrary, opera is a living, dynamic art. After decades of seclusion, it is abroad again, finding new and larger audiences and evolving in a manner reminiscent of the exciting days of Gluck and Wagner. The employment picture for American artists continually improves, and for the talented, creative performer there are exhilarating opportunities to participate in the premieres of new works as well as in revivals of the classics.

Along with the opportunities come challenges posed by new kinds of opera and by the demand of audiences that performances reflect vivid imagination and fully integrated performance skills. These challenges are remarkably different from those that earlier generations of performers faced, and they may be more than some of today's artists can meet. Further, those with the potential to thrive in this bustling arena will need a performing technique that allows them to focus every bit of their talent and energy on the work at hand. Wesley Balk's approach puts such a technique within the reach of able and dedicated artists, and so the publication of *Performing Power* could not come at a better moment.

The need for such a new approach to training became abundantly clear at a June 1980 colloquium of the National Institute for Music Theater in which Balk played a principal role. Taking part in that colloquium were leading representatives of the educational and professional production communities who sat down to compare perceptions of the desired end product of training for the lyric stage. These "hirers" and "trainers" approached their task with zeal because the bottom line was better opportunities for graduating students and better casts for the producers.

They concluded that new curricula must be devised that would allow students a thorough mastery of all of the basic skills of the singer actor: musicianship, reliable vocal production, inventive dramatic imagination, and control of the body's nonvocal means of theatrical communication. Moreover, these skills must be fully integrated into a technique free from tensions and inhibitions. Understandably, the breadth of this concept presented difficulties for some, but one who probably understood better than anyone present was the author of this book, as the training goals set up in *Performing Power* reveal.

Wesley Balk has many interests in life: music, theater, performance, pedagogy, and various aspects of physiology, health, and psychology. He has studied, taught, and practiced physical education, music, and acting; and he has studied the workings of the human body, mind, and spirit — the inseparable, interdependent elements of our beings. It is a remarkable diversity of interests and abilities to find in one man, and it is precisely this diversity that enabled Balk to write a book that reflects a full understanding of the physical and spiritual needs of music theater performers.

At the core of Balk's approach is his understanding (demonstrated over the past two decades in his productions, classes, and previous book — *The Complete Singer-Actor*) that the integration of highly developed though disparate abilities is the keystone to effective performance, whether on Broadway or in the opera house.

Performing in music theater (and especially in opera) is one of the most difficult disciplines humans have devised to amuse themselves, and it's not surprising that few of the existing texts on music-theater performance deal satisfactorily with the issue. Some take a simplified "outside-in" approach, offering gestures, interpretations, lazzi, or routines that have worked in the past for someone or that appeal to the author's imagination. They offer little comfort to the artist who is attempting to develop and integrate his or her own abilities and to assemble a distinctive artistic personality.

Others offer adaptations of popular spoken-theater acting techniques, such as "The Method" (a corruption of Stanislavski's techniques). The objective of these techniques, however, is to assist spoken-theater actors in bringing a believable, personal touch to their use of timing, pitch, and inflection. In music theater, of course, these elements are controlled by the composer; the adapted methods are, at best, of little value and, at worst, counterproductive.

Performing Power stands on firmer ground partly because its author recognizes that music theater is a distinct art form with special demands and partly because he has developed effective methods of combating the tensions that seem always to arise in artists assaying this monumentally difficult art form. It is a new approach and will require careful study, strong motivation, and real talent to master. But that is to say only that its demands are no different from those of a career in music theater. I hope it will find the eager and able users it deserves: we need them onstage.

Break a leg!

Preface

Books are always products that grow out of a process. Some of them are also parts of a continuing process, a slice of which is fixed in time and place to resemble a product—a kind of in-action snapshot as opposed to a still-life pose. *Performing Power* is such a snapshot, and this preface describes what happened before the picture was taken, what is happening now, and what sort of pictures might be taken in the future.

Four years ago I encountered the concept of the perceptual modes and began exploring their projective parallels. That exploration led to *Performing Power*, the writing of which was completed a year and a half ago. Since that time, the next volume in the sequence has begun to take shape. Tentatively entitled *The Synergistic Performance: Performing as an Enlightenment Process*, it will form a trilogy with *The Complete Singer-Actor* (2nd ed.; Minneapolis: University of Minnesota Press, 1985) and *Performing Power*.

From my present perspective, the title for the trilogy might well be: *Transcending Duality in Music-Theater Performance*. This theme was touched upon in *The Complete Singer-Actor* in discussing the concept of opposites. In both life and performance, opposites must partake of each other for maximum vitality. In performance, for example, to choose between relaxation *or* tension, freedom *or* discipline, singing *or* acting does not release a performer's true potential. Both factors must be integrated: the singer-actor becomes complete when the dualities established by the either/or verbal formulation are brought together in a single process.

The difficulty of achieving that integrated state is heightened by the unique energy makeup of each performer and by the tendency in us all (encouraged by academic training) to find the right answer in verbally

definable terms. Performer *A* is a bundle of performance tension for
whom a state of sloppy, released relaxation may contribute a vital step
of awareness in achieving a balance between tension and relaxation. But
she frustrates her goal by focusing on the *product* of relaxation rather
than on the *process* of finding a vital state of readiness that is neither
relaxed nor tense. She tries to overcome her tension by gravitating to the
opposing duality. Performer *B*, on the other hand, who is already sloppily
relaxed (a rare condition among opera singers), hears the suggested exercise for Performer *A* and applies it to himself, increasing his already overrelaxed state; or he may receive an appropriate exercise for his state of
being and be pulled from there into the tension end of the spectrum.

The dualistic nature of language, which is based on the separation
of word and referent, may lie at the core of performers' pendulum swings
between extremes as they try to grow and develop. Language is reasonably
accurate in describing either end of any energy spectrum (such as tension
and relaxation), but it is less clear in describing the nondualistic states of
being between those extremes (readiness? poised vitality?). We can
become what we can describe. To attain what we cannot clearly
describe—particularly if it lies between two opposing descriptions—is
more challenging.

Performing Power examines the duality of external energies of performance vs. their internal motivation. The projective modes—the external information that we are able to send to other people—become the
focus. They are not more important than what is occurring internally, but
they have been neglected and are badly out of balance with the internal
aspects. The aim in *Performing Power* is to attain a more useful balance
between the two.

From its beginning, this century has seen an intellectual search for
internal answers. It has been called the psychological century; along with
producing a large body of useful information about our mental and
emotional processes, it has created an imbalance in perspective that has
affected all the arts. As the stress on verbal-intellectual analysis has increased, the singer-actor has been especially affected. Unlike other arts,
in singing-acting the performer is his or her own instrument. The mind,
which is an integral part of that instrument, is asked to focus on itself.
The result is a tangle of self-conscious, judgmental control patterns that
diminish the performing power of countless performers.

One young singer-actor described the balance between internal and external aspects of performance this way: "When I first began with the modes technique I said, 'Thank God for a way of work which doesn't try to get you to spill your guts all over the stage.' But after I got comfortable with the idea of working with the external energies, I began to realize that things were also happening on the inside in response to the externals. But unlike the old internals, they were *good* things, *real* things, and I could encourage them and make the connection between the inside and the outside even stronger." This is an unusually clear experience of the unity that can overcome the almost universal separation of externals and internals, of expression and feeling. By exercising the hitherto neglected end of the spectrum and being aware of its potential for integration with the other end, we can find a relationship that is undefinable in words but stunningly palpable in experience. It is the relationship of synergy.

Synergy is sometimes described in mathematical shorthand as $2 + 2 = 5$. It refers to the relationship in any system in which the parts of the system mutually enhance each other's power and create a whole that is greater than the sum of its parts. In music, for example, many separate notes played simultaneously create a chord in which they all coexist, attaining a greater whole than if each was played alone.

The Complete Singer-Actor and *Performing Power* are devoted to exploring the synergy that can be released when working with separate aspects of the singing-acting process. In the third book, the exploration will deal with the unified field of singing-acting. The greater the number of synergistic parts in a system, the proportionately greater the whole. Opera and music-theater involve a great many parts—more than any other performing art. In addition, research into group dynamics suggests that in a synergistic system involving human beings, the whole may be seen as equal to the square of the sum of the parts: rather than $2 + 2 = 5$, we have $2 + 2 = 16$. This supports what we sense intuitively about the opera and music-theater form: that its potential power as a performance experience is unrivaled and rarely realized. We have yet to tap the true synergistic potential of the form, a potential that is largely contained within the performer. The performer who attains a state of performance enlightenment has, by definition, realized the synergistic potential that lies within.

The Complete Singer-Actor, which began the search for the realization of that potential, continues to serve as a philosophic working base. *Performing Power* begins a new and crucial step in the unfolding of the journey toward the enlightened performance. I have worked with the technique expressed in the book for several years, and it has evolved as a fundamental key to the synergistic performance. Using the technique, I have witnessed unprecedented performer growth; I have also received numerous validations from outside observers—and the growth continues. I tell each new group of performers that the technique is available, and it works. Practice it, play with it, persist in it, be patient with it (and with yourself), and always treat it as what it is—a process. For that is what you are, and the quality of your growth depends upon the degree to which you honor that fact.

H. W. B.

Performing Power
A New Approach for the Singer-Actor

Introduction
A Report from the Laboratory

For the past fourteen years I have been in charge of a research laboratory for acting and singing-acting. With this laboratory, which is my own creation, I am able to do experimental work wherever there is a piano, a coach, and a singer-actor willing to make the effort. In a typical experiment, I add a complication to the singer-actor's performance—a challenge of some kind—and then carefully observe what happens. This challenge is followed by another one, further observation of the ensuing performance, and notation of the results.

The laboratory is unique in its outreach to both the educational and professional worlds of theater and music-theater. It has moved from place to place: Aspen Music Festival, Wolf Trap Farm Park Festival, San Francisco Opera Merola Program, Central City Opera Festival, and many other workshops and demonstrations throughout the country. During these years, it has been based at the Minnesota Opera Company, the opera's Studio Training Program, the Minnesota Opera Institute, and the University of Minnesota Department of Theatre Arts.

The laboratory has also dealt with an extraordinary range of talent and skill, from singers who have never acted to actors who have never sung, from advanced, professional singer-actors to those who are just beginning. The goal of the laboratory has been to learn the art of singing-acting through exercise and experiment with actual performers. Many ideas emerged that formed the basis of my previous book, *The Complete Singer-Actor*. Since that time (1977), I have worked to refine the basic theory. In 1981, however, I encountered the concept of perceptual modes, which gave me an entirely new perspective on the challenge of performance and led to the most stimulating tool for performer growth in my experience. More on that below.

3

The concept of the moving laboratory allowed me to develop a technique and philosophy involving the total spectrum of acting and singing-acting performance. Working with both beginners and experts has also encouraged me to search for the unifying principles underlying all performance. How do human beings use their energies when they perform? How can we help them become masters of those energies? These questions have informed the search, and because they can never be fully answered, the work will go on. The insights I set down here are not final conclusions but part of an unfolding process.

The Elephant and Rose Challenges

Two challenges arise when one helps performers to use their energies more effectively: getting rid of interference with the energy flow and increasing the energy flow. I call these the elephant and rose challenges. Let me explain. If one asks a person *not* to think about elephants, that

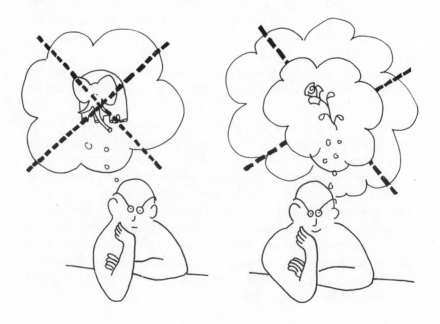

person will think about them in the very act of trying not to do so. Similarly, in trying *not* to do something that we know interferes with our energy flow—for example, releasing physical tension in the body—the very act of trying not to be tense may increase the tension. But we can replace the effort *not* to do something with the effort to *do* something: to avoid thinking about elephants, for example, we can choose instead to think about roses. Where physical tension is a problem, concentrating on communicating more energy with the face might release the superfluous tension in the body. Although we may be able to exorcise an elephant by using only the negative challenge (extreme shoulder tension sometimes relaxes simply because of awareness), it is always useful to tackle a problem from both fronts at once—to counter an elephant with a rose. In the course of this book, I will identify as many elephant blocks and suggest as many replacement roses as possible.

One elephant, however, has developed into a veritable herd in the twentieth century, and that elephant is the fear of judgment. This fear and its various offspring do more to block the free use of artistic energy in the performer than any other single factor. The plague of judgmental fear seems to be more pronounced in this century than in any previous time. Like the plague that afflicted ancient Thebes and destroyed Oedipus, it involves knowing too much. We know what we want to be (or what we think others want us to be), we have a product in mind, and we judge our present state in view of that potential product. We know what is good and what is bad, what is of value and what is not, what is in and what is out, what is clever and what is not. We are surrounded by critics telling us what our opinions should be, and the judges outside and inside of us sing in unison: you should be this, you shouldn't be that, you should be thin, shouldn't be fat, should eat this, but never eat that, and so on in all aspects of our lives.

We want to be different (that is, a different product) than we are, and this is the basis for growth. But if we focus too strongly on the product we want to become, we lose touch with the process of what we are, and become unable to change and grow. Knowing too much about what we want to be, we judge ourselves harshly because we know too little about what we truly are. We must balance our knowledge of becoming with our knowledge of being if we are to escape the plague of judgment.

This crisis in comparative judgment began for all the arts at the end of the nineteenth century. Professional criticism—the evaluation of product and the essence of judgment in its most refined and brutal form—was born through the efforts of G. B. Shaw, who, by simultaneously intellectualizing and vulgarizing the craft of criticism, turned it into an art of its own. His intellectual brilliance was unquestionable, yet to win a point he would resort to shamelessly entertaining tricks. He amused as he criticized, and his cleverness with words—the principal judgmental tool—gave those words precedence over the artistic experience itself. At about the same time the manifesto mania emerged. Critical, analytical words made statements about artistic philosophy that defined what the product was to be and then sought to control the processes in music, architecture, and painting in an attempt to attain that product. Verbal, intellectual theory began to precede the creation of art, and intellect began to dictate to and supersede sensibility. The writings of Tom Wolfe and Henry Pleasants concerning this trend in painting, architecture, and music provoked outrage from those whose livelihood is founded on the preeminence of the analytical intellect in the world of art—namely, critics and museum directors.[1]

A similar pattern of subordinating process to product arose as realism became the vogue in theater and the literary arts. In science, this orientation was expressed in efforts to determine the "real" nature of human beings and their place in the universe. Darwin, Marx, Freud, and Einstein were dominant figures in that search, but it has been a century-long phenomenon that continues today. Because the subject of investigation was humanity, it was of great interest to the student of acting. Perhaps it was the smell of intellectual respectability—so long denied the theater world—that encouraged the idea of making acting a science. In any case, a new interest in *why* people behaved as they did and in the laws governing that behavior began to pervade the work of acting theorists.

This new science grew also from the impulse of comparative judgment, giving birth to the figure of the director. If an actor is trying to be "real," he or she is trying to be "lifelike"; but that demands the presence of someone who watches and compares, who judges whether the attempt is accurate. The next step is supremely logical: the judge naturally attempts to tell the actor how to be more lifelike, and the director thus becomes indispensable to the actor who is trying to be "real." The actor as person-being-compared-and-judged became a permanent phenomenon. In short order, a concept of acting was created that made a science of the art of being real as an actor. Had Stanislavski not lived, he would have had to be invented to fit the need for an aesthetic theory to make acting more lifelike.

As in the other arts, a verbal definition was created that has placed enormous judgmental burdens on actors since that time. Painters painted, architects designed, and composers composed to the tune of aesthetic manifestos, and actors made a similar attempt to practice their art according to a verbal program. This tendency was especially strong in America, where its complexity was compounded by the fact that the manifesto was created by a Russian. A small part of the total concept was translated into English, leaving numerous important facts, nuances, and cultural understandings behind in the process.

Many of the new "scientific" findings upon which these acting systems were based were those of a science still in its infancy. Even today, psychology, psychoanalysis, psychotherapy, and other sciences of the mind lack the specificity of knowledge to be true science. New methods of psychological treatment arise yearly from the continuing research into the physiology of the brain and from new and imaginative "maps of the mind."[2] A comprehensive science of human behavior is still in the early process of formation.

Along with the director/Pygmalion who sculpts the actor into a life-like representation, we find acting schools and teachers springing up like weeds, all helping the actor to achieve reality on the stage. The implication that the actor is not real without such judgmental midwives to help give birth to self is absurd, but the fallacy continues to mislead thousands of young actors. Once that comparative, analytical approach gained a foothold, it was no longer enough to seem to be the character: one had to *become* the character, inside and out. The total being of the actor, including the internal workings of the mind, had to be brought into organic interplay by means of the newly minted discoveries of psychology and psychoanalysis. For some reason, especially in America, the outer being—the aspects of performance that can actually be described and worked with by the actor—became of less interest than that fascinating mystery, the inner being. The *why* superseded the *how* in importance.

The trend has persisted to the present day. Directors and teachers of acting are often seduced into the roles of amateur psychologists, mind readers, and psychoanalytic dabblers. Academic acting departments present Gestalt therapy, EST, transactional analysis, reality therapy, and other therapy-based approaches as the keys to acting growth. The American student of acting has become, in many cases, a feedback dependent. Rather than working independently, the actor must have a coach, teacher, or director to judge, advise, and help in artistic growth. The generalized truth that all action originates in the mind has been taken to mean that the working of the mind is what one attends to in the teaching of acting, rather than the means used to communicate those mental processes.

This approach to the acting process would not be so daunting were we to confine ourselves to theatrical realism or naturalism. Actors are highly skilled at faking naturalism when it is useful to do so — which is much of the time. But we are addressing the challenge of becoming a singer-actor. This person is not an actor who sings or a singer who acts, but one who wishes to develop the capacity to deal with a maximum production of energy in all the channels available, whether singing or speaking; who wants to learn to communicate peak experiences comfortably and convincingly; and who looks forward to using the physical, vocal, and emotional systems to their limit in spoken theater or musical theater or opera. These singers and actors represent the maximum development of human potential in serving the arts of theater and music-theater.

What, then, about the *singer* who approaches the art of singing-acting? We have discussed some of the burdens felt by actors in the theatrical world; what about those experienced by singers in the musical world? For musicians, the judgmental challenge has always been an issue. There is a musical score with which to compare their efforts (unless they are improvising), and it is a simple matter for a knowledgeable musician to tell whether the singer's efforts are right or wrong relative to the score. The function of the conductor as we now think of it also emerged at about the same time as the other judgmental figures in the arts.[3] A whole new breed of interpretative musical judges thus became a permanent part of the cultural milieu. If you are a singer, the conductor is the person who can judge with ease whether your interpretation is in agreement. It is a short step from being "in agreement" to being "correct"; once that step is taken, the judgmental circuit is completed.

Musical training seems to impose a far greater judgmental burden than theatrical training. In my university classes, it is easy to tell the music students from the theater students. As a group, the music students are more controlled and disciplined, a result of the highly judgmental aspects of their training. The inhibitions of theater students are more cleverly hidden because that is what their art is about: disguising from the observing audience what is really going on in the mind. But combine these two concerns about product in the singing-acting training process, and the judgmental temperature rises. New burdens are added to the right-wrong baggage they already carry. Actors think they cannot sing and are terrified of being criticized for it; singers think they cannot act and are equally nervous about revealing it.

Fortunately, both actors and singers are beginners at their respective new challenges of singing and acting, and they have no acquired habits created by fears of performance criticism. Thus the singers often make enormous acting strides, astonishing the trained actors; and many of the actors develop as singers with comparable rapidity. But the judgmental burden on the singer-actor remains a huge one, inhibiting the performance growth that could happen.

The crisis of misplaced intellectualization, of judgmental interference with life processes, has been widely recognized in books that try to help artists, athletes, and people in everyday life "zen" their way out of the judgmental bind. Zen and the Art of Almost Anything You Care to Name has been the topic of dozens of self-help books in the past three decades, beginning with the progenitor of them all, *Zen and the Art of Archery* by Eugene Herrigel. Perhaps best known is Tim Gallwey's adaptation of the zen of nonjudgment to tennis and skiing, beginning with *The Inner Game of Tennis*. Others have used similar approaches to golf and athletics in general, whereas Robert Pirsig's *Zen and the Art of Motorcycle Maintenance* relates to life processes as a whole. A book of particular interest here is Eloise Ristad's lovely volume, *A Soprano on Her Head*, which deals with musical performances of all kinds. These useful and stimulating books are highly recommended.[4]

One must have a technique, however, with which to apply the Zen, nonjudgmental, detached-observer approach.[5] True students of Zen never get involved with the Zen of what they are doing but with the thing itself, with what is being done. The Zen of it is the *doing* of it. As Eugene

Herrigel puts it in *Zen and the Art of Archery*, "Far from wishing to waken the artist in the pupil prematurely, the teacher considers it his first task to make him a skilled artisan with sovereign control of his craft." Zen is manifested through a technique, whether it be archery, flower arranging, tea serving, motorcycle maintenance, tennis, skiing, golf, singing, acting, or singing-acting (and life itself, if the Zen of any of the preceding activities is comprehended). If the technique of the art or activity is not specifically understood and practiced on all levels, there is no vehicle through which to manifest the Zen of performance in that art or activity. And the Zen of performance in any art is, by definition, the best possible performance the artist can give with whatever technical skills that artist possesses.

Let us remind ourselves that knowledge of the technique precedes its effective use. It would be silly to tell a person who has never touched the instrument, "Just allow yourself to play the violin" (although it would be a better first lesson than many, and it could be followed up with great effect by an enlightened teacher). Nonetheless, the aspiring artist must learn the techniques of playing the instrument, and in the *how* of practicing and performing—in the performer's physical, mental, and emotional relationship to those techniques—is found the Zen of the art, or its best performance.

The case becomes more complicated when approaching acting or singing-acting. Not only are many judgmental figures involved, but the actor or singer-actor is his or her own instrument. The technique of playing that instrument is intertwined with the subjective aspects of the instrument. The singer-actor-instrument is played and has reactions to *how* that instrument is played. But the singer-actor-instrument has been made dependent upon someone else's reaction—the directors, conductors, coaches, and teachers who watch the performance. Their perceptions of the performance are filtered through their observational capacities, interpreted, and translated into words that necessarily reduce the complexity of the original experience. Those words are then spoken to the performer, filtered through the performer's mental processes, combined with the performer's own reactions, and retranslated into some sort of behavioral change. After that many translations and interpretations, it is a wonder that any beneficial changes are made.

To make matters even more difficult, the singer-actor has no agreed-upon set of techniques for achieving what is desired, nor even a clear vocabulary for talking about the issues surrounding the technique. Comments made by otherwise expert observers or listeners are often subjective and vague, intensifying the judgmental burden on the performer. The frustration can be enormous, with the performer unable to judge the product and rarely given clear techniques with which to work. This is not to say that individual skills used in singing-acting performance may not be clearly defined. Movement instructors speak with great specificity about how the physical being should be used. I have heard master coaches define the musical requirements in staggering detail. But there is little clear, precise feedback about the interaction of these details as they relate to the total art of singing-acting. Because one cannot touch a single aspect of the singing-acting system without affecting all the other parts, this is a serious problem for those who aspire to complete singing-acting performances. We have not yet developed a way of discussing the whole system, particularly the acting aspect.

Instead, one hears quotes like the following (taken from actual directing or coaching situations): "show me more feeling," "really listen," "let down the barriers," "be more vulnerable," "react to what's happening," "get involved," "show some guts," "let it all hang out," "there's not enough humanity," "you don't seem to be feeling it." This kind of imprecise verbal communication is a monumental challenge to a performer's composure and coherence, not to speak of artistry. The comments scratch the judgmental nerve of the performer: the observer clearly had something else in mind, and in comparison the performer is found wanting. Yet the performer is given no clear descriptive means of making the desired change. This undefined, judgmental burden has been placed on virtually every one of the hundreds of young performers I have encountered in the past fifteen years. A few have found intuitive answers that have enabled them to zen their way out of the dilemma on their own, but the rest interfere with their own performances by trying to respond to such unclear descriptions. Even worse, they are usually unaware of what they are doing to themselves, and their lack of awareness increases the helpless frustration they feel. They have robbed themselves of performing power by their attempt to respond to evaluations of their art that are unclear, undefined, unspecific, and therefore strongly judgmental.

The twentieth century has also endowed us with powerful internal judges. Generalized descriptions of performances often lead to negative interpretations by the performer. The observer says, "That was good," and we think it was good for the wrong reason. We place more emphasis on that reason in succeeding performances—for example, tense shoulders—and end with something that is no longer "good" in the eyes of that observer. No wonder we are confused. The observer says, "Be more vulnerable," and we think, "He hated the scene, I'm shallow, I don't have any feeling." But we can avoid misleading and judgmental generalizations almost entirely by specific, accurate description. To say something is "clumsy" is inaccurate and strongly judgmental. To describe the actual action is more difficult: "Your arm movements were spasmodic," "your shoulders were lifted and appeared tense," "the movement did not seem to flow," "your pace was rapid, but it appeared to be jerky." But in making that extra effort, one has given the performer a series of descriptions that are less judgmental and also lead to greater awareness. By telling the performer exactly *how* he or she did the action, the performer is able to concentrate on changing the description rather than worrying about whether it is good or bad. One can do the same thing with other aspects of expression as well. Instead of saying, "You looked uninvolved, it was boring," you can say, "I wasn't receiving any messages from your face—I got it from the words, but not from your face"; or, with reference to the voice, "Your voice sounds high pitched and intense," rather than calling it "shrill and unpleasant." Judgment will not be eliminated from the performer's mind, of course. Performers are very good at hearing what they don't want to hear; they are perfectly capable of placing negative connotations on almost anything one says to them. But we want to make it as difficult for them to feel judged as possible, and we can do that with accurate description. If we, the judges, describe accurately, performers will learn to describe their behavior to themselves in different terms. We all know performers who condemn everything they do before they do it, creating self-fulfilling prophecies as they go. If we can use our energies for accurate description rather than for creating judgmental patterns, the performers we are working with will begin to do the same, and we can all strive to change the description rather than warding off the critical blows.

A prime way to escape the judgmental bind, then, is to change the verbalization of the judgment, to make the description more accurate, and thus to make change and growth available to the person described.

The Performer's Dilemma: Analyzing the Art

Much of this book is devoted to finding new ways of describing the singing-acting performance, thus giving us the perceptual and verbal tools to communicate clearly and specifically with the singer-actor. Before we do that, however, let us see how generalizations, as unconscious thought processes, affect our views of life and the art of performance.

Judgments are generalizations—another name for bad descriptions—and generalizations are the enemy of good performance. They are product-oriented labels: "good," "bad," "noble," "vulgar," "intelligent," "stupid," and so on. They are reductionist security blankets that we use in coping with the overwhelming complexity of life and art. Generalizations rescue us from the chaos of multiplicity, and in this sense they are useful; but because they also remove us from the power of that multiplicity, they are to be used with care. Acting systems, for example, begin as reductions of human behavior into describable patterns, which are further generalized as they are used in acting classes. When acting theories filter down to directors, teachers, and performers, they are inevitably reduced to sets of rules about human behavior. They are academicized, pigeonholed, and categorized until they lose contact with the very life from which they arose. The creators of acting systems were brilliantly and ingeniously responsive to the overwhelming complexity of life and art. In deriving generalizations from that chaos of vitality, they necessarily left out portions of the confusion in order to make systematic sense. But in passing those generalizations on by word of mouth or printed page, the generalizations became substitutes for the life that gave them birth rather than flexible means of achieving a lifelike art. They become dogma, holy writ, and systematic methods that no longer respond to their source.

How do we balance the need for specificity with the equally important need for generalizations? How can we return to life for a new kind of specific description without losing the generalizing usefulness of the existing acting systems? How can we make a new description of life and

art without creating the verbal reductionist dilemma for which we are trying to compensate in the first place?

The description of the acting process with which we have lived for some time focuses on the movement from the internal motivation to the external manifestation. Especially in America, we continue to cling to the view that "you gotta feel it first." Some descriptions of the acting process suggest that if the thought process is "correct," the external communication will also be "correct" and will reflect the internal thought process perfectly. This is obviously not true. To assume that what is in the mind corresponds with what is communicated externally is not only untrue, it would be disastrous if it were. Every actor has thoughts not to be shared with the audience during a performance. The inner workings and the outer behavior are seldom if ever in a one-to-one relationship, and any description of the acting process that implies otherwise—as do many interpretations of the Stanislavski system—leads performers into attempts to control their thought process or to imitate those of someone else. More sophisticated is this description by Peter Brook of internal process working its way out to external expression:

> Acting begins with a tiny inner movement so slight that it is almost completely invisible. . . . What happens? I make a proposition to an actor's imagination such as, "She is leaving you." At this moment deep in him a subtle movement occurs. Not only in actors—the movement occurs in anyone, but in most nonactors the movement is too slight to manifest itself in any way: the actor is a more sensitive instrument and in him the tremor is detected. . . .In early theatre rehearsals, the impulse may get no further than a flicker—even if the actor wishes to amplify it, all sorts of extraneous psychic psychological tensions can intervene— then the current is short-circuited, earthed. For this flicker to pass into the whole organism, a total relaxation must be there, either god-given or brought about by work. This, in short, is what rehearsals are all about. In this way acting is mediumistic—the idea suddenly envelops the whole in an act of possession—in Grotowski's terminology the actors are 'penetrated'—penetrated by themselves.[6]

This is an inspiring and articulate description of what Brook perceives as the acting process at work. But it is not hard to imagine one's reaction as a young actor when given this brilliant analysis of the process-to-product sequence. Almost immediately one will begin trying to "show," consciously or unconsciously, that one is going through the "mediumistic" process. Or self-observation will be used to decide whether one is truly going through the process described. "Am I 'penetrating' myself? Is the 'flicker' there in the first place? Is it working its way out as Brook describes it?" One is, in short, doing everything to subvert the very process one wishes to experience.

This outcome is true for every mind-reading description of the actor's ideal internal process: no matter how brilliant the description, it tends to focus the performer's attention on his or her own internal process in order to compare it with the description. The very act of analysis introduces a self-consciousness into the process that stops it from producing the result desired. It does not matter how true, accurate, articulate, or inspiring the description is: so long as it calls into play an intellectual focus on the nonintellectual internal process, it is self-defeating.

Mind reading is a two-way process for the performer and the observer: the mind reader is trying to guess what is going on in the performer's mind, while the performer is trying to show what is going on in his or her mind, or at least what the performer would like the mind-reading observer to think is going on. Now the latter is a good description of what an actor must be able to do: communicate to an audience what the actor wants them to think is going on in the character's mind. But if the actor thinks that what is communicated is *actually* going on in his or her own mind, the actor is perpetuating a delusion that will lead to further confusion.

We have fostered a view of acting in which performers try vainly to match their own thought processes against some ideal model that has been described to them. It is an example of the elephants dilemma: the harder you try to do the task, which is to think only certain thoughts and not others, the more you interfere with the task. Some roses are desperately needed to give a new focus to the effort.

Quantum physics offers us another metaphor for this inability to observe our thought process and make it conform to a desired product. The indeterminacy principle of quantum theory tells us that we have no way of predicting the precise future location of any subatomic particle. If we determine its position by observation, we cannot know the speed of its movement; and if we determine the speed at which it is moving, we cannot know its position. The act of observation affects the thing observed. We cannot know both speed and location because observation of one excludes knowledge of the other. The future position of the particle must thus remain unknown or indeterminate.

If we observe Brook's flicker—that initial impulse of dramatic response within the actor—we may be able to define what it was, but it will no longer be there; and if we try to define its movement, we cannot know what it is. If we try to force the flicker to end up as we wish, we snuff out its life in the process. And if we try to maintain it as it is, we smother it. Awareness focused on the internal process is awareness of awareness; the thing observed is part of the process of observation, and therefore it can never be what the observer wants it to be. Like playing Pirandello within the psyche, it becomes impossible to determine which level is the real one because the observer is part of all levels.

When the mind-reading approach misses fire and we guess wrong as to why actors are behaving as they are—which will be a good share of the time—they tend to become defensive, and understandably so. Mind-reading comments made to actors are invariably hackle raising: "Really *think* about what you are saying" (as though the person was trying not to); "Get involved" (as though anyone is being purposely uninvolved in acting a scene); or "Show more commitment" (as though one is purposely uncommitted in performing a scene). Instead, one can make the point in a positive and descriptive way: "I know you are thinking [or are committed, or involved, or whatever the need may be], but it doesn't appear [or sound] that way because. . . . " and then follows the vital but difficult step of describing what has actually happened.

Mind reading also leads to *indirect* directing. In this approach, the director never says what is really wanted but tries to trick it out of the performers by giving them suggestions that change their behavior without their being aware of what they are doing. (After twenty minutes of rarefied directorial verbalizing, the actor says, "You mean you want me to say it louder?") The indirect director holds on to control: the secret is internal, and if the director plays psychological sleuth properly he or she finds the right internal suggestion to get the performer to do everything the way it should be done, "organically." The right thought will make the tension go away, the voice sound better, the somber face beam with joy. This transformation almost never happens, but the pursuit is fun and has an air of mystery about it precisely because it is unknown, and it keeps the director in a position of power. As in other parts of our psychological quick-fix mania, if you know the secret—the right intellectual method, the magic bullet—you too can create actor change in the twinkling of an eye.

This places yet another burden on performers, who are forced to prove that their mental processes are real and are functioning as they should be. But they are given no clear description of how to communicate those processes. They become responsible for the mind-reading guesses of observers: if they guess wrong, the performers are at fault because their minds are not doing what they should. Yet performers know, intuitively, that observers cannot actually read their mind—they are only guessing. It turns into a game with unspoken rules: performers try to convince the director-sleuth that they are thinking the right thoughts (or the character's thoughts), while the director becomes a belief barometer as well as a judgment detective who finds the missing motivation to reveal that truth.

Performers respond to the sleuthing in a logical but unspoken way. "If you're going to blame my acting problems on my thoughts, so am I. But, like it or not, only I know what is *really* going on in there. It's my secret and I'm not going to alter it just because you have a bright idea. I think I know what you want, but I have to figure out how to show you that without forcing my mind to play the games you want it to play. So I'll tell you I'll work on it on my own so that I don't have to do it in front of you." The problem is moved to the future, preventing any useful work from being done on the spot. Control, which was taken away from the performer when the judgmental mind-reading began, is also moved back to the performer.

Unfortunately, all that homework that actors supposedly do in private seldom changes their performance because they also are caught in the mental manipulation trap. When we try to control the mind so that it will produce the proper behavior, our intellectual-judgmental approach scuttles the basis for intuitive, natural behavior. The performer is failing to work with the actual problem, which is *how to express* what he or she already understands, not how to understand it better or differently. Performers become more concerned about their internal mental processes than about the communication of those processes through their external resources. Guilt builds up as they compare what is with what they think should be, and even a strongly communicating performance fails to give them joy because they have been judging the internal process and have found it wanting. In a classic vicious circle, judgment of the product diminishes its quality, which in turn intensifies the negative judgment of the product, and so on.

Uta Hagen counsels the young actor to keep certain things a secret, a mystery that is never revealed or talked about.[7] This rare piece of wisdom should be extended to include more of the realm about which acting classes attempt to verbalize. Words describing the internal processes of an actor are like imaginative fiction: the story may ring absolutely true, be incredibly stimulating, be the best description of what one perceives in an acting performance, but it is fit reading for nonactors only—unless the actor can read it and then continue to perform without succumbing to comparison. The actor must focus on sharing, on giving energy to fellow performers and to the audience. That energy must be drawn from a well of intuitive mystery, a well that can easily become clouded and muddied by intellectual analysis.

Actors, then, are in a difficult position. They are asked to "show" something to prove that their internal processes are functioning, that the flicker is working its way out. But they are not given an accurate description of what to show and how to show it, only descriptions of mental processes that are supposed to lead to the external product. They watch other performers who are said to be manifesting the process and imitate those models, but this approach makes them totally dependent upon the quality of the product: impersonate a good performer and the exercise can be useful; if not, it isn't.

But even the impersonation of good performers can turn into product generalization. Marlon Brando, through enormous talent and a specific personal process growing out of his training in the Actor's Studio, created a stunning portrayal of a Tennessee Williams character named Stanley Kowalski. The result? A whole generation of young actors aped either the final generalized product or treated the perceived process as a product in itself, to be communicated by various physical or psychological mannerisms that demonstrated adherence to the faith.

In the decade of the sixties, when Jerzy Grotowski's influence was being felt in the land, many young actors attended Grotowski-oriented workshops and came home attempting extraordinary physical exercises as they performed their scenes or soliloquies. Almost two decades later, during the writing of this book, a fine young actor in one of my classes performed an extended Grotowski exercise while delivering a Shakespearean soliloquy. The exercise demanded great physical skill and strength, as well as the kinesthetic bravura that we associate with much of Grotowski's work. The actor wanted to know how he could make it better, how to turn the exercise into a product. It took lengthy discussion to tell him that, while I admired his physical prowess in coping with the demands of the exercise and found the exercise itself to be an interesting and useful challenge, it was simply that — an exercise. It was one of many possibilities, not an end product in itself. Rather than practicing that specific exercise until it was "perfect," I suggested that he find a similarly challenging exercise for both the vocal and emotional systems and practice them each time he exercised the physical system. In that way, he would be developing his total performance capability rather than only one part of it to the exclusion of others. The actor-instrument should be able to serve more than one style; it should learn to deal with any style appropriate to the performing situation. Developing this capability is a more useful task for the young performer than concentrating on mastering a single stylistic generalization. Again, process and product are confused.

There is nothing wrong with impersonating performers and styles as an acting exercise. Short of actual mind reading, it is the only way to emulate another performer's process. If that attention to the descriptive detail of one performance is extended to dozens, if young actors were to impersonate fifty great performers or styles instead of only one, it would be a rich approach to the acting process and one suggestive of the techniques we will be discussing.

The Theory of Perceptual and Projective Modes

To help the performer avoid the twin traps of generalization and limited role-modeling, let us return to the idea of description, placing it in a broader context. Every great advance in human thought has been preceded by a new description of the nature of man, as in the views created by Darwin, Marx, and Freud. Artists have responded to these views with corresponding artistic descriptions of humanity and art that have changed the ways in which we think about ourselves, our lives, and our culture. In theater and music theater, the great creators—Shakespeare, Monteverdi, Mozart, Verdi, Wilde, Shaw, Brecht and Weill, Tennessee Williams, and others—have provided descriptions that not only changed the way we see humanity but also altered the arts of theater and music theater themselves. On a still more modest level, Stanislavski, Meyerhold, Vahktangov, Artaud, Copeau, Chaikin, Grotowski, Strasberg, and others have created new descriptions of the human being as performer that have changed the way actors approach their art. This art uses the artist as the instrument with which to describe another human being. But once these new and potent descriptive generalizations are accepted, they are soon labeled, categorized, and devitalized.

To reverse this tendency, we can either return regularly to life for information to add to the existing generalizations or we can create a fresh description that can combine with and expand upon the old one. This book follows the second course, drawing upon information from psychology and psychotherapy to derive a subtle but significantly different view of the human being as a performer.[8]

People, as communicating beings, have five senses or modes of perception: hearing, seeing, touching, tasting, and smelling. Only the first three are used for interpersonal communication, when we hear, see, and feel (physically touch or empathize with) other people. Thus, we have the hearing mode, the seeing mode, and the kinesthetic mode. Corresponding to these *perceptual* modes, we have three *projective* modes that communicate with their perceptual parallels. We speak and sing; we project mental and emotional messages facially; and we move, gesture, and touch with our bodies. These projective modes may be called the hearing/vocal mode, the facial/emotional mode, and the kinesthetic mode. All sensory communication is based on some interrelationship of these three perceptual and projective modes. Not just acting, but any art involving human communication would profit from knowing how the communicating power of each mode, both perceptual and projective, can be enhanced.

How does this description of communication differ from previous descriptions of acting systems? Whereas acting systems have tended to concentrate on internal, mind-reading problems, the description based on perceptual and projective modes aims for as much objectivity as possible. It concentrates only on what can be seen and heard in observing and listening to performers, on what can be objectively agreed upon by anyone present at the performance. Initially, of course, some observers will be more aware than others. Once that awareness is shared, however, all observers realize that they have all perceived the phenomenon in question—they just have not noticed it. There are only three possible means of communicating—with the voice, the face, or the body. These three means can interact in a multitude of ways, both positive and negative, but the messages they deliver can be accurately and objectively described and agreed upon. It simply takes practice.

What cannot be described and agreed upon is *why* the person is delivering those messages. There are too many possible reasons why a person never smiles, or talks in a monotone, or holds the body stiffly, or has a facial twitch, or stammers or fidgets and so on. To spend time trying to guess which reason is the right one is to play the mind-reading game. It may be fascinating, but it is seldom useful and is often destructive. Even if the guess is correct, that knowledge will seldom change the behavior; the voice will continue to be monotonous, the face grim, the body tense. Psychoanalysis has proved this repeatedly: an intellectual understanding of the psychological reason for a behavior problem does not necessarily solve the problem. It may provide motivational understanding to help fuel the energy for change; but if behavioral problems were that easy to solve, the person would long since have done it alone.

In contrast with finding the motivational cause of a behavior, I have yet to work with a group that did not agree unanimously on the description of the behavioral message. Each group also had an amazing variety of mind-reading explanations for the behavior. Some guesses were accepted by performers and some were not, but very few guesses changed the messages delivered. Mode descriptions, on the other hand, are easy to understand, and changes can be created on the spot by simply changing the projective mode messages. Time and exercise may be needed to make those changes comfortable and convincing, but they are there to be worked with freely and without defensiveness.

An audience is convinced that it knows a character's mind by what it perceives through the external means of communication. These audience descriptions can be communicated precisely to the performer for correlation with that performer's unique internal processes. Rather than rules for what must be thought, there are only descriptions of what has actually happened externally, and these happenings can be changed to communicate the internal process more effectively.

Although this book emphasizes the development of external communicating capacities, the internal and external relationship is a unity. I do not intend to denigrate the internal half of that unity, nor to create a false duality by separating the two. The internal intent and the external message form a whole so far as their relationship in time is concerned. In most cases, as we will see, there is a virtual simultaneity of occurrence. Only interference between the modes causes this simultaneity to go out of synchronization. Because the external is the grosser part of the two-way system, it can block the internal flicker; that flicker, however, is much less likely to block the external expression except by inhibition. External capabilities create the environment within which the internal flicker can grow; only if the environment is in a proper state will the flicker occur. When the external process is prepared to communicate clearly, precisely, and truthfully, the internal process will also be ready. But whereas the external part of the system projects only one set of messages, the internal system contains many awarenesses and perceptions that are not communicated. Any attempt to stamp out those extra internal energies can lead to frustration and failure.

Brook's description of the flicker process suggests another way of viewing the issue. The system through which the flicker works its way to overt expression must be prepared to express not only that flicker but all possible flickers. The channel for the mediumistic passage of energies must be clear and responsive to the needs of the flicker. The body, the face, and the voice must all be prepared through exercise to be possessed by the flicker and to express its meaning. The medium through which the flicker expresses itself is the external system of communication, and until that system has been properly prepared, many flickers will die aborning. In fact, the capacity to express a given flicker may often determine whether that flicker will originate in the first place. For the actor, the external and the internal form a true system in which the capacity of each affects the other. Our power of conception is interrelated with our power of projection.

The projective modes—the voice, the face, and the body have minds of their own apart from the verbal, intellectual mind that tries to control them. As human beings we have three nonverbal, nonintellectual minds: the mind of the voice (and the music it makes in speaking or singing, apart from the words themselves), the mind of the emotions, and the mind of the body. These are the mode minds. As the verbal, intellectual mind tries to control these other minds, it interferes with their operation, blocks the flow of their communication, and inevitably reduces the range of their communication.

We cannot, however, do without the verbal, intellectual mind: we must enlist it in the task of transcending itself. The intellect does the actual describing of the modes in operation because it is the only part of the mind that has the resources, the words, to do so. Accordingly, it must be deeply involved in helping performers to increase their own descriptive awareness. The kind of in-depth and specific description we seek will challenge the most acute intellect; but this task is something that most of us will have to learn and practice diligently, particularly how to do it in a nonjudgmental way. Each of the mode minds—the voice mind, the facial/emotional mind, and the body mind—must be allowed to function and to develop the capacity to communicate. To do so, however, they must become more self-aware, which involves both intuition and careful description. That well-worn word *intuition* here describes the specific, nonverbal mental processes of the mode minds as opposed to the verbal mental processes of the intellect. These intuitive capacities must be expanded, exercised, and developed with the help of the intellectual mind. Words are still our major means of communication with one another, however ambiguous, imprecise, reductionist, misleading, or generalizing they may be with respect to the three mode minds.

As we use our intellect in this process, we must be alert for the traps of prediction, judgment and overcontrol that are automatically called into play when using the intellect. The intellect will try to predict the outcome—the product that it wants to emerge—and then try to control the process by which that product is to be attained. In doing so, it blocks the intuitive flow of the three processes that create the product and diminishes the quality of that product. By trying to control the intuitive processes, the intellect reduces the complexity of their energies, robbing them of part of their flow and life. How to speak to all the issues surrounding this interrelationship between intuitive and intellectual resources—possibly the most fundamental challenge facing the performing artist—is the task of this book. How to develop the three intuitive minds and to coordinate their efforts, with the help but not the interference of the intellectual mind—that is the Zen of singer-actor performance.

Chapter 1
Exploring a New Description

I arrived at the concept of projective modes and their use in teaching actors and singer-actors during an exciting sequence of events that I find useful to review when approaching a new group with the concept. I focus on it and the performer-in-action with a "beginner's mind," just as I did in the initial explorations.

When first encountering the idea it may seem too simple, too pat, or almost a truism. It appears commonplace and lacking in intellectual depth, so that it is easy to wave it aside and miss its substance. The simplicity is deceptive, however, because the concept is foreign to the traditional way—the academic "method"—of perceiving the performance process.[1] Yet when the perception, diagnosis, and prescription of projective modes is practiced, it creates performer changes that are unique in my experience or in my observations of the work of others.

When working with the modes concept one is virtually compelled to perceive and describe in terms of process, which in turn may be perceived as a product at any given stage. For example, my own process of learning about the modes concept and its application to the performer is represented at one of its stages by the product that is this book. But the book is part of a continuing process that extends beyond itself—and must so extend for everyone who reads it if it is to be of any real use. This book must either become a part of your own process of exploring the modes concept or it is simply another product: stimulating and suggestive, but lacking the continuing development and fulfillment it could attain.

With that invitation to join the process, let us begin where it began in the fall of 1980. At that time I was teaching classes in acting and directing for music-theater at the University of Minnesota and singing-acting classes in the Minnesota Opera Studio training program. These classes were based on the philosophy and concepts I had developed before encountering the idea of the modes. I should stress that the point of view developed in my previous book, *The Complete Singer-Actor*, is not contradicted by the modes concept but rather given a new and powerful tool with which to work.

Mode Domination: How We Perceive the World

The theory of perceptual modes states that of the five major channels of input (or modes of perception) by which human beings receive information from the world about them—hearing, seeing, touching (body sensations in general, which I call kinesthetics), tasting, and smelling—the first three are the most important.[2] Hearing, seeing, and touching are our most significant sources of information about life in general, and particularly about other people. Interpersonal communication is almost totally governed by those three modes. Thus far, nothing in the concept creates any special interest. The trigger factor is the idea of mode dominance, which holds that human beings tend to favor one of the three modes of perception in processing information from their environment. They tend to perceive life dominantly either through what they see, what they hear, or what they touch (or kinesthetically feel). They learn or understand best if the information is communicated either visually, auditorily, or through physical-spatial means.

When learning to spell, the seeing mode child will *see* a word spelled and that will be sufficient. The hearing mode child will *hear* it spelled and understand. And the kinesthetic mode child will understand how to spell the word best by writing it out. The best teachers relate to all three modes in teaching spelling: writing it on the board, saying the spelling out loud, and asking the kinesthetic student to come up and write it on the board. The kinesthetic mode response may be empathetic: that is, the kinesthetic person may respond to another person's gestures or movements without actual touch, or may respond to a structure in space. For example, the kinesthetic student may understand how to spell a word by watching the teacher write it out physically. Each of us has a favored way of gaining information about the world around us, and if those communicating with us use a different way, we literally may not perceive the information. Some children are considered dullards by one teacher, but they blossom under another. The difference is often in the match or mismatch of the communicating mode of the teacher and the perceiving mode of the student.

When I first encountered this theory in the work of psychotherapists Richard Bandler and John Grinder, it seemed particularly relevant to my work as an opera director.[3] In the performing arts we have long known that audiences tend to divide into the music crowd (hearing mode dominants), the theater crowd (seeing mode dominants), and the dance crowd (kinesthetic mode dominants). Opera is not included in the division because it straddles the dominance issue depending upon who is doing the producing and who makes up the audience. The music crowd resents theatrically active stagings of opera because they interfere with their hearing mode interests; the theater crowd resents theatrically passive opera productions because they don't give them enough to "see."[4] It is a relatively small audience that is able to integrate their modes of perception, appreciating each separately or in combination and enjoying the complexity of interplay among them.

The theory made me more tolerant of opera audiences and critics who were unable to absorb the difficulties of a totally conceived opera production. Those who attend opera consistently tend to be made up of hearing mode dominants for whom visual meanings are simply an interference with their favorite mode of perception. The leading conductor and artistic director of a major opera company was quoted as saying he didn't have time to worry greatly about "the visuals," meaning the acting and scenic elements. And sometimes those who resent "the visuals" are correct. Theatrical action and musical action are obviously unintegrated in some productions, each making separate statements that interfere with each other, and with audience perceptions. But the real problem occurs when the same annoyed audiences and critics are confronted with a production in which the integration *has* been thought through and carried out. Because the new, integrated experience is still a complex one, demanding an interplay of perceptual capacities, it is rejected on the same basis as the previous, unintegrated one: that there is simply "too much visual distraction, too much action."

We could, of course, view the problem of unsympathetic audience dominance as another kind of handicap. One cannot blame a blind person for not appreciating a picture, or a deaf person for not appreciating a symphony. In the same way, one cannot blame a kinesthetic dominant for not being strongly responsive to a nonrhythmic, nonkinesthetic piece of music, a seeing dominant for not finding compensating pleasure in the music of opera when visual excitement is lacking, nor a hearing dominant for being offended by what is perceived as visual distraction while trying to listen to some beautiful operatic music. It is a matter of helping the audience develop its integrative capacities over a period of time so that they may come to enjoy the greater complexity of perception involved. In my experience with opera audiences, once the perceptual modes have attained a higher capacity of integration in perceiving opera, the audiences are no longer satisfied with a less complex substitute. Operatic performance that is only a hearing mode experience is simply not sufficient when one is able to integrate all the modes of perception. While this may be gratifying to proponents of total music-theater experience on the operatic stage, there is no clear way of helping audiences to attain that higher level of perceptual integration except to encourage them to keep trying and to provide them with productions that allow them to do so—sometimes against their wishes.

ANECDOTE: As I write this, during the run of an opera I directed (Carmen), I am struck by a perfect example of mode dominance affecting the judgment of the audience and critics. This performance was in the Guthrie Theater in Minneapolis, Minnesota. The theater has a thrust stage that places the performers almost literally in the laps of the audience. As a result, there is a much stronger emphasis on the kinesthetic and seeing modes than is usual in opera.

The tenor was tall, handsome, and well built. He was singing the role of Don Jose for the first time and experienced some vocal difficulty in doing so. The audience in Minneapolis, a city with a striking amount of good theater available, has a great many seeing and kinesthetic dominants—or at least audience members who have been trained by experience to demand good work in those modes. Although the tenor was having vocal problems, the audience gave him as strong an ovation as anyone, including Carmen, who gave an outstanding performance both vocally and dramatically. It was as though a great many members of the audience liked so much what they saw and what they kinesthetically felt that they also heard what they saw and felt, or at least were able to ignore what they heard because of the other pleasures.

The critics, on the other hand, who were hearing mode dominants—the usual case with opera critics—roasted the tenor for what they heard as vocal inadequacy. Because they literally did not respond to what the seeing and kinesthetic dominants did, that aspect of the total performance could not affect their judgment.

Neither group was perceiving the whole truth.

From the mode dominance perspective, it was fascinating to be approached by bewildered audience members who genuinely enjoyed the performance of the tenor and simply could not understand the vituperation of the critics. The critics might have been equally puzzled, though possibly a bit disdainful, had they discussed the issue with those same audience members.

In time, I hope it will be possible to enjoy opera critics who have integrated their perceptual modes and who are capable of responding as sensitively with their eyes and their kinesthetic senses as with their ears; and to have audiences who have achieved the same integration whatever their original mode dominance. This kind of deficit training *(see below), although peripheral to our work with the performer, could do more to increase audience size for what is glibly called total music-theater than all the publicity in the world.*[5]

Matching Projection with Perception

Although the modes concept clarified audience responses to opera and music theater, it was not the primary issue. The real interest for me lay in the relationship of the concept to the performer. Like the teacher of spelling, the performer should be concerned about communicating with everyone in the audience, not just those who share mode dominance. One does not have the option of labeling an audience member inadequate or lacking in intelligence because that member does not perceive our messages—unlike the unfortunate child who *is* often labeled when his or her mode makeup does not match that of the teacher. Instead, the performer should try to expand the scope of communication to relate to all perceptual modes. If this is the case, are there modes of *projection* matching the modes of perception? If so, does the concept of mode dominance apply to these projective modes as well?

Let us first try to identify the projective mode equivalent for each perceptual mode. Two of the hypothetical projective modes are fairly easy to define. For the hearing mode the projective equivalent is the voice, whether speaking, singing, or making nonverbal sounds. For the kinesthetic mode, the projective equivalent is the movement of the body and its appendages, which are seen and responded to empathetically by the viewer. (Touch, except as empathetically perceived, can be omitted in considering the performing arts because performers rarely touch anyone in an audience and cannot rely on touch as an important means of audience communication.) That leaves us with the seeing mode and its projective equivalent. If we wish to project to an audience that is seeing mode dominant, what are the means we would use to do so?

The hearing mode deals with all the sounds that are made with the voice and heard by the ears. The kinesthetic mode deals with all the information seen with the eyes that is communicated by the body and its appendanges through physical stance, head and torso movements, and movements of the body through space. Any communicating resources left over necessarily involve the seeing mode. Of those resources only the face and the eyes remain, which clearly deal with the communication of thought processes and emotion independently of body and voice. If it is possible for the face to communicate without any physical or vocal contribution, then it must be considered as a separate communicating channel. While it is true that facial musculature and eyes communicate through physical movement as well as stillness (and thus are technically part of the kinesthetic system as a whole), the gross movement messages of the body—from the arms, the shoulders, the legs, and even the head—are distinct from the messages that are communicated by the face alone.

Anyone encountering this concept for the first time will doubtless raise the same questions that my students and I did when we first considered it. But we noted that it did have the virtue of corresponding to my previous classification of the three components of singing-acting communication: the physical, the emotional, and the vocal. Translating that concept to the new terminology, the physical component is now the kinesthetic mode, the vocal component is the hearing/vocal mode, and the emotional component acquires for the first time a specific means of projection, designated as the facial/emotional mode. The emotional component had been undefined projectively and was a generalized term for an internal process that one talked about but that was too elusive to discuss clearly. That may be why it took us so long to agree upon a defini-

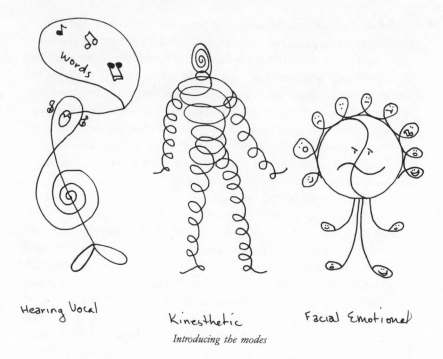

Hearing Vocal   Kinesthetic   Facial Emotional

Introducing the modes

tion of the facial/emotional mode: we all had definitions, but none of them were specific enough to talk about. It took weeks of discussion and debate before continued observation of performance convinced us all that the concept made sense and was useful in creating growth in the performer.

One of the difficulties in arriving at a projective equivalent of the seeing mode was that both the kinesthetic mode and the newly designated facial/emotional mode are perceived with the eyes. We see an actor's face with our eyes, which is also the way we perceive a dancer's body. But we understand the dancer kinesthetically, translating the kinesthetic messages (with the aid of words, music, and context) into emotional meanings, and we understand the actor's face emotionally. The dancer's communication may also involve emotion, but that conclusion is based on information separate from the kinesthetic message itself. We respond to dance with kinesthetic empathy, and we respond to an actor's face with emotional empathy. More specifically, it is clearly possible to separate the messages delivered by each of the two systems, which is, in fact, what clearly identifies them as separate communicating systems. The face may be sending intense emotional messages while the body is in a state of passivity, neutrality, or readiness; and the body can be going through astonishing displays of power and flexibility while the face remains in a relatively passive, neutral, or ready condition.

An actress in a full-body cast with only the face exposed can send messages of grief and anger (or joy and excitement, or anything.) A classical ballet dancer can seem to defy gravity and physical logic with his body, while his face is capable of remaining poised and even masklike. Although we perceive both sets of messages with the eyes, the sending, projecting systems are clearly separate. This does not mean that they operate independently as a natural tendency; it takes a great deal of training. But where the dancer's body with the isolated face is often a standard part of dancer training, the reverse is not true. The capacity of the face to send powerfully charged messages independently of the body has never, to my knowledge, been defined as a specific discipline to be learned. Yet, as we will see, it may be one of the most significant and vital aspects of the modes concept. There is a strong tendency for the kinesthetic mode to interfere with the facial/emotional mode in performance. One of our principal training efforts will be to help the performer achieve an independent but interrelating stance between those two modes.

Another obstacle to defining the facial/emotional mode is its relationship to traditional acting systems; this psychological obstacle is discussed at length in chapter 5. The modes concept treads upon a private preserve of American acting methods, a supersensitive area to be approached with extreme care from the inside only, while using a mind-reading point of view: "Play around with facial manipulation, with technical, emotional facial indicating and you risk being phony, insincere, and an actor who *mugs* — and that is the ultimate sin!" The warning, though perhaps not explicit, seems to have become a sanctified but unspecified command for actors everywhere. I trespassed into that hallowed area by focusing on the external, technical means of communicating emotion, calling it the facial/emotional mode and actually exercising it. But I was insistent (I had actually been trespassing there for years), and my students followed with growing enthusiasm as they saw that it not only made intellectual sense but also helped them become stronger, more believable communicators—and therefore better performers.

Having defined projective equivalents for the perceptual modes, a process that lasted several months in the actual exploration phase, let us return to the question of mode dominance as it relates to the projective modes. We can put that question another way for each mode.

If we are kinesthetically dominant in our perceptions, will we also favor communication with our kinesthetic system? If we are hearing mode dominant, will we also have a dominant need to communicate with our voice? If we are seeing mode dominant, will the face be our favored means of communication? I could only answer those questions by testing the concept in my classes and rehearsals (the laboratory described in the introduction) and by sharing the question-asking process with students in a mutual and continuing exploration. I invited the actors, singer-actors, and singers with whom I was working to continue the dialogue as we investigated the implications of the modes concept in action.

We began by trying to understand our personal perceptual dominances. We exchanged insights, compared anecdotal evidence, and took tests devised to ascertain perceptual mode dominance.

ANECDOTE: While attempting to determine our individual mode makeup, a group of students from the class were discussing course offerings in the university catalogue. A student said, "Here's a course in writing about the nonverbal arts—what would that be about?" One of the group replied that it would be about music, another thought it would be about dance, and a third thought it would be about painting. As a group, they suddenly realized that the three opinions were those of a hearing dominant, a kinesthetic dominant, and a seeing dominant, respectively. Their mode dominance had made their interpretations for them, although their intellect had seemed to be the source. As it turned out, the mode dominance indicated by these reactions was verified in class exercises with the projective modes.

With the heightened awareness gained by this self-examination, we began observing performance exercises to ascertain mode dominance in the projective modes. At first we simply tried to connect a performer's perceptual mode dominance with what we were able to perceive in that person's performance. If a performer with a perceptual kinesthetic dominance performed a monologue, we simply watched for what that might mean in the performance. It was remarkable to sense the expansion of awareness made available by the concept. It gave us all a new set of perceptions with which to watch, to listen to, and to feel a performance. The insights came too rapidly to record in detail, but that was of little importance: lists of ideas are of less significance than the process of observation. The modes concept is a perceptual tool for the increased awareness of performance. Performance itself is a process, and each observation with a new perceptual tool is also a process. There are no hard and fast rules, only an ever-increasing specificity and flexibility of awareness in describing the performer's uses of energy. It has been my experience that the insights keep recurring, but always in a new context that gives them fresh meaning.

As we had suspected at the beginning of our performance observation, perceptual and projective dominance tend to be the same in any individual. A hearing mode dominant will tend to be a hearing/vocal mode dominant.

ANECDOTE: One of the means of determining the dominant mode of perception is how one relates to tiny babies. Does one make faces at them? (Seeing mode) Does one make sounds at them? (Hearing mode) Or does one reach out and touch them? (Kinesthetic mode) One may do all three, of course, but one of them is a more immediate urge.

This was a key question for me in determining my own dominance, which happens to be kinesthetic. In mentioning to a group of young singers that my own immediate urge is to touch the baby and that that was an indication of kinesthetic dominance, one of them seemed startled and said, "That's what I do, I always want to reach out and touch my little baby boy." He may have been startled because most singers tend to think of themselves as hearing mode dominants, feeling perhaps that being singers they should be.

Whatever the case, the startled young singer also happened to have a long-standing problem with gestural tension. His arms seemed to insist upon reaching out in a tense and awkward manner while he was singing, regardless of the subject matter of the song or the appropriateness of the gesture. He had been told about the problem, he was aware of it, and had been repeatedly reminded of it, but he seemed unable to do anything about it.

It seemed likely that he was a kinesthetic dominant, given the need to do something all the time he was singing and his reaction to the baby test. I explained to him that because of that dominance, he had a need to communicate physically while singing, but that the means he chose were not always appropriate and often were counterproductive. I then asked him if, knowing that, he could ask the kinesthetic mode to turn the communication burden over to the hearing/vocal mode and allow it to do the work. And somehow, now that he had a reason for the insistent behavior of his arms and body and could understand the possible cause of it all, he was able to sing an aria without the annoying gesture tension for the first time in his life. In one brief session, with the aid of the modes concept, he made greater progress than he had made all year.

But we soon realized that it really made no difference whether there was a direct correlation between perceptual and projective dominance. One could identify the performer's projective dominance by observing the performance, and performance was our main concern. It makes little difference whether the performer is a seeing mode dominant perceptually

but a kinesthetic dominant projectively because our interest is performance behavior, not perceptual orientation. If, on the other hand, a consistent, positive correlation can be established between perceptual and
projective dominance, it might speed the process of identification and
change. In fact, a high correlation appears to be present, which provides
a positive answer to our question about correspondence between perceptual and projective dominance.

Developing the Weaker Modes

Another question emerged from the exploratory process, suggested by
the classroom spelling lesson in which a teacher tries to reach children of
all mode dominances. If each child is assumed to have a dominant mode,
there are, by implication, two weaker modes. If that idea is true for the
projective modes as well, performers will have a stronger, dominant mode
and two weaker modes that are less likely to be used. A person who is
a hearing/vocal dominant may be less likely to use the kinesthetic or
facial/emotional modes in communicating. Or, to put it another way, if
we do not perceive kinesthetic messages as our favored mode, we may be
less likely to use the kinesthetic mode to send messages.

The weaker projective modes, however, are much easier to determine
than the weaker peceptual modes. The emphasis is also very different. An
educator tries to determine the dominant perceptual mode of each child
so that the proper mode can be used to communicate with that child.
That approach plays to the child's perceptual strength and leaves the
weaknesses as they are. But our concern is the reverse: we want to determine the performer's dominant projective mode so that we can develop
the weaker modes. A good performance implies balance between the
projective modes, each communicating with comparable power. Educators may have tried this approach with perceptual modes, strengthening
the weaker ones through deficit training, but the training has not been
successful, and the stress has shifted to teaching methods that relate to
all three perceptual modes and thus reach all the children.

We came to see, however, that deficit training for the projective
modes was absolutely vital. Instead of accepting the projective weakness

and compensating for it, we tried to help the performer expand and strengthen the weaker modes as well as the total mode system. This preparation would allow the performer to communicate with everyone in the audience and to play any character, not just modal duplicates of one's self. The performer is his or her own instrument, able to develop the capabilities of that instrument. We must accept the perceptual limitations of the audience, but we can take charge of the development of our projective modes. This is an idealistic challenge, but experience has demonstrated its feasibility. Growth and change are possible to a degree I had not imagined.

But why is it possible to develop the projective modes when it has been so difficult to develop the perceptual modes? One answer may be that we *do* nothing in order to perceive—that is, we do nothing overt or manipulative. We simply see, hear, and *feel*, but we don't seem to be *doing* these things or performing a special act to accomplish them. The process of perception is largely unconscious and therefore difficult to alter. But we *do* things to use the projective modes: we move our arms, our heads, our torso, we move through space, we make a variety of sounds with our voice, and we use our face in varying ways to communicate feelings and thought processes. We do these things consciously—or can learn to do them consciously—and can therefore become increasingly aware of how we do them. Drawing on that awareness, we can alter the way we do those things. What we can define in action, we can change; but we have great difficulty changing what we cannot define in action, and perception is difficult to define in that way.

We should thus be able to create projective exercises that would change the perceptual system and educate audiences (as well as critics) so they would develop integrated perceptual modes. My students and I certainly have found our perceptions expanding in significant ways as we worked projectively with the modes concept; by concentrating on the understanding of projective modes, we found ourselves perceiving life and performance in new, expanded ways.

The director-actor interplay of perceptions and projections is an important consideration in expanding mode capacities. The director is first the perceiver and the actor is the projector. But this relationship reverses when the director comments on what the actor has done and becomes the projector, at which point the actor becomes the perceiver. The director perceives in a certain way because of his or her perceptual makeup and then speaks to the performer in terms of that makeup; but if the performer has a different mode makeup, the response arises from perceptions that are consistent with that performer's own makeup. It is the teacher-student spelling lesson all over again: coaches, conductors, teachers, and directors can all benefit from awareness of their own perceptual and projective systems as they work with performers and students.

ANECDOTE: A coach took a class in singing-acting from me after having played for several of my other classes. He felt that he must get to know what performance was like from the other side of the piano. It was extraordinary having him in class, and his insights were compelling to us all. He commented almost immediately that those exercises oriented to the development of the seeing mode (and the facial/emotional mode) were extremely difficult — "It feels like learning to walk all over again." And when he was performing, his hands kept wanting to express themselves just as they did when he was playing the piano. The best part of all was that he did not feel defensive about his underdeveloped seeing-facial-emotional modes, nor about his ineffectively active kinesthetic mode. Neither did we feel judgmental about it. They were simply capacities to be exercised and developed. Would that all coaches, directors (there was also a director in the class who had done little performing and she too was an inspiration to the singers), and, yes, conductors would place themselves in that kind of open learning situation with respect to the art of singing-acting.

A long speech of instruction delivered to a kinesthetic dominant performer will accomplish little except boredom on the performer's part and an inevitable misunderstanding and mistranslation of a large share of those verbal instructions. Conversely, a kinesthetic demonstration to a hearing mode dominant may similarly misfire and even lead to active antagonism. Communications from one channel are not picked up by the intended receiver because that person is tuned to a different channel.

Mode mismatches probably produce more missed communication in theater and in life than any other factor. It is comparable to the wife who is hearing mode dominant who says that her husband doesn't love her, even though he hugs and caresses her, because "He doesn't *tell* me he loves me." Or the reverse: the husband who is hearing mode dominant who tells his kinesthetic wife repeatedly that he loves her but doesn't show it physically, so she doesn't believe it either.

This phenomenon occurs constantly when a scene is performed and is followed by comments from the class. The reactions of the observers run the gamut of opinions, some relating to the voice, some to the feelings, others to the physical energies of the scene. The teacher is then supposed to select the appropriate options from all these divergencies because his or her perceptions are supposed to be the 'correct' ones. And those of us in the position of group leader sometimes fall into the trap of thinking that we *are* always on the mark. How often I have attributed the inability of students to perceive what I did in a scene to a lack of training, sophistication, or perception on their part. It was indeed the last of these, but not in the way I had always thought; for though they may have been weak in a perceptual area in which I was strong, the reverse is true in other modes. We sometimes think of people as dull, obstinate, or imperceptive when they do not relate to the same thing we do in a performance. It has now become a fascinating exercise to try to understand the mode makeup and dominance that is responsible for a student's reaction (or for audience reactions in general) to a performance. Students and performers can become *our* teachers in the best sense of that word. Instead of bemoaning their lack of insight, teachers can search for the insight and perception in them that can help develop our own. If they do miss a significant point, it presents an opportunity to help them perceive what they missed by appropriate exercise of our own projective channels. It is also instructive to sort out and improve the projective and perceptual matches between directors and performers.

*ANECDOTE: On two separate occasions about a week apart, a
director in my Acting for Music Theater class made
kinesthetically oriented suggestions to actresses performing eighteenth-century soliloquies. One actress was
a kinesthetic dominant (although we were not aware of
that at the time) whom we were trying to help to a
stronger language musicality: more vocal variety, more
changes of process in pitch, rhythm, and speed. But no
matter what kind of musicality we asked for, nothing
really changed. Then the director in question suggested
that she play the role like a hip-swinging slut. Everything changed for the better, including the language
problem we had been addressing directly.*

    *A week later, another actress (a hearing/vocal
dominant, as it later turned out) was having what
seemed to be facial/emotional communication prob-.
lems. Again, we were addressing that issue directly with
little success. The same director made another kinesthetic character suggestion—this time that of a bounc-
ing, fluttering, high-spirited soubrette. But this time
the suggestion made absolutely no difference in the
performance. It was not until we determined that the
actress was a hearing/vocal dominant and isolated that
mode (a procedure to be covered in chap. 4) that any
real change occurred and genuine growth became possible.*

In both instances, the director was speaking from his dominant
kinesthetic mode. When he spoke to a similarly dominant actor, the
communication was successful and created exciting change. But when he
spoke in the same way to a hearing/vocal dominant, no connection was
made and there was no change. When there is no connection, directors
who do not make an adjustment in their projective mode communication
are left with two choices: repeat the suggestion with variations using the
same projective mode makeup, or give up, condemning the actor men-

tally or audibly as an incompetent. Actors in a similar state of frustration, being told what they were doing as performers but unable to quite perceive what the message is, will either suffer silently, defend themselves, or give up.

ANECDOTE: Shortly after writing that sentence, I encountered a very gifted young actor who had been working at one of the country's leading regional theaters under the direction of an internationally known director-designer. When I asked the actor about the state of things at the theater, he replied, "Oh, Mr. X [the director] and I don't work together anymore. I told him that if I had wanted to be an acrobat I would have joined Ringling Brothers." I commiserated with the actor and found that instead of acting he was teaching in a small college. Not that there is anything wrong with teaching in a small college (I would be the last to impugn the idea of teaching acting), but this particular person was a brilliant professional actor who should have been practicing his art as well as teaching. How sad, I thought, that a simple matter of mode makeup and dominance should lead two brilliant theater talents to go separate ways rather than blending their gifts. For the director-designer was a European kinesthetic dominant with seemingly little concern for the hearing/vocal mode (his productions, although usually visually brilliant, were marred by a shouting, insensitive use of the language) and the actor was an American facial/emotional dominant who also possessed excellent hearing/vocal capacities, which is rare for American actors. The two had never connected, and neither seemed to understand why. If the actor had been able to understand the gap, and then treat the working relationship as an opportunity to expand his own mode capabilities, to develop flexibility of mode interrelationships and sense-making mode capacities, not only would he have enjoyed the

work (and still been employed in his art) but he would
have grown as a performer.

Early in our exploration, we realized that there is a relationship between the instrument potential of the mode, skill in the mode, and mode dominance. One can have the instrument potential, in terms of a well-proportioned, well-coordinated and attractive body; or a strong, wide-ranging, and attractive voice; or a compelling, strongly communicative and attractive face. One may also be dominant in any of these areas, in having the urge to express oneself through the body, the voice, or the face. Finally, one can develop the skill to use any of these three communicating instruments. The accompanying chart expresses this relationship.

Instrument	Dominance	Skill
Body	Kinesthetic: Urge to communicate physically	Physical training, dance, ballet, tai chi chuan, martial arts, acrobatics, gymnastics, etc.
Voice	Hearing/vocal: Urge to communicate with voice by speaking or singing	Musical coaching, voice lessons, diction, rhetoric, speech classes, etc.
Face	Facial/emotional: Urge to communicate emotionally with the face and eyes	Acting lessons, therapeutic work involving the expression of emotion, opening of the personality, etc.

Clearly, the three factors are not necessarily related. Dominance in a projective mode, for example, does not mean that one will have the appropriate instrument or skill to project the dominance. One can be fat and ungainly (with neither the instrument potential nor the skill) and still have a dominant urge to express one's self kinesthetically. (One is reminded of the dance of the hippopotamuses in Walt Disney's *Fantasia*.) Or one can have a superb, natural voice (instrument potential) without being a hearing/vocal dominant, or without the skill training to use that instrument. (I once heard a brilliant operatic tenor voice coming from a gymnasium. But when I investigated, I found that it was the hockey coach yelling at his players. A wonderful hearing/vocal instrument potential trapped inside a kinesthetic dominant). Or one can have the

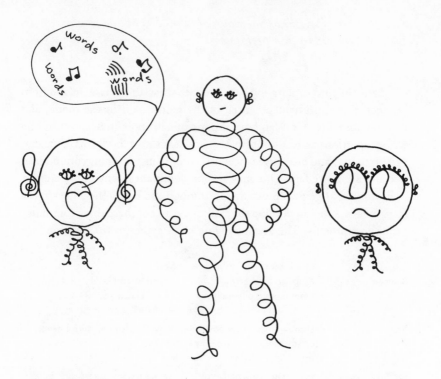

urge to express one's self through the facial and emotional resources without those resources being naturally communicative — they are sometimes trained by life experiences to be neutral or passive — and without the skill training to use the existing resources effectively. (I am reminded of the many actresses I have known whose eyes simply burn with emotion, but whose face as a whole remains relatively neutral.)

There are any number of other possible combinations of instrument potential, dominance, and skill. One can have the instrument potential with or without either the dominance or the skill; one can have the skill with or without either the instrument potential or the dominance; and one can have the dominance with or without either the instrument potential or the skill. Some singers with glorious natural voices (instrument potential) have no musicianship (no dominance) and must labor to acquire the musical or vocal skills to become an artist. Some pretty faces (instrument potential) seem to express nothing with them (no dominance) and must work at developing their expressive skills.

ANECDOTE: A young woman in one of my classes was the daughter of a well-known choreographer-dancer. The young woman had a fine dancer's body — a good instrument potential. She also had a great deal of training in dance and ballet — a good level of acquired kinesthetic skill. But she chose to be an actress against her mother's wishes and contrary to her seeming capabilities. Only when she learned that she was strongly dominant in the hearing/vocal mode did she realize why she had gone against her mother's wishes and become an actress rather than a dancer. Although she was not aware of it at the time she made the decision, her dominant projective mode was making it for her.

The Performer as an Individual

I suggested in the Introduction that the concept of modes helps to liberate performers from the judgmental treadmill. In the educational world, judgment, overcontrol, trying to do it right, obeying the tyrannical "shoulds" of art are the greatest barriers to genuine growth and creative use of energies. Somehow, using the concept of modes to deal with, talk about, and perceive the use of the physical, the emotional, and the vocal energies is remarkably liberating. Why?

One of the reasons I suggested was its power of specific description. One avoids judgmental inference by describing an action with total specificity. But perhaps there is another reason for the freeing quality of the modes concept. It could be the way it relates to each person as an individual. We pay universal lip service to that ideal, of course, but it is seldom practiced. We talk about "individual differences" and "personal needs" and the desirability of relating to each person's unique talents and abilities. In spite of this, however, teaching often becomes an imposition of generalized patterns on all individuals regardless of proper fit. Even more significantly, much subject matter is taught from the perspective of one mode only, depending on the dominance of the instructor. For example, in an acting class the kinesthetic mode teacher relates everything to the physical, the hearing vocal mode dominant to the voice, and the facial emotional mode dominant to the "inner feelings." Each approach relates to only a portion of the class.

Most acting classes that I have attended or observed tend to speak to actors as though they were all the same, as though they all functioned as communicating human beings in the same general way. Everyone was expected to think about or deal with the problems of acting in much the same way. They had to have a mental image that informed their acting, or they all had to "feel it." The image approach seems to relate to the facial/emotional mode via a seeing mode visualization, while the "feel it" technique tends to promote an entanglement of the kinesthetic and the other two modes.

When I began teaching, my classes followed the same pattern. I talked about the singing-acting problem from the perspective of my own mode makeup. But I was soon forced out of that rut by the fact that my classes covered a much broader range of pure technique and stylistic challenge than is customary in American acting classes. I had to deal with everything from opera singing to naturalistic acting. Nonetheless, I still approached my students as though they were homogeneous in their way of perceiving, as though they shared my mode makeup and dominance. The modes concept changed that. I became aware of perceptual mode dominance and how it filters and defines not only *what* one is able to perceive and *how* one perceives it, but also the effect it has on the way one communicates with others. I was compelled to be specific with actors in entirely new ways—ways that have proved to be clearer in understanding, easier to work with, and less likely to become judgmentally threatening than any method I had previously encountered.

I can no longer talk in the same way to all performers, nor to insist on the specific way a performer should think about the problem of performing. I have learned to recognize and avoid the mind-reading approach, in which actors are either told what they were thinking as they were acting a scene, or what they should be thinking if they want to act it better. Instead of enforcing any point of view on an entire class, I have changed to an individual approach: learn the nature of each actor's mode makeup and exercise that makeup according to its needs, strengthening the weaker modes and developing their cooperative relationship. To approach all students in the same way is to impose a generalization on the specifics of life. Generalization has been called the greatest enemy of good performance; it may also be the greatest deterrent to the teaching of performance. If so, the modes concept offers a superb tool for fine-tuned specificity.

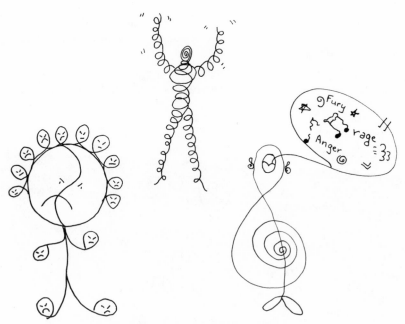

Mode cooperation-negative messages

The modes may either cooperate or interfere with one another in communicating. Cooperation can work in several ways. All modes can function simultaneously, sending messages that are in agreement—all sad, all happy, all neutral. Well-timed gestures that punctuate and clarify verbal statements, or smiles that accompany a warm greeting are other examples of mode cooperation. Another kind of cooperation is mode readiness: one mode does the communicating while the other two remain ready to assist at any time, yet communicating nothing specific beyond the capability of action. An example would be the voice speaking threatening words in an angry way while the face and body remain poised for action, neither tense nor totally relaxed, but ready to funciton at an instant.

The other side of cooperation is interference between modes, which is literally that: one mode blocking or distorting the communication of another. An example is the actor allowing the kinesthetic mode to gesticulate so wildly that the listeners cannot understand what is being said. Interference can also be created if the kinesthetic mode tries to communicate through the medium of another mode, creating vocal or facial tension in the process.

I will also use the term *entanglement* to describe the habitual and mostly unconscious relationship between the modes that draws them all

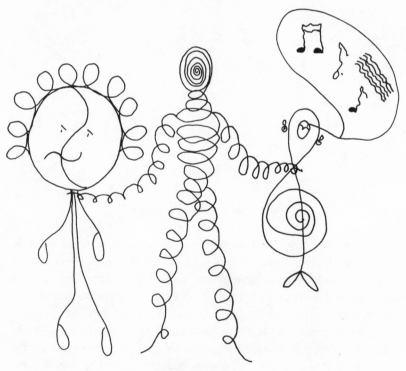

Kinesthetic interference

into play when one of them goes into action. As small children, we are deeply entangled: when we are excited, everything is excited, and use of one projective mode inevitably calls the others into play. As we mature, this projective mode entanglement becomes untangled to varying degrees depending upon environment and awareness. But virtually everyone remains entangled to some extent, and it is this entanglement that creates the interferences and blocks when singing-acting (or any other strong use of projective energies) is attempted. Bringing to awareness and releasing those entanglements in each performer is an integral part of the growth process.

In chapter 7, I explore the concept of congruency or incongruency between modes. For now, we can see that the possibilities of mode interplay can be either voluntary or involuntary, conscious or unconscious, on the part of the person communicating, but the professional communicator must make them conscious and voluntary. The difference between the artist for whom communication is an art and the ordinary person who simply communicates (or fails to do so) as a matter of acquired habit lies largely in the capacity to make a greater number of choices among communicating possibilities. All the potential of the interrelating system of modes and meanings should be made available for the artist's communicating needs. In rehearsal, the performer must be able to make choices from the total gamut of possibilities and create a performance from those choices. Few actually attain this ideal, but the attempt leads to continual growth. The modes concept offers a systematic way of approaching the choice-making challenge. By perceiving the three modes as three separate and independent ways to send messages, rather than one interlocked gestalt, a vast range of choices is made available. By making a different choice for one system, we are affecting all the other systems. A choice made in the kinesthetic mode, for example, alters the possibilities available to the other modes. We set up a creative flow of choices by accepting the idea of three separate but interrelated processes.

All these ideas—the development of weak modes, cooperation, interference, congruency and incongruency—stem directly from the concept of mode dominance. By giving rise to new ideas, the modes concept becomes freshly compelling. It has certainly been the chief stimulus to self-examination for me and many of the performers with whom I work.

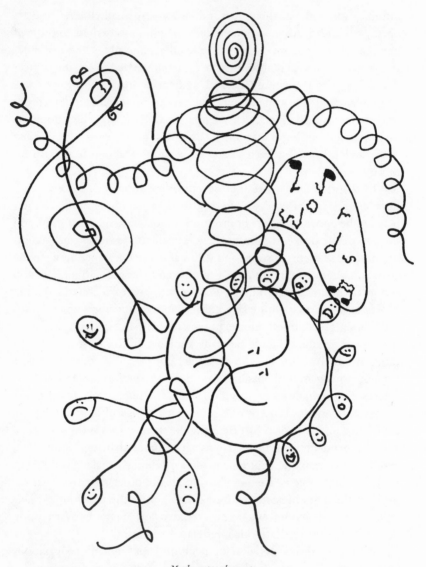

Mode entanglement

ANECDOTE: *Although I am a kinesthetic dominant, many
years of helping actors and singer-actors work with the
body, the voice, and the emotions in various combina-*

tions have helped me to integrate my three modes on the perceptual level. I have had to develop my perceptual capacities in each area in order to teach and direct effectively. Although this integration is less advanced for my projective modes, it has taken a greap leap forward since I began working with the modes concept. (I wish I had been able to work with the concept when I was singing and acting.)

When I realized that I was kinesthetically dominant, it illuminated the reasons for many of what I thought were simply personal choices. My directing, for example, has always been characterized by a great deal of physical communication, and I have a strong need to understand theater and music-theater through the physical. As a performer, my dominant need to communicate kinesthetically interfered with my vocal efforts, creating tension in the voice that was occasionally extremely harmful. At the time, the tension seemed necessary (on a nonverbal level) to communicate the emotion more strongly. I can still recapture the feeling of physical tension that my kinesthetic mode generated during attempts to make a Shakespearean line "feel" right to me. I also remember too well the way my singing voice was damaged in the process — cracking at a most embarrassing time doing a solo in a Christmas concert less than a month after the play closed.

My long-term awareness of physical tension as an interfering factor for singers and actors is a result of kinesthetic, perceptual, and projective dominance. Knowledge of that dominance began to free me from my kinesthetic interference with voice and face the day I realized it. It takes practice, persistence, and patience (the three P's of growth, as I tell my classes), but once the mode awareness is set in motion, the performer (and the person) is put in charge of his or her own evolution as a communicator. No longer a captive of habit,

circumstances, and history, the performer has been
given the tools with which to become an artist — simply
the ability to make whatever choices are desired in cre-
ating a performance. The first step in achieving that
ability is awareness of one's mode makeup, the second
is balancing the strength of the three modes, and the
third is developing their interrelating capacities.

Mode Dominance in Acting Systems

As explorations proceeded in my classes, we began reexamining acting
theories in light of the modes concept. Awareness of one's personal mode
makeup and the habitual uses of one's communicating energies are often
obscured in an acting class by what one "thinks" one should be doing (or
saying or seeing.) Acting systems in general insist upon ways of viewing
the performer that isolate certain values, ignore others, and place a negative judgment on still others. By the time my students encounter the
mode's concept, they have usually had years of acting training and performance that have established firm attitudes about what acting should be
and do. Acting systems in themselves are strongly oriented to one of the
modes. Each system concentrates heavily if not exclusively on the factors
that relate to its dominance. As a result, actors dominant in one of the
other two modes are frustrated and less effective than they might be.

The American adaptation of the Stanislavski system is a case in point.
According to those who specialize in such things, America has been described as a nation that is dominant in the seeing mode; the equivalent
projective mode is the facial/emotional mode. When American acting
teachers first became acquainted with the Stanislavski method, they re-
lied almost exclusively on his first book, *An Actor Prepares*, which stresses
the internal emotional life of the character in almost mystical ways. This
revelation to the American acting tradition took place in the 1930s and
was not balanced until years later by the second and third volumes in the
series. As a result the first book was treated as a total system in itself,
producing a method that dovetailed neatly with the increasing American
interest in theatrical realism and naturalism. It also coincided with the

mushrooming popularity of movies, which are par excellence a seeing mode medium. Both cinematic acting and naturalistic stage acting stress personal, nontechnical emotional performances that have relatively little concern for the kinesthetic and hearing/vocal modes. They depend instead almost entirely upon the facial/emotional message system, which was addressed specifically by that first volume.

Although only a branch of the total system was grafted onto the American tree, it soon blossomed into the phenomenal success of the Actor's Studio, through which many important actors have passed. Whether their talent was nurtured by the passage could be questioned, but for years it was the place to study naturalistic performance in New York, and any performer who was anybody at all had to have been there. One should not blame Lee Strasberg, who constantly fought for a more complex view of the Method than its more facile proponents, but there is no question that the important aspects of Stanislavski's work were and are largely ignored in practice by the American acting tradition. Stanislavski's later investigations of the acting problem (part of *his* continuing process of exploration) dealt at length with the use and development of the kinesthetic and hearing/vocal modes. But the Americans who brought us the Stanislavski Method perceived only what their mode dominance permitted, or perhaps what the cultural mode dominance found aesthetically and commercially acceptable. They created a method that still fails to deal adequately with hearing/vocal and kinesthetic mode skills.[6]

We are not concerned, however, with attacking or replacing other systems. The modes concept is not an acting method, nor is it a path in itself; it is conceived as an aid to all acting approaches, allowing each to do more effectively and powerfully what they wish to do. No matter what the style or the aesthetic point of view, we found as we explored the modes in action that they could be applied to any and all approaches.

←Start

Chapter 2
Determining Mode Makeup

Our century has been labeled in many ways: the age of anxiety, of the bomb, of technology, of the computer, of communications, and the like. It could also be called the "know thyself" century. There has never been a time when so many people have spent so much time trying to figure out who they really are. Every magazine has a test to determine something about one's self: aptitude, lovability, intelligence, stress quotient, happiness quotient, health, quality of diet, artistic capability, and so on and on. The century was initiated by several practitioners of intense self-analysis, which changed the way we think about ourselves. Freud is perhaps the best known of these. His self-analysis established a view of the mind that has changed human consciousness. Dozens of other psychological offshoots have sprung up in response to Freud's impetus and continue to evolve today. F. Mathias Alexander did the same thing for the physical being, spending seven years simply analyzing the way his physical being worked by observing himself in a three-way mirror as he spoke the words of Shakespeare. From his analysis he evolved the Alexander Technique for psychophysical reeducation, which is a significant method for the performing artist as well as human beings in general.[1] The technique also became part of a continuing exploration by psychoanalysis of how we function physically, giving us such methods as Rolfing, Feldenkrais, Bio-energetics, Reichian Therapy, Trager, and others. Stanislavski analyzed his performance as an actor and explored acting as an offshoot of human behavior. In so doing, he established the basis for the many acting techniques that inform acting training today.

The modes concept is part of this overall effort to know ourselves better. Like most psychological and psychoanalytical explorations, the theory of perceptual modes help us to understand the way our mind works. We want to know *why* we behave as we do, which has placed the emphasis in the past on mind reading, on ferreting out the reasons behind the behavior. We have been continually fascinated by why we behave as we do, with the behavior itself being of lesser interest. The intellectual mystery about the *why* feeds the century's voracious intellectual appetite. Interest has grown in the *how* in past two decades, as in books on body language and in Desmond Morris's popular analyses of the comparative behavior of people and animals, but the dominant concern has remained with the why.[2]

By examining the concept of perceptual modes from the point of view of their projective parallels, we are placing the emphasis on the *how* rather than the *why*. But in analyzing the how of projective behavior, we must understand *why* we perceive what we do. The answer to that question lies in an understanding of our perceptual dominance and mode makeup. To deal effectively with the performers we observe as teachers, directors, and coaches, we must be able to perceive how their projective modes are functioning through an expansion of our own perceptual awareness.

Those of us who try to help performers also express our dominance in various ways. Eloise Ristad reveals the soul of a true kinesthetic dominant in her excellent book, *A Soprano on Her Head*. She may be a double dominant, because she is a music teacher, but she consistently gets at the problem of performance by finding ingenious kinesthetic exercises, and she suggests by implication that everyone is a closet kinesthetic. I have known many performers, however, who simply do not respond to that mode—it only made them work harder. I had to search instead for a way to free their unique mode makeup from kinesthetic interference. I do not deny the value of a strongly kinesthetic approach like Ristad's, but we can expand upon its concepts to relate to the needs of individuals in each of the modes.

As teachers-directors-coaches, our understanding of the projective modes of our students is also conditioned by our own perceptual mode makeup. The changes we make in our perceptual awareness as observers directly affects the potential changes the performers will be able to make in their projective capabilities. The relationship between the projective and perceptual modes is a system in itself: we help performers make changes in their projective mode systems in proportion to our perceptual awareness, and performers who heighten their perceptual awareness affect their projective awareness as well. Performers who realize that their projective performance growth is closely connected with the growth of their perceptual awareness make remarkable progress as performers. They also become excellent coaches of their fellow performers. The same principle is true for teachers-directors-coaches: they can help the performers with whom they are working in proportion to their increased perceptual awareness. Performers can become their own teachers on the same basis.

The interaction of the perceptual and projective modes is a two-way street that relates to both the why and the how of behavior. We behave as we do because of the conditioning of our perceptual makeup. We developed our behavior patterns from age one to age seven by imitating what we were able to perceive in others. Knowing the perceptual mode makeup that helped create our projective mode behavior allows us to begin altering that behavior; changing that behavior in turn begins subtle alterations in our perceptual capacities as well. For example, once we know we make certain choices because of kinesthetic dominance, we can make the behavioral choice of projecting in other modes with greater energy. As we do, we heighten our awareness of those modes as they are used by other people. It is a process of continual feedback.

To exercise our projective modes effectively, we must identify our mode makeup. Although identification can only take place person to person in an actual class situation, let us examine some of the principles behind it. Diagnosing the mode makeup of performers involves observation, discussion with them about their own sense of perceptual mode preference (which may not always be accurate), and tests that may provide clues. In the end, projective mode makeup is a complex and tangled human energy system that cannot easily be labeled or pigeonholed. It resembles a set of psychophysical fingerprints: each personal combination is unique, with differing strengths and interrelationships. Differences between combinations is both tangible and specific. Like fingerprints, there should be as little qualitative judgment as possible.

The identification of mode makeup is not as important as the attempt to do so. The process of analysis will do as much to heighten awareness and promote growth in both performers and directors as anything else. Because the process is the important thing, it is vital that the description of individual differences in mode makeup be nonjudgmental and nonpejorative.

The concept of mode dominance and makeup must stay flexible and playful with little categorizing and labeling. Performers are apt to take anything as criticism, even the suggestion that they may be dominant in a mode. It is like the old question that reflects a person's life attitude — Is the glass half full or half empty? Being a kinesthetic dominant means you are not a hearing/vocal dominant, and a singer can view this as a serious shortcoming; a dancer who was not a kinesthetic dominant might respond the same. As soon as labels come into the play, the half-empty syndrome arrives right along with them. Little should be made of the dominance issue, and much of the development of the total system. Mode dominance is what already is — a product; but development of the weaker modes, a balancing of the total system with a flexible interplay of all the modes, is what can be — a process that will continue to unfold the rest of one's life.

A testing device for elementary school children uses plastic shapes and memory of patterns to determine perceptual mode makeup. It is called the Swasse-Barbing modality testing kit, and one of its attractive aspects is the fact that its measurement of mode strengths always adds up to 100 percent. Thus, any combination of mode strengths or weaknesses is good. Each individual's mode personality is what it is, and no combination is superior or inferior on that basis. And we are seldom speaking of large differences in mode strengths; differences of more than 5 percent are regarded as significant. An individual is likely to have mode strengths varying, on a percentage basis, from 29 to 33 to 38 at most, with occasional 25-35-40 combinations. However, the Swasse-Barbing modality testing kit is less useful for adult performers than for elementary school children. In a class of university acting students, one attained a perfect score in all three modes. Yet it was evident from the student's work in class that she was not a triple dominant projectively, nor did her perceptions of acting and singing-acting performances reflect that unity and evenness.

Another significant distinction between perceptual and projective modes is how they can be tested. Perceptual mode evaluation is a mental process that can be written down and analyzed as in any other academic

testing situation. But projective mode evaluation depends on observation: the perceptual modes have to perceive the projective modes in action and come up with a description. Subjectivity thus enters the picture, making objective evaluation more difficult. Accurate description of the projective process becomes vital to compel objectivity and expand the objective awareness of those making the description. However accomplished, the purpose of the evaluation is to determine what the individual needs to do to develop individual performing power, which modes to strengthen and which mode relationships to release from interference. Once these two steps are accomplished, all three modes can be reintegrated as freely cooperating partners.

The diagnostic process should involve every member of the class, not merely the teacher-director-coach. I worked with a class in directing that met simultaneously with a class in singing-acting. This arrangement helped develop the communication process between actors and directors, as well as providing a broader range of diagnostic opinions. The more a performer uses the modes concept to heighten personal awareness of what other performers are doing (or not doing), the more that performer becomes aware of his or her own use of energy, how it is blocked, and what is possible as a performer. As teachers-directors-coaches are specific in describing what performers are doing and what they might be able to do, they facilitate change in those performers. Teaching-directing-coaching is a two-way communication process. If the teacher-director-coach is perceiving and projecting through a mode dominance that is unrecognized, that teacher's best work will be done with performers who are similarly oriented. Other performers will simply be frustrated: "He doesn't understand me!" (Translation: He doesn't hear what I hear, see what I feel, or respond to my kinesthetic statements.) Or, "I don't understand her!" (Translation: I don't see what she feels, hear what she hears, or respond to what she does kinesthetically.)

Almost all people who encounter the modes concept for the first time begin analyzing their own makeup immediately. It is vital for the teacher-director-coach to do so.

ANECDOTE: *It was a revelation to discover how my own kinesthetic dominance had influenced my teaching, my directing, and my communication processes. I have always had a strong tendency to overexplain concepts to classes, to repeat an explanation in different ways. Although I was aware of it, it kept happening. I regarded it as one of those bad habits I needed to kick. But I never did. Then one of my assistants (also a kinesthetic dominant) observed that I would stop talking when I received a kinesthetic signal from my students that told me that they understood. After discussing it with my classes, they quickly learned they could stop additional explanation (if it was not needed) by sending kines-*

*thetic signals of understanding — head nodding, agree-
ment masks, and the like. They also learned that they
could keep the talk going if they needed more explanation (or if they didn't want to perform) by giving kinesthetic signals of puzzlement, frowning masks, head
shaking, and the like. It was a small but very useful
awareness to have developed. And even though I knew
the technique of kinesthetic agreement was being used
to affect me, I still responded to it. Technique works as
communication even when we know it does not reflect
the inner subjective truth. We appreciate and respond
to a technically genuine smile even though we know it
does not reflect the person's "true" feelings — which may
be sorrow, anger, or distrust. We put the two ideas
together and the smile becomes, not a false role, but an
attempt to deal with sorrow or anger or distrust rather
than dumping those feelings on us. And for the person
who doesn't know the "real" feelings, the smile is
simply a welcome gift on its own terms. The same lesson can be applied to all relationships between the
inner state of being and what one actually wishes to
communicate. There are several questions here: Are we
to be the victims of our inner states of being, or participants and masters of what we wish to communicate?
How can we affect and change that inner state of being
by acting upon it with appropriate mode choices?*

*Developing this end of the external-internal feed-
back process (as well as strengthening the relationship
between the two) is one of our continuing themes. The
modes are fundamentally external projective channels
that can reflect the internal, ignore the internal (and
sometimes begin to change it as a result), or contradict
the internal (augmenting the change of the internal).*

*My directing has always been characterized by
strong physicalizations of the verbal and musical meanings. Working in opera and theater has forced me to
develop a relatively well-coordinated perceptual system.*

As a result, physical action that is arbitrary or does not relate meaningfully to music, words, and emotional meaning offends me. I would rather leave out the kinesthetic messages entirely in such cases. A concert version of opera in which there is clear-cut hearing/vocal dominance with some assistance from the facial/emotional mode seems better to me than a so-called realistic version in which the kinesthetic action and the music have nothing to do with one another.

Besides increasing my personal awareness as a teacher and director, the modes concept has improved the level of communication in my classes and in my professional directing even while reducing the level of defensive resistance. In two recent cases, the modes approach enabled me to deal effectively with professional singing-acting problems that might otherwise have been very difficult to handle. Both artists were highly gifted singers who interfered kinesthetically with their acting performances. Both artists were trying (or rather their bodies, their kinesthetic systems were trying) to express things that could not be appropriately expressed kinesthetically. The effort turned into held tensions that adversely affected both their singing and their acting. In both cases, a few simple demonstrations of the ineffectiveness of this kinesthetic interference, a bit of discussion as to its possible origins, and then lots of practice in releasing the dominating interference in rehearsal enabled the artists to give stunning performances. The performances they would have given would have been acceptable, but the final result was the difference between being a fine performer and a truly great singer-actor.

My kinesthetic dominance may explain my strong awareness of misplaced or faulty use of kinesthetic resources in a performer. (Chap. 8 gives a specific example.) Because of this sensitivity to kinesthetic problems, my classes came to believe from my comments

during the diagnostic process that I did not like kines-
thetic statements in general. The reverse is true, but it
is a good example of how the mode makeup of the
observer influences his evaluation of the mode makeup
of the observed, which in turn affects their attempts to
exercise that mode makeup. It also demonstrates the
propensity of the performer to convert all evaluations
into negative judgments.

When I first began working with the modes concept, I was not aware of any specific testing procedures for determining mode makeup in general or mode dominance in particular. After introducing the concept as a part of a master class for singer-actors in San Francisco, synchronicity struck again. A college teacher in the audience told me that she was deeply involved with mode testing for elementary teachers and students, and she referred me to literature and tests that dealt with perceptions. One of them, a book called *Teaching through Modality Strengths*, includes a set of checklists for dominance characteristics in each mode. The checklist applies to the observation of elementary school children, but many of the characteristics also apply to adults. It is a useful tool for heightening awareness and beginning the process of personal evaluation for the performer.

I stress again that this is not a labeling process. There is already enough of that in life and education. Mode diagnosis of performance is simply a specific way of understanding how the communication process works for each performer. Mode makeup is seldom a simple matter of mode dominance; rather, virtually every case includes some sort of interference by one mode with another and interplay between modes that reflects the personal background of the performer, the character being portrayed, and the situation in the scene.

Because any sung or spoken performance involves the use of all three projective modes, each performer is first asked to deliver a soliloquy or song. It should be a "normal" version of the piece, with no attempt to alter usual performance behavior. During the performance, certain general phenomena occur regularly that help in evaluating the performer's mode makeup. Note that some of the negative characteristics can be

Swassing-Barbe Checklist of

Area Observed	Visual
Learning Style	____ Learns by seeing; watching demonstrations
Reading	____ Likes description; sometimes stops reading to stare into space and imagine scene; intense concentration
Spelling	____ Recognizes words by sight; relies on configuration of words
Handwriting	____ Tends to be good, particularly when young; spacing and size are good; appearance is important
Memory	____ Remembers faces, forgets names; writes things down, takes notes
Imagery	____ Vivid imagination; thinks in pictures, visualizes in detail
Distractibility	____ Generally unaware of sounds; distracted by visual disorder or movement
Problem solving	____ Deliberate; plans in advance; organizes thoughts by writing them; lists problems
Response to periods of inactivity	____ Stares; doodles; finds something to watch
Response to new situations	____ Looks around; examines structure
Emotionality	____ Somewhat repressed; stares when angry; cries easily, beams when happy; facial expression is a good index of emotion
Communication	____ Quiet; does not talk at length; becomes impatient when extensive listening is required; may use words clumsily; describes without embellishment; uses words such as see, look, etc.
General appearance	____ Neat, meticulous, likes order; may choose not to vary appearance
Response to the arts	____ Not particularly responsive to music; prefers the visual arts; tends not to voice appreciation of art of any kind, but can be deeply affected by visual displays; focuses on details and components rather than the work as a whole

Walter B. Barbing and Raymond H. Swasse, *Teaching through Modality Strengths:*

Observable Modality Strength Characteristics

Auditory	Kinesthetic
____ Learns through verbal instructions from others of self	____ Learns by doing; direct involvement
____ Enjoys dialogue, plays; avoids lengthy description, unaware of illustrations; moves lips or subvocalizes	____ Prefers stories where action occurs early; fidgets when reading, handles books; not an avid reader
____ Uses a phonics approach; has auditory word attack skills	____ Often is a poor speller; writes words to determine if they "feel" right
____ Has more difficulty learning in initial stages; tends to write lightly; says strokes when writing	____ Good initially, deteriorates when space becomes smaller; pushes harder on writing instrument
____ Remembers names, forgets faces; remembers by auditory repetition	____ Remembers best what was done, not what was seen or talked about
____ Subvocalizes, thinks in sounds; details less important	____ Imagery not important; images that do occur are accompanied by movement
____ Easily distracted by sounds	____ Not attentive to visual, auditory presentation so seems distractible
____ Talks problems out, tries solutions verbally, subvocally; talks self through problem	____ Attacks problems physically; impulsive; often selects solution involving greatest activity
____ Hums; talks to self or to others	____ Fidgets; finds reasons to move; holds up hand
____ Talks about situation, pros and cons, what to do	____ Tries things out; touches, feels; manipulates
____ Shouts with joy or anger; blows up verbally but soon calms down; expresses emotion verbally and through changes in tone, volume, pitch of voice	____ Jumps for joy; hugs, tugs, and pulls when happy; stamps, jumps, and pounds when angry; stomps off; general body tone is a good index of emotion
____ Enjoys listening but cannot wait to talk; descriptions are long but repetitive; likes hearing self and others talk; uses words such as listen, hear, etc.	____ Gestures when speaking; does not listen well; stands close when speaking or listening; quickly loses interest in detailed verbal discourse; uses words such as get, take, etc.
____ Matching clothes not so important, can explain choices of clothes	____ Neat but soon becomes wrinkled through activity
____ Favors music; finds less appeal in visual art, but is readily able to discuss it; misses significant detail, but appreciates the work as a whole; is able to develop verbal association for all art forms; spends more time talking about pieces than looking at them	____ Responds to music by physical movement; prefers sculpture; touches statues and paintings; at exhibits stops only at those in which he or she can become physically involved; comments very little on any art form

Concepts and Practices, © 1979. Reproduced by permission of Zaner-Bloser, Inc.

positive for those with opposite characteristics. The tense performer, for example, can profit from releasing tension totally and learning what an unenergized stance means, even though that is not the final goal. Moving between opposite states of being in this way is sometimes an intuitive response on the part of the overly tense or unenergized performer. It creates what I call the pendulum effect, or the swing back and forth between a state of tension and a state of relaxation. Neither state feels appropriate, which sets up movement between them as the performer searches for a comfortable way of being. The goal is a state poised somewhere between the two opposites—neither tense nor relaxed, but vital. We refer to this state of optimum capability as a state of readiness. It is an athletic state of being in which one is capable of doing whatever needs to be done swiftly, spontaneously, and immediately. Because one is capable of doing whatever needs to be done does not mean that the capability has to be exercised. True readiness is as comfortable doing nothing as doing something. As we will see, it is a concept that can also be applied to the facial/emotional mode and the hearing/vocal mode.

The accompanying checklists are useful for mode diagnosis of performance. Some of the terms in the checklists are explained in detail in the chapter describing that mode.

Performance Behavior in the Kinesthetic

Negative characteristics
1. Unenergized stance that lacks vitality
2. Standing with weight back on the heels
3. Standing with weight on one leg
4. Sitting back on the hips
5. Locked knees
6. Shifting of weight back and forth from one leg to the other
7. Excessive hand, finger, arm activity
8. Lifting of the shoulders
9. Held tensions perceptible in any area of body
10. Excessive facial movement or tension (any action or hold that calls attention to itself but communicates nothing specific relative to the performance)
11. Eyebrow lifting or forehead wrinkling repeatedly
12. Wandering eyes, darting eyes

13. Any physical activities or ways of being that call attention to themselves and do not communicate anything specific relative to the performance

Positive characteristics
1. Sense of readiness, vitality
2. Sense of flow and alertness in the physical being
3. Sense of balance and centeredness
4. Feeling of kinesthetic potential without tension
5. Ease of quick transitions from one physical state to another

Note: Some of the negative activities listed above, especially 10, 11, and 12, relate to the facial emotional mode; but they are evidence of kinesthetic interference with that mode.

Performance Behavior in the Facial Emotional Mode

Negative characteristics
1. Deadpan quality that never changes
2. Seeming inability to smile naturally
3. Seeming inability to convey any emotional feeling
4. Overly active, nervous face; darting, nervous eyes, tension in any part of the face, any held quality that calls attention to itself
5. Little or no communication of what is going on in the mind

Positive characteristics
1. Strongly projective face with emotional states, both positive and negative, easily perceived by the observer
2. Facial mobility in general, as distinguished from kinesthetic interference patterns mugging or indicating
3. Face that seems alive, interesting, compelling, fascinating, charismatic
4. Strong communication of thought process by the face
5. Sense of the person visualizing what is talked about, or seeming to *see* what is talked or thought about

Note: A lack of any of these positive qualities can be regarded as a negative characteristic, or as something that should be added to the performer's facial emotional arsenal.

Performance Behavior in the Hearing/Vocal Mode

Negative characteristics
1. Continually cadenced endings of phrases
2. Flat or monotonous phrasing
3. Lack of pitch inflective range

4. Lack of range in tessitura
5. Glottal tension when delivering emotional passages
6. Vocal indicating in general (interference with vocal production by the kinesthetic system that makes the voice "sound" emotional: this technique is discussed in greater detail on page 85)
7. Artificially produced speaking tone quality ("Shakespearean" voice or "cultured sound") that is unlike the speaker's normal voice
8. Sameness of rhythm, speed, pitch, lack of tonal variety, (as with the "cultured" voice above or with a continual flat or nasal or breathy or hollow quality)
9. Heavy breathing, gasping, gasp-laughing continually when dealing with emotional material

Positive characteristics
1. Voice that feels alive and free, betraying no interference
2. Voice that manifests easy flexiblity
3. Voice that is able to make sudden changes of process with ease
4. Voice that is unpredictable
5. Voice that has variety in its coloring, in its use of rhythms, speed, volume, and musicality
6. Voice that is used in a way that sounds and feels natural, as the person uses it in life, only with greater energy

Note: Several of these negative hearing/vocal mode phenomena are also evidence of kinesthetic interference, especially 5, 6, and 9.

The next diagnostic step is isolation of the modes in performance, allowing each to dominate in turn while performing a speech or song. Each member of the class performs three versions of a soliloquy or song, isolating in turn the hearing/vocal mode, the facial/emotional mode, and the kinesthetic mode.

If time is limited, there is a quicker diagnostic version in which the performer moves from one mode dominance to another while performing the piece. Although a complex exercise for young performers, no matter how skilled they may be, it is a superb means of heightening awareness. The mode-to-mode approach can be used in songs, speeches, scenes, and ensembles. It is a superb, all-purpose Nautilus, a name I borrow from universal exercise machines to describe all mode exercises that develop performer power.

Even when the modes are isolated, all are functioning at all times. There is no such thing as a nonstatement: the face, the body, and the voice are always projecting some kind of message, whether it be boredom, indifference, excitement, apathy, or tension. But isolation of one mode simply means letting that mode be the dominant communicator. Consequently, for two of the three versions the performer is asked to portray a person with a mode dominance different from his or her own. Those with a hearing/vocal dominance will be asked to portray characters who are facial/emotional and kinesthetic dominants, and similarly with performers dominant in the other modes. Successive mode dominance is a way to test the relative strength of each mode, of determining the performer's capacity to isolate the modes, and of perceiving any entanglement within the mode system.

This process of isolation sounds a great deal easier than it actually is. In practice, surprisingly few performers are able to distinguish between the vocal, physical, and emotional delivery systems. American acting classes tend to relate to the concept of being "natural," or to how it "feels." Little attention is paid to selective musicality of language (for fear of sounding artificial, phony, or unbelievable) or to specific selection of gestures and physical statements (for fear of looking artificial or feeling uncomfortable). And the last thing the American actor wants to be concerned with is what the *face* is doing (the horror of mugging!). But even experienced performers can develop awareness of the modes system and can profit from understanding and working with the idea of three distinctive and independent channels of communication.

Performers should be reassured, however, that mode entanglements are inevitable for everyone, regardless of their dominance. Entanglement is a natural part of learning to communicate. When we are very young our bodies, faces, and voices often work simultaneously in communicating. They interfere with one another, and habits of entanglement are established. These habits may persist throughout our entire lives, or they may be unconsciously altered (for better or worse) as we imitate our parents or other authority figures. But some sort of entanglement remains for almost everyone, especially when attempting to communicate under pressure. Developing the capacity to unentangle these habits at will or to use the modes in any combination in a coordinated fashion is an essential skill for the professional communicator.

As performers try to isolate each of the modes in succession after their "normal" performance, observers should attend to the following questions.

Is there any change in energy in the hearing/vocal mode as the other modes becomes less active? For example, as the kinesthetic energies are placed in readiness rather than put into action, do the vocal energies increase or decrease?

When the facial/emotional energies are made the dominant communicators, how are the other two modes affected?

Do the hearing/vocal energies increase or diminish with a corresponding use of the facial/emotional energies?

Do the kinesthetic energies increase or diminish, or does tension set in as the facial/emotional energies change?

How are the facial/emotional and hearing/vocal energies affected when the kinesthetic mode is made the dominant communicator?

Does the face begin mugging or indicating as the kinesthetic mode is engaged?

Does the voice become tense, or does it lose or gain energy as the kinesthetic energies increase?

The attempt of observers to answer the questions is an excellent diagnostic of their perceptual awarenesses. They also expand their perceptual strength, which is vital to their projective awareness and to their growth as performers. It is fascinating to hear young performers describe what they have perceived in a performance. The mind-reading approach is common: "Their thought processes weren't connected"; "they weren't feeling it"; "he didn't seem involved"; and similarly unhelpful comments. But the insistence upon describing what actually happened to communicate those thoughts, feelings, or attitudes quickly leads the observers to a new point of reference: they begin looking at the facts of emotional communication, at the way the facial/emotional system visibly, *describably* functions to communicate its messages; they begin listening to the facts of vocal communication, to specific ways the musicality conveys its messages; and they begin observing the facts of physical communication, the way the body and its appendages convey their messages. "Ah ha!" expressions appear as the observers are released from the mind-reading necessity. They find that they are able to talk about the facts of performance and that when they do so, change and growth take place immediately.

One of the continuing themes of this book is the idea of systems theory as it relates to the modes concept. Systems that work best have one specific characteristic in common: the parts of the system work in a mutually supportive relationship with each other and with the whole. Each part of any system has both assertive, individual needs and integrative, holistic needs. All systems involve an interplay between the assertive and integrative needs of each part of the system. When this interplay is operating effectively, it is often described by the word *synergy*, derived from the Greek *syn-ergos*, meaning *to work together*. High synergy within a system indicates a healthy system, one that is functioning at its best. It also means that the assertive and integrative needs of each part of the system are being satisfied even as they work together in harmony for the greater whole.

Each modes system has its own communicating function to realize, its own assertive needs. The kinesthetic system, for example, wants to communicate messages with its specific skills. But for maximum synergy, for its own higher needs as well as those of the larger, total modes system, the kinesthetic mode needs to integrate with the other two modes. In this case, maximum synergy means maximum communication. The same principle holds true for the other modes: they have their assertive needs as individual communicating systems, but their integrative needs must also be served if the total modes system is to achieve the highest possible synergy and thus the clearest and most powerful communication.

We can look at the perceptual and projective mode systems from this same synergistic perspective. The three individual modes together form a larger projective system, and that system in turn combines with the perceptual system to form a still greater whole. Each of those two systems also has assertive and integrative needs. It might seem that perception is basically a receiving system and projection a sending system, but the perceptual awareness of the performer can focus on the projective system of the performer and give information to that system. The projective system can then receive that information and alter its own workings.

For the singer-actor, the systems of perception and projection can be truly synergistic in their relationship. With mode awareness, the perceptual system is focused on the projective system of other modes as well as on its own. Their perceptions become specific in their focus, rather than generalizing about performance. As the perceptual system becomes more specific in its awareness, so will the projective system become more specific and defined in the way the three modes send messages. Again, the greater the synergy between the two systems, the greater the growth in the performer's communicating capacity, in performing power.

An immediate challenge of heightening this synergistic relationship between perception and projection is self-consciousness. One can over-monitor one's voice, face, or body in early stages of the work, but it is often a necessary phase and not to be feared. The Zen concept—"First there isn't a mountain, then there is a mountain, then there isn't a mountain"—refers to the sequence facing any artist attempting to master a technique. The young actor, for example, often begins with an exuberant, unself-conscious naturalism (there isn't a mountain); and then is confronted with techniques of various kinds that can seem to be overwhelming and certainly bring on self-consciousness (there is the mountain); but finally, with practice, these techniques become natural, unself-conscious resources (and, once again, there isn't a mountain).

Even in the initial phases of modes exercise, my experience indicates that the negative effects of self-conscious overmonitoring is less than one would have anticipated, and it is always more than compensated for by the growth in the performing power of each of the modes as they release their entanglements, develop strength individually, and learn to cooperate more freely. If there is a degree of potentially negative overawareness at first, that is part of the mountain phase, and it is relatively easy to release. In any case, the awareness, even if excessive, is part of the growth process and must not be mistaken for an impediment to that process.

One of the gratifying things about the modes approach is the relative ease with which change can be stimulated in the performer. It arouses an enthusiastic, sympathetic excitement in observers as they see a familiar performer make immediate and obvious improvement. As one of my students said after two months of class, "It's as though little miracles happen every day." They happen because of the simplicity and specificity of the modes concept.

Although we have used the term diagnosis and have suggested a specific analysis of each performer, nothing so cut and dried happens in actual practice. Each new exercise, each new Nautilus raises its own set of complications and its own specific needs. Performers confront themselves anew in each exercise. Regardless of individual dominance and makeup, the overall process is the same for each Nautilus: isolate the modes and free them from mutual entanglement, develop their power as independent units, and then exercise them in combination.

One of the many benefits of the modes view is the ease with which one can specify the essential problems. I told an advanced performer who wanted to take the class, "At one time I would have hesitated in working with a highly experienced actor in class, but now I would feel comfortable with Olivier." (A slight exaggeration, but the modes approach makes teaching on all levels so simple and exciting that it leads one to hyperbole.)

After the first round of diagnosis, one can begin working on each mode in succession. But any sequence suggested in this book is an example rather than a routine to be used in every case. The modes approach demands an individual sequence of exercises for each performer, which is one of its primary strengths. Each exercise in any given sequence serves a different need. One performer needs a kinesthetic mode isolation, another a facial/emotional isolation, the third a hearing/vocal isolation, while a fourth needs a mode-to-mode Nautilus. The modes concept demands constant attention to the needs of the individual at that moment; as performers grow in their capabilities, their needs change and so must the exercises.

For the purposes of this book, however, we begin with the hearing/vocal mode, the only one that makes specific statements almost continually. A scene can exist without physical movement or facial expressivity, but—with the rare exception of mime—words being spoken or sung are required for a scene.[3] The hearing/vocal mode is not the usual first step in the American academic acting tradition, which stresses internally oriented, facial/emotional acting. This emphasis is intensified by the increasing concern with film and television performance. Despite efforts in the sixties and seventies to bring greater emphasis to the kinesthetic mode, the concentration on facial/emotional energies has continued. The efforts to stress the kinesthetic, however, aggravated a common pattern of kinesthetic interference with the hearing/vocal mode. Let us take a moment to explore that relationship in detail.

The opinion that film and television acting must be small in scale to be believable may seem to be logical: the facial/emotional mode is subtle and easily interfered with, and large-scale use of the voice and body often creates facial distortions for the inadequately trained performer. But such distortions are not necessary. Performers can be trained to deliver powerfully and freely in all three modes, as repeatedly demonstrated during the last decade on the BBC's Masterpiece Theater. For me that demonstration began with *I, Claudius* and has continued with little interruption in succeeding years. Large-scale vocal work is not only compatible with the intimacy of television, it is absolutely integral to some of the most exciting work seen (and heard) on that medium since its rise to prominence as a public attraction.

Why were those actors able to achieve that kind of performance? The basic technique simply demands the ability to use the hearing/vocal mode with no kinesthetic interference or accompaniment, entanglements that can be seen and heard in any beginning acting class. The average untrained actor delivering a speech with stronger than customary energies becomes a veritable "feast of kinesthetic excess," as one of my students described it after observing some relatively advanced actors do the American body dance that so often accompanies large and unaccustomed vocal energies. If the voice uses greater energies, so must the body—or so it seems. And if those additional energies are not manifested by body accompaniment—lifted shoulders, waving arms, and jabbing head—we will see them in the face. The facial/emotional system is called into kinesthetic play, dancing its own dance to the tune of the vocal energies. The superfluous accompanying energies lend the performance an amateurish feeling unless the combination happens to be appropriate for the characterization. Even then, however, it should be the performer's choice to do so and not the incapacity to do otherwise. A voice locked into correspondence with the kinesthetic pattern may also be deprived of true flexibility and communicating power. The body is a grosser instrument that limits the voice severely if allowed to impose its own speed, flexibility, and patterns of change on the voice. Kinesthetic interference with the vocal process usually comes into play simultaneously with kinesthetic accompaniment. The ability to use maximum vocal energy from a state of physical and facial readiness is an essential skill for the singer-actor, and it must be exercised specifically as such.

ANECDOTE: *After beginning my exploration of the modes concept, it was instructive to watch a typically brilliant hour of Masterpiece Theater followed by an episode of Steve Allen's Meeting of the Minds. In both cases, a certain style and elevated use of the language was called for. Without denigrating Mr. Allen's laudable program, the problem on that particular night was strikingly evident. There was a huge contrast between the acting level of the BBC show and the Allen show, disparity created almost entirely by the incapacity of the American cast of bewigged historical characters to isolate the hearing/vocal mode as did their British counterparts. I realized for the first time the reason for the vaguely amateurish air of the Allen show: the intrusion of the kinesthetic mode in subtle but significant ways when language of any stature or an elevated style was called for. If the use of the language is accompanied by the kinesthetic dance—body or face—it invariably brings to mind the stereotypes of children, clowns, and bumblers (or amateur actors), and unless one is portraying characters of that nature, the kinesthetic accompaniment to the hearing/vocal energies simply reduces both the level of the characterization and the proficiency of the performance.*

I do not mean to elevate one kind of performance over another, but only to clarify the problem that arises when the mode demands of a performance style are not matched by the mode capacities of the performers.

In another context, those same American performers might have acted their British counterparts into the ground. I doubt it, however, because if one can isolate mode energies, one can also combine them; but if they are entangled to begin with, it is very difficult to use any individual mode with greater energy without dragging the others along. That is the real issue, not the comparison of performance products per se.

Nor is it my intention to elevate one mode over the other, to say that the hearing/vocal mode, for example, is the most important mode to the actor or singer-actor. But it is the mode without which the others cannot exist, and thus the foundation mode to which the other two must relate. All three modes are important, and it would be folly to base an acting tradition exclusively on any single mode (as many acting systems do).

Theoretically, it may be easier to move from a hearing/vocal foundation to a skillful and artistic use of the other two modes than to move from, say, a facial/emotional foundation to a use of hearing and kinesthetic modes. British actors have been able to incorporate the best of the American facial/emotional mode tradition into their hearing/vocal work with relative ease, but American actors have either not tried, have not been taught, or have failed to make similar artistic use of the British hearing/vocal skills.

The hearing/vocal mode is a convenient starting point to begin our progress toward the real objective, which is the strengthening and coordinating of all three modes. Regardless of the mode makeup of individual members of the group, it is a logical introduction to the idea of modes for all students, even though the exercises that follow will be responsive to the needs of the individual. Some individuals in the class will undoubtedly be hearing/vocal dominants, but they do not necessarily possess either instrument potential or skill in using the mode. In any case, the words of the scene or the song must be given utterance before our work can properly begin.

Chapter 3
Implications of the
Hearing/Vocal Mode

The hearing/vocal mode is probably the least popular of three modes in America. Words themselves, written and spoken, have become increasingly subject to abuse on both scholarly and popular levels. At least one popular book each year is concerned with the declining standards of literacy and the debasement of language by bureaucratic misuse, scholarly indifference, purposeful manipulation, and general ignorance. Jargon is on the march, literacy is in retreat, and language, written or spoken, can no longer be trusted. Concern with the abuse of language is reflected on the mass level by an increasing mistrust of words and of those who speak well in using those words. And it is in speaking and singing words that have been written by others that we encounter the crucial difference between the hearing/vocal and other modes.

The Musicality of Language

The hearing/vocal mode deals with *what* language says, but it also deals with *how* it is said, with the musicality of language. In a kinesthetic gesture or physical statement of any kind, the gesture *is* the meaning.[1] It can contradict messages from the other two systems or even deliver two contradictory messages within itself, but the nonverbal statement of the gesture has meaning that is independent of verbal definition. Although the relaxed body can conceal murderous intent, the statement "The body is relaxed and is not currently tense" is true for that moment. Similarly with facial/emotional statements, where a smile has its own meaning even though it may conceal other meanings.

Only the hearing/vocal mode contains the possibility of separating what is said from how it is said. The double-bind concept of Gregory Bateson is a specific instance of the mode incongruency concept discussed in the introduction. ("Of course I love you," snarls the parent to the child, sending two contradictory messages through the same system.) As an example of the many possibilities contained within the hearing/vocal mode, those words—"Of course I love you"—could be spoken with a language musicality that conveyed any one of the following possibilities: annoyance, boredom, anger, hate, indifference, passion, spite, sarcasm, and a host of mingled shades of emotional meaning. These are in addition to the literal meaning of protesting love, which is the verbal meaning apart from the musicality with which it is spoken. The words could also be spoken congruently, with a tenderness and compassion matching the positive potential of the words.

The kinesthetic and facial/emotion modes may join the hearing/vocal musicality in agreeing with, contradicting, or otherwise defining the message of the words. For the moment, however, let us stay within the hearing/vocal mode and examine the many opportunities to exercise this unique capacity of the mode for internal incongruency. The ideas of agreement, contradiction, or difference without contradiction help to clarify how the mode can be exercised within its own sphere.

Each verbal statement has a cluster of potential musicality attitudes that agrees with its meaning, a cluster that contradicts its meaning, and a cluster that adds complexity without agreeing with or contradicting the literal meaning of the words. This in itself suggests the exercise: simply saying the words with as many different kinds of musicality as possible. But this tends to call the other two modes into play, which can be a vital part of the total message but does not help in developing the strength of the hearing/vocal mode as an independent communicator. An important way of doing this is by giving it the opportunity of being the dominant mode, isolating its efforts from the other two and observing the kinesthetic and facial/emotional modes for unintended interference or participation. We cannot emphasize this basic point too strongly: unless each mode can be exercised in isolation from the others, it will be difficult—even impossible—to develop its potential power.

In performing the exercise of varying musicality attitudes, many of the most unlikely combinations prove to be performance worthy. All exercises, however, must be regarded as such and not as final products. Orientation toward product begins to scuttle the potential of the growth process. Judgment joins the game, spoiling what *could* happen by its concern for what *should* happen. Especially in working with the hearing/vocal mode, which alone among the modes contains the verbal-intellectual-judgmental center, we must remain mindful of the importance of process exercise as opposed to product judgment.

We have two goals in isolating the modes. The first is cultivating the ability to work with maximal energy in one mode without interference or assistance from the others. The second is strengthening and extending the capabilities of the mode itself. A problem related to this concept has arisen in recent years in American training of the speaking voice. It is common to encounter vocal training that develops and frees the voice by encouraging interaction with the kinesthetic mode. Theater voice classes often resemble movement classes; the theory on which they are based stresses the interrelationship of the voice with the entire body, not just those parts used as a vital breath support system. These theories try to make vocal instruction a holistic system by interrelating vocal energies with total physical energies. In theory, the interrelationship is vital: we have already stressed the importance of the holistic view implicit in the modes concept. But the healthy functioning of any system depends upon balance between the assertive and integrative tendencies of the subsystems that make it up. It is a mistake to overstress the integrative tendencies between the vocal and kinesthetic subsystems and to neglect the assertive (isolating) tendencies, which allow the voice to function interdependently with the physical energies. The systems view allows us to perceive this imbalance more clearly and to avoid the mistake of polarizing our choices. The great law of opposites—which says that the greatest vitality is found in the synergy between opposing values—holds here as elsewhere.

On a practical level, the actor must be able to use maximal vocal energies without depending upon the active engagement of all physical resources. Opera singers, for instance, are physically static much of the time during a performance, yet they are able to produce vocal energies of amazing power and flexibility. It may be necessary to use a full-body response to develop the vocal breath support system (though this seems questionable), and it may be useful to learn to release physical tensions through full-body release. But the singer-actor must be able to sing and speak with full power and with the breath support system functioning perfectly without the rest of the body doing an accompanying kinesthetic dance. A singer may sing better while lying on the floor, waving arms, dropping the body over, being given a tension check, or any number of other physical activities during a lesson; but eventually, the singer must learn to achieve the release of tension that allows the vocal energies to flow freely without depending on kinesthetic exercises.

The acting teacher needs to develop a sensitivity to vocal tension of any kind. We have no term to describe the vocal equivalent of the facial tensions that lead to mugging or indicating. I have coined the term *vocal indicating* to describe the tension interference with the vocal process that is induced to indicate or show emotion. Since coming to the modes concept, I realize that what I call vocal indicating can be simply explained: it is the kinesthetic mode interfering with the hearing/vocal mode in order to convey emotional intensity. Once one is aware of the process of vocal indicating, it can be heard very easily; but it has been accepted as viable and necessary for so long that it can take an actor months simply to become aware of the damaging habit (which is often practiced in life as well), and much longer to undo it. It is one of the first and certainly the most common form of kinesthetic interference that comes into play when an actor attempts to use greater vocal energy.

Why should vocal indicating be such a common phenomenon? Why should actors interfere with their vocal process (albeit unconsciously) simply because they are asked to use greater vocal energy? One possible explanation is that the interference is an attempt to justify the use of greater vocal energy in advance by creating a physical feeling of intensity and emotionality. The actor who is not accustomed to using vocal energy on that scale is afraid of sounding unmotivated, phony, empty, inorganic, or lacking in inner truth — all cardinal sins for the American actor. Having grown up in an acting tradition that places the supreme condemnation upon the sin of phoniness and that has associated the sin with artificial acting, elocutionary schools of correct speech, and the British tradition, the actor must "do" something apart from using the language itself to give that language feeling, emotion, motivation, or guts! Rather than letting the musicality of the language — the volume, speed, rhythms, pitch — create whatever emotional meaning is appropriate, the actor tries to control the way the voice creates meaning, to show the intensity of emotional speech through generalized vocal tension. The actor uses the glottis to partially block the voice, to force the sound through the constricted vocal mechanism with abdominal pressure and thus to create a strong sense of "doing" something that requires great

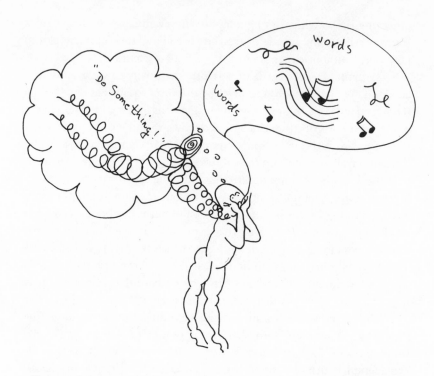

effort and brings the sound of vocal turmoil. Unfortunately, the performer suffers vocal damage in the process. If the interference is encouraged by default, it can easily become a habitual way of showing emotion, a habit that is defended to the death by actors who grow to associate that kind of vocal pressure and injury with "emotional truth." It has nothing to do with emotional truth, of course, nor is it an exciting way to use the voice; it prevents the true energies of the voice from being used, it limits the range, volume, flexibility, nuance, and musicality in general, and it offers nothing but vocal attrition and unfulfilled performance.[2]

"Justification by tension," or mistaking repression of energy for the expression of emotion, will be an ongoing theme in this book. Chapter 6 explores the phenomenon in detail, but at this point we can note that the kinesthetic system is the principal means for creating tension interference with the other two modes. The tension interference is invariably involved with the communication of strong emotion, but it actually communicates the repression of the emotion rather than its expression. It also interferes with and damages the working relationship of the entire modes system.

For the singer-actor, the interplay of the words and the musicality used to express those words is both simpler and more subtle than for the actor. The music of the words, how they are to be delivered, has been established by the composer, and the amount of variation available within that context (although significant and seldom exercised to full capacity) is far more limited than for the actor. A performer's stylistic freedom in this area varies by composer and period. Operatic singing, for example, has less stylistic latitude than musical comedy singing. Almost any kind of voice can be used in musical comedy, and the musicality of the score is often subordinated to the capabilities and personality of the performer. Communication of both textual meaning and performer personality is vital to musical comedy. In opera, the musicality and use of the voice is strongly conditioned by the demands of the score and the energy demands placed upon the voice itself. Use the operatic voice unhealthily and you destroy it; violate the traditional style and you won't be hired.

Most style decisions for the singer-actor are guided or dictated by musical coaches or conductors, particularly in the formative stages of one's career. An exception is Rex Harrison's performance in *My Fair Lady*, which may be the most famous and influential example of score modification by a singer-actor. The decision was dictated by Harrison's inability to sing well in traditional fashion, necessitating a free use of extended or semi-intoned spoken inflections. Many observers attribute the decline of singing in the Broadway musical in the past twenty years to this specific example. Harrison made a great success of his nonsinging performance; in fact, I find his melodic inflections preferable to the score as composed. But he was a hearing mode dominant, British actor who had a brilliant command of the spoken language, allowing him to make spoken music that rivaled or surpassed the composed score in interest and subtlety. Unfortunately, his example gave permission to a host of other producers to use nonsinging stars in leading singing roles in other musical comedies. Very few of these stars—most of them Americans—had the language skills of a Harrison, and the next two decades heard some appalling singing that was excusable on no grounds to any self-respecting hearing mode dominant.

The Left and Right Brain of Performance

The word-music dichotomy inherent in exercising the hearing/vocal mode relates as well to the concept of left and right brain. This concept of left and right hemispheric functioning in the brain has been grossly oversimplified in the past decade, offering a view of mental functioning as distorted as the conscious-unconscious division at the beginning of the century.[3] Cliché uses of the concept are being attacked by researchers who correctly insist upon the underlying complexity of the brain. Nothing in life is as neat and tidy as the left-brain/right-brain dichotomy would indicate.

Nonetheless, the opposites presented by the theory are a meaningful metaphor for much of life's activities, and they are especially apropos to music theater. The concept intersects revealingly with the concept of modes.[4] The right hemisphere—the repository of noverbal, intuitive, spatial, imaginative, creative, artistic, holistic thinking—is the home of the kinesthetic mode and therefore of all athletic and artistic physical activities. It is also the home of emotional reactions and musical impulses.[5] Most of the performer's projective communication, through the kinesthetic and facial/emotional modes, is governed by the right brain, which is nonverbal and nonintellectual in its approach. The only aspect of the total performance act that is directly related to the left brain is the language. Consequently, hearing/vocal mode is the only one governed in part by the left brain—the words themselves, which are sung or spoken—and in part by the right brain—the musicality with which those words are spoken or sung.

This insight helps us to understand one of the interference problems mentioned above. When one asks an actor to do something unusual with the musicality of the language (or merely asks a singer to sing a song), one is asking for increased right-brain involvement in the process of using the voice. Almost inevitably, one sees an increased amount of both physical and facial activity as an accompaniment to that increased vocal energy. Perhaps calling on one of the right-brain functions (or one of the mode minds) excites the other two into action, the energizing of one portion of the brain creating a potential in adjacent areas. An exception that increases the likelihood of the rule is the performer who grows up in a hearing/vocal culture that trains the isolating capacity from the beginning.[6]

ANECDOTE: Peter Brook gives a brilliant description of the art of Sir John Gielgud as a hearing/vocal mode dominant who actually rejected the other two modes and concentrated on the interrelationship between the intellectual meaning of the language and the musicality that makes those meanings clear: "His art has always been more vocal than physical; at some early stage in his career he decided that for himself the body was a less supple instrument than the head. He thus jettisoned part of an actor's possible equipment but made true alchemy with the rest. It is not just speech, nor melodies, but the continual movement between the word-forming mechanism and his understanding that has made his art so rare, so touching, and especially so aware."[7]

How fortunate that Sir John grew up in a hearing mode dominant culture where the choice he made was both appropriate and accepted! But how much better if actors in every culture could develop the mode most appropriate to their personal mode makeup, without giving up the ideal of developing the capacity of each mode to its maximum. How many hearing/vocal dominants in this country have not found an outlet or even the proper training for their skills in this country? One could even adapt the old "mute Milton's" idea for the modes. Each mode not only has a mind of its own, but a genius of its own. It is possible to be a genius in any mode and yet to lack the environment necessary to allow that genius to bloom. The mode dominance of each country no doubt suppresses capabilities in many

*of its potential artists without meaning to do so. How
useful it would be to recognize this factor and make
allowance for it.*

We need a way of exercising the left-brain/right-brain partnership.
The logical and verbal left brain discriminates between the right-brain
functions that are appropriate to the circumstances in question. It may
call upon that right-brain function and then allow it to work without
overcontrolling it, observing but not interfering. For example, the intellect may call the musicality of language into play, but it must then relin-
quish the control and allow the hearing/vocal mind to take over. It must
allow the right-brain system to do whatever needs to be done, trusting
it while remaining in an observing, nonjudgmental role. The same pattern applies when working with the other modes as well: the left brain
summons greater kinesthetic energies into play and gives them performance challenges, such as an extended gesture assignment, and then
turns the assignment over to the kinesthetic mode mind for execution.
Or, in working with the facial/emotional mode, the intellect asks for a
burst of beaming, facial/emotional joy and then allows that energy to
function naturally without interference.

This concept of calling into play, then allowing yet not controlling
will be a continual theme as we exercise the modes separately and in
combination. Mode minds governed by the right brain *know* what to do
and how to do it; they only need to be allowed to do what they know.
But the left-brain intellect must make decisions about when and how
much of that doing and knowing should be summoned up and allowed
into play. The left-brain resources are generally nervous and inhibited
about what the right brain can and should be allowed to do. Rarely do
we see a performance in which the right brain is allowed too much freedom; but it is depressingly common to see performances in which the left
brain is exerting too much intellectual control over intuitive, right-brain
functions. Our exercise of the modes attempts to develop a more equal
partnership between the two sets of resources.

The hearing/vocal mode contains this struggle within itself. It is the
paradoxical union of opposites and a personal battleground as we try to
intellectualize and control performing energies that are essentially non-

intellectual. In the Introduction, I called the overintellectualization of the arts the primary aesthetic disease of the twentieth century. The rise and fall of acting systems in our century demonstrates this struggle to bring under intellectual control a process that is not intellectual in the first place. An unspoken rule underlying acting theories says that if you understand the theory on an intellectual basis it becomes part of your acting capabilities. No one says that out loud because it is obviously untrue; but each time an acting teacher advises students to read a book on acting (as I have done and will continue to do), it sends a message about where the answers are to be found. Books are helpful and necessary—I would hardly be writing one if I didn't think so—but the answer lies beyond them, beyond the verbal reduction of experience into words. The left brain explains and rationalizes the irrational, inexplicable energies of the right-brain mode minds. It intellectualizes the nonintellectual and makes logically verbal that which is nonverbally logical.

The books we write set down the rules whereby all those freewheeling, fantasizing, mystical, magic-making energies can be categorized and brought under conscious control.[8] In the process, those activities are often robbed of the very qualities that made them desirable in the first place. Kinesthetic energies, emotional processes, and the musicality of language are all subjected to intellectual scrutiny, and unless they are allowed to function freely once again they are inevitably reduced to lifeless techniques. The paradox arises, however, because we can only grow by change and we can only change usefully through awareness; but in awareness lie the seeds of self-consciousness and judgment that may undermine the whole endeavor. We must confront this paradox in each mode and search for ways to circumvent that sequence of analysis to judgment to self-consciousness. Without the attempt there will be little growth except for the intuitive few, many of whom flee acting schools to escape the very real dangers of the analytic sequence.[9]

Because the left-brain factors of analysis and control are intertwined with the hearing/vocal mode, altering the musicality of language is always a great challenge to the performer. Overcontrol is inevitable when first attempting hearing/vocal exercises. Instead of giving an assignment to the hearing/vocal mode mind to make sense of—for example, fast and staccato—the intellect tries to assert control over the process. Most beginning efforts thus sound stilted, unnatural, and self-conscious. Because

they are overcontrolled, they are not complex enough to be natural. The fast, staccato assignment ends up as someone going fast and staccato. Such renditions lack the seasonings to make them palatable: they need the oregano, thyme, salt, and pepper of the rest of the musicality resources (rhythm, speed change, inflective variation, change of process, pause) to make them taste of meaning. This complexity can only be achieved by the holistic, intuitive, right-brain capacities of the hearing/vocal mode mind.

Acting is the only art that, for all practical purposes, has no history. It must be created anew by each new generation of performers. Like civilizations, actors who do not study history are condemned to repeat it: each generation of actors must rediscover for themselves the relationship between external and internal process. They can be aided by descriptions and assisted by directors and teachers whose on-the-spot observations help untangle the web of internal-external interplay, but each actor is a unique complex of skills, urges, instrument potentials, and mind sets. No verbal description, no matter how articulate, can totally unravel the complex web of good performance. Discussions of the mask-face, of external-internal opposites, have occurred in every period in which there has been theater, as have arguments about naturalism versus style. The final statement comes from the performers themselves as they demonstrate the art that is impossible to reduce to verbal terms.

Cole and Chinoy's excellent historical anthology of acting commentary gives a generational reanalysis of the acting dilemma. To cite one pre-Stanislavskian example from the nineteenth century, the actress Fanny Kemble wrote brilliantly on this issue of intellect versus instinct (or, as we would call it, left-brain versus right-brain resources). She knew nothing of our current understanding of the brain, but she clearly perceived the difference between verbal-intellectual understanding of a role and communication of that understanding (and much more) in actual performance. Her thesis was simple: the person who has the intuitive capacity to perform a role brilliantly is unlikely to have the intellectual capacity to write an equally brilliant analysis of that role.

There is no reason whatever to expect that fine actors shall be necessarily profound commentators on the parts they sustain most successfully, but rather the contrary. . . . Mrs. Siddons' analysis of the part of Lady Macbeth is to be found alone in her representation of it . . . the two treatises she left upon the characters of Queen Constance and Lady Macbeth — two of her finest parts — are feeble and superficial.

If that great actress had possessed the order of mind capable of conceiving and producing a philosophical analysis of any of the wonderful poetical creations which she so wonderfully embodied, she would surely never have been able to embody them as she did.

> The dramatic faculty lies in a power of apprehension quicker than the disintegrating process of critical analysis . . . , and the persons endowed with this specific gift will hardly unite with it the mental qualifications of philosophers and metaphysicians. The reflective and analytical quality has little to do with the complex process of acting, and is alike remote from what is dramatic and what is theatrical.[10]

This view does not call in question the intelligence of actors, but only specifies the *kind* of intelligence that serves them best. Vocal, body, and emotional intelligence are equally vital to the functioning of performers and human beings. And since there are three mode minds and a single verbal-intellectual mind, their importance as independent entities may outweigh that of the intellectual-verbal. They might be a better guide in the long run, not only to artistic activities but to the rest of life as well.

We must ask whether the analytical, verbal intelligence that is prized in academic situations is not antithetical to the synthesizing, intuitive, nonverbal necessities of actor performance. The intellectual fourth mode, by its very nature, may be an impediment to the first three modes. If so, the performer is likely to fight back with the principal weapons of academia, the verbal-intellectual tools.

Where do we find outselves, then, but in the middle of the paradox, trying to analyze in verbal-intellectual terms the very thing—the acting process—that is not subject to that kind of analysis and may even be impeded by it. That becomes the task for acting classes everywhere: finding a productive confrontation between the opposites of analysis and intuition, discipline and freedom, personality and characterization, naturalism and style, and text and subtext (which includes musicality of language, physicalization, and emotion). We cannot know whether the confrontation is useful or not. Many outstanding actors have never taken an acting class or have left acting school without finishing.

If the teacher-director-coach is to be productive, however, he or she must communicate with and bring into play the right-brain functions (physicality, musicality, and facial/emotionality of the mode minds) without allowing the judgmental, left-brain capacities to dominate. To call the intuitive functions into play the teacher must use words, which are still the primary means of helping performers increase their awareness. But in awareness, the performer runs the risk of listening to self, watching self, and controlling self to such an extent that spontaneity is lost along with the possibility of genuine growth and discovery. The actor's art, as Fanny Kemble said, "has neither fixed rules, specific principles, indispensable rudiments, nor fundamental laws. . . . . The mere appearance of spontaneity . . . is its chief merit."[11]

Achieving Awareness without Overcontrol

As we explore the hearing/vocal mode, we have a paradigm in miniature of this larger issue: the words, and all the intellectual control that accompanies them, on one hand, and the musicality with which the words are spoken or sung on the other. When the music of language or the musical score is overanalyzed, it becomes pompous and pedantic; if it is ignored, the musical capacities of language and song will tend to remain what they are. In our nation, which is not hearing mode dominant, the resultant naturalism may be appropriate for the actor if the style of the role already matches that of the actor (assuming that the actor is truly able to use his or her own musicality in performance.) But it makes inaccessible a vast range of characters and styles. As we seek to achieve awareness and growth without self-consciousness and overcontrol, we must find ways of communicating clear language challenges to the hearing/vocal mode mind and allowing that mind to play with those challenges with little judgmental interference.

In *The Inner Game of Tennis*, Tim Gallwey sets up the self 1, self 2 metaphor, which corresponds roughly to the left-brain, right-brain concept. Self 1 (left brain, intellectual control center) interferes with the body-knowing, intuitive freedom of self 2 (the right brain system) by imposing judgmental opinions. I have found it useful to ask self 1 and self 2 to engage in a creative dialogue. Instead of self 1 criticizing and judging the actions of self 2, self 1 is asked to create alternatives for self 2 to execute in its own way. Self 1 knows the usual patterns that self 2 would use in reading a line, for example, and in knowing this can also conceive of different ways of delivering the line. Self 1 can then allow self 2 to execute that variation, altering it in any way necessary to make musical meaning of it. Any metaphor like this that allows the intellectual resources to analyze the situation, suggest the means, and then get out of the way of the process is useful in dealing with the paradox of performance.

The connection of the hearing/vocal mode with the intellectual-verbal spectrum can be seen in our stereotypes of high intelligence, authority, and power. The ability to allow the mode to be the dominant channel of communication is almost always associated with high intelligence or authority or power.

ANECDOTE: *The association of British culture and acting with isolation of the hearing/vocal mode often interacts with American culture and acting with its emphasis on the facial/emotional and kinesthetic modes. The American actor Arthur Hill, who worked with the British director Sir Tyrone Guthrie, relates an incident that reflects one of these interactions.*

Hill was acting in The Matchmaker, *directed by Guthrie, who said to him on one occasion: "In the theatre, if you want to concentrate your power, the less of your body you use the more concentrated it will be." Hill continues, "And he was right. If really want to say something dead serious, don't move one limb, move only your jaw. And suddenly everything stops dead and everybody says, 'This is serious, this is important.' "[12]*

Our culture has granted more and more weight to the power of the word, as opposed to physical actions and emotional feelings, in the past few centuries. The power of the isolated hearing/vocal mode is doubtless the result of its unique connection with words and the intellect. Whatever the implications of that power, the ability to isolate the hearing/vocal mode from entanglement with the other modes is an important means of characterization for the performer. A useful observational exercise is to study people in life for pronounced dominance in any mode and for the ability to isolate in that mode. What we call characterization, one can see, is based precisely on varying mode dominances and combinations of mode strengths. These combinations are virtually infinite in their variety, but they can be described with great specificity. Once described and exercised, each can be used as the basis for a characterization.

In developing the hearing/vocal mode, one of our immediate tasks is to expand the potential musicality for each performer.

ANECDOTE: Lest one think that this expansion of language musicality be confined to the beginning actor, witness Sir Laurence Olivier's reply to the following question from Kenneth Tynan: "When you came to play Othello, did you feel physically equipped for it in every respect?" Olivier: "No, I didn't. I didn't think that I had the voice for it. But I did go through a long period of vocal training especially for it, to increase the depth of my voice, and I actually managed to attain about six more notes in the bass. I never used to be able to sing below D, but now, after a little exercising, I can get down to A, through all the semitones; and that helps at the beginning of the play, it helps the violet velvet that I felt was necessary in the timbre of the voice."[13] As a student, I heard Olivier perform the Othello, and the shock on hearing his 'new' voice after being so familiar with what I thought of as a brilliant brass trumpet was profound.

Development of musicality beyond the actor's normal range means that the actor can use his or her voice to make a unique contribution to the performance. The playwright contributes the words themselves, but the performer creates the score to which the words are set. The performer becomes a composer and a player at once by creating the language score or musical characterization and then playing that score on the instrument of the voice. The playwright has already done the left-brain work creating the logic and analytic structure that make the meanings clear. All the performer has to do is understand that logic, not recreate it. There is often a confusion about this concept of re-creation: the thought of the playwright in creating the character is one thing, involving all sorts of understandings about unconscious motivations that are not part of the character's thought process; the thought of the character is a different concept from that of the playwright, and it is expressed through music as well as words. This music is the performer's primary creative contribution. The words and the music *are* the meaning, regardless of the performer's actual thought process.

The creation of the score by the performer depends first upon the musical capacity of the performer's instrument. Sometimes, as in the case of Olivier and Othello, the performer's instrument capabilities need to be expanded. (If Olivier's did, whose does not?) Next is the composing of the "notes" themselves, the musicality with which the language is spoken; last is the ability of the performer-instrument to play that score with authenticity, believably and naturally. No matter how unusual the score—regardless of the bumps, the pops, the sensual words, the sudden changes of process—and despite the virtuosity of the performer, the actual performance must sound authentic.

For the singer-actor, the process is similar but one step removed. Because both words and music have been created, the singing-acting performance is totally re-creative, making it more difficult to sound authentic. The performance may sound correct, logical, and precise, but it must also sound convincing. Spontaneity and naturalness are difficult to attain in proportion to the technical difficulty of the music, yet the performer must sing the words and music in a way that is both technically proficient and convincingly authentic. It is the same challenge faced by the speaking actor—simply more technically challenging.

In all performance we confront this set of opposites: the cluster of ideas around the word *authentic*, including believable, honest, convincing, natural, real, and true; and the cluster around the word *interesting*, including theatrical, compelling, varied, energized, exciting, and fascinating. The manner in which a person talks in life is, for that person, natural/honest/believable. The manner in which the character talks in performance must be those things, but it must also be interesting/energized/theatrical. We can give up neither demand, but it is clear that we exercise the first continually in our everyday life. But the singer-actor has no model in life on which to base the singing-acting performance. We don't sing in life as a habitual process, and we have no paradigm in life for singing-acting performance—only other singing-acting performances. To ask a singer to be natural with the voice is a contradiction in terms, yet we know singers who sound more natural than others.

One of the great challenges of acting technique is how to use on the stage what we already know how to do in life without interfering with it. In the Zen of tennis playing, one already knows how to play tennis and must simply allow the body to do what it already knows how to do without getting in its way. But the actor has another challenge: to expand the range of things done freely, without interference, even while continuing to function believably. To return to our metaphor, once the tennis player has learned the techniques of playing tennis and how to allow those techniques to play themselves through the body, he or she has to learn to play the same game in many different styles—a net-rushing style, a backcourt volley style, a soft-shot style—and to play them all with equal authenticity. The "music" of the game would have to be enlarged to include all possible kinds of strokes and strategies—fast and slow paced, rhythmically varied strokes, hard and soft strokes, change of pace, timing, attack and lay-back approaches, all with both forehand and backhand skills. The very best players do precisely this: they are able to alter their style to deal more effectively with an opponent. Sports is filled with lessons about teams or individuals losing or winning insofar as they are able to adjust to or exploit their opponent's style. Sports reporters also talk of the art of a player, or the artistic manner in which victory was achieved. Here again is authenticity, the sense that the performer has mastered the style of the game so well that it is played with supreme grace, which translates to believability and naturalness. Authenticity comes when the skills required for a style are mastered so completely that they seem natural to the person doing them. If you can perform anything with great ease, it tends to be convincing on that basis alone.

One of the skills the actor must acquire is the sense of interconnectedness between external and internal resources, with feedback between the two alive and responsive. It is not enough to be glib and flexible with the language—it must also *sound* as though it comes from a genuine thought process. The crucial difference between sports and acting here is the relative importance of authenticity. In sports you may have no authenticity or style whatsoever, but if you defeat your opponent you have won. For the singer-actor, skill and authenticity are of equal importance. For example, the greater the range of musical capability, the greater the range of characterizations the performer can create; but that range will be useless if the performer cannot use it with authenticity. Nothing will have been "won."

One cannot practice authenticity without first mastering the skill itself. To impose the demands of authenticity before mastery of skill is to interfere seriously with the process of mastery. In expanding hearing/vocal mode capabilities, we concentrate on skills and their mastery with the understanding that, although authenticity is vital to the final product and may be the key aspect of the actor's performance, premature demand for it can short-circuit the growth process that produces it. When the instrument has been properly exercised and prepared to receive the music of the character, one must nurture that flicker of authenticity with great patience and love; overconcern with technique may even snuff it out. But if the flicker of authenticity has no access to an instrument able to express it, it will never grow. We stand poised between opposites, partaking of the energy of each for maximum vitality.

Chapter 4
Exercising the
Hearing/Vocal Mode

Our hearing/vocal mode mind makes the speaking music it does without thinking about it intellectually—it simply plays the tune that *feels* right. Even the words we say are not planned out in advance in most cases, but are thought and spoken simultaneously without intellectual prejudgment and control. Normal everyday speaking is a process that we modify and guide as it occurs, not stopping before each phrase to decide how we wish to structure it verbally for maximum meaning. If we did stop to decide, our speaking would be unimaginably dull. The choice of words is an intuitive process, and how much more so is the choice of musicality with which we speak them? The control is in-process rather than predictive, dealing with the flow of energy as it moves rather than predicting it in advance and forcing it into that predicted pattern. If we allow the left brain to assert predictive, judgmental overcontrol, the delivery becomes stilted, pretentious, and ultimately unbelievable.

Mindful of those dangers, however, we often need to make the techniques happen when we are expanding the range and communicating power of our natural musicality. In the initial stages of exercise, we must simply do the new musicality skills without worrying whether they work or make sense. Demanding the final, successful product too quickly reinforces the kind of product thinking that keeps us from growing. However strange, uncomfortable, or foreign the technique may feel at first, however much it may pinch or irritate, we must first *do* it until we can handle it easily. We can then begin playing with the techniques, allowing them to happen in response to the flicker of inner meaning and making them a part of the intuitive process. Yet even that intentional *doing* can be infused with the idea of allowing; the real goal is to do and allow at the same time.

Describing Language Musicality

Because musical terminology is relatively precise, we will define these techniques—the hearing/vocal mode skills for speakers as well as singers—in musical terms. As we do so, let us keep several things in mind. First, spoken human language is far too complex musically to score accurately, and even if it could be, the score would be too complex to read. The musical definitions we will use are broad generalizations that must be seasoned with the infinite variations of which the human voice is capable. Second, any device that creates change in the performer's language musicality, whether spoken or sung, is useful. The more precise our description of what already is and what is desired in its place, the more likely the change will occur. The suggested descriptions are useful beginnings, but one should not feel restricted to them. The only description to avoid is one that is too subjective: for example, "Say it with more feeling" (or anger or sarcasm or pleasantness) is a description that commits the mind-reading fallacy and that can lead to varying degrees of vocal-indicating.

Before proceeding to the definitions, let us distinguish between the speaking voice and the singing voice. The singer works from a score in which a great share of the musicality is already defined. Speed, rhythm, volume, and pitch are specified, and the singer works within a far more restricted range of choices than the speaker. But choice is there, and more use can be made of it than is usually the case. The singer is hemmed in by authority figures, many of whom are more intent on correctness than on expression. Getting it right is important, of course, but there are many different ways to get it right. Every conductor has a different way in mind, and the singer has to be flexible enough to execute any one of them authentically. I have a running request of the musical coaches with whom I work: prepare the singer to give five completely different interpretations each with authenticity—a Muti version, a Karajan version, a Mehta version, an Ozawa version, and a Marriner version. The flexibility and understanding they acquire in such a process serves them better under any circumstances than the "one right way" approach that is so common. It is a rare coach, however, who can give up one favorite interpretation to teach several possibilities. Those working for different conductors do so automatically, of course, but I speak here of the training process. (Many singers are slow in coping with a single interpretation, let alone five; but perhaps mastery would come quicker if they understood it from the perspective of alternative choices in the future.)

As we discuss language musicality, I assume that the same changes on a more modest scale can be exercised by the singer and coach: songs can be sung faster and slower, louder and softer, more legato or more staccato, more intensely or more relaxed, along with attention to the other expressive aspects of language musicality. The singer who investigates the meaning of language musicality in depth and develops a sensitivity to it acquires an understanding of the composer's use of musicality in setting words.

Let us begin with an objective list of ways one can describe language musically. One can speak a sequence of words

Fast	or	Slow
Loud	or	Soft
Staccato	or	Legato/Smoothly
Intensely	or	Relaxedly
High pitched	or	Low pitched
Disconnectedly	or	Connectedly.

Each of these ways can also be used with a variety of tone colors or voice placements, and with progressions (fast or slow) within each of the categories. (One can move from loud to soft to loud, for example, doing so either rapidly or gradually.) Using these basic musical descriptions, one can describe, and thus change, a person's characteristic musicality. One cannot speak at all without using each of these descriptive categories— speed, volume, pitch, rhythm, intensity, and the rest. I call these "in-time" categories. In asking a performer to change an in-time category, one is not asking for something new or foreign; rather one is asking the performer to give attention to the musicality, make a change in it, get comfortable with that change, until finally the new usage is available as a communicating technique. The important thing is that the performer becomes more specific about the choices made.

The ability to describe another person's language musicality is vital to the growth process. It is like coaching in music: the more the performer is aware of the musicality techniques of another performer, the more readily they can be used for his or her own performance. Hearing/vocal mode learning is a matter of perception as well as projection, and the two may be related in ways that defy separation. What we are able to perceive we can learn to project, and vice versa.

Several "out-of-time" categories help to define the shape of the in-time flow. These include pauses (significant or tactical ones), nonverbals (all sounds that are not actual words), pops and bumps (momentarily touching the highest and lowest notes in one's range), sensual words (words given a special coloration or intensity), and noncadencing (avoidance of a downward inflection at the end of a line, thus connecting and sustaining phrases). Other out-of-time categories, with which we will not deal, are accent, diction, and dialect skills.

Two aspects of the hearing/vocal mode are to be developed: one is the strength of the mode itself and the other is its ability to work independently of the kinesthetic and facial/emotional modes. The third step—the ability of the hearing/vocal mode to work in a flexible partnership with the other modes—is discussed in chapter 7. To achieve the first two steps, the performer must be given challenges that carry the hearing/vocal mode beyond its normal functioning. These challenges strengthen the mode and test its capacity to function without the assistance or interference of the kinesthetic and facial/emotional modes. We focus attention on both issues: how the hearing/vocal mode is responding to the challenge of the exercise, and how the other two modes are relating to those responses.

The ideal condition or state of being for the kinesthetic and the facial/emotional modes during the exercise of the hearing/vocal mode is a state of *readiness*. Although readiness is a somewhat subjective idea, it is very tangibly and objectively perceived by observers. It refers to a physical and facial state of being that is alive, alert, and totally prepared to communicate or act in any way. Neither tense nor relaxed (opposites that must partake of each other to create a state of readiness), it is rather the preparedness to respond freely and quickly to anything that may occur. In athletic terms, readiness is the state of being of an athlete prepared for action. Described as a poised, vital, ready-to-act condition, it is also the ideal mental state for the performer, making one ready for any contingency, flexibly prepared to deal with whatever might occur.

Readiness is also essential to the hearing/vocal mode, but there is a significant difference in the ability to perceive it. In the facial/emotional and kinesthetic modes, one can see or sense the readiness. In the hearing/vocal mode, however, one can only hear the state of being, which means that there is no way to determine mode readiness before it is in action making sounds. There will always be physical holds of some kind when the hearing/vocal mode is not in a state of readiness, but they will often be too well disguised to detect. When they are released, however, the difference will be seen and felt as well as heard, even though it may not be easily describable. In any case, readiness in the hearing/vocal mode is an in-process condition that tells us retrospectively what the state of being was prior to singing.

The tricky thing about this state of being, this readiness, is that in a highly skilled performer its absence can be so cleverly disguised that one is not aware that the performer's full potential has not been realized. The highly skilled performer has such careful control over the product that it is generally acceptable and often very compelling. As long as the performer is creating the product in the usual way, it is difficult to sense the interference. Only when an exercise of some kind *reveals* the interference or *removes* it do observers realize what the performer has been doing to prevent full power from coming into play. When product orientation is given up and the performance is attempted with higher levels of energy, the interference culprit is left with his or her hands in the energy cookie jar. By trying to use more energy in any mode, the performer's habitual control-interference pattern has to work that much harder to deal with the new energies, and the struggle will be clear to everyone including the performer.

Most control-interference patterns to which we have habituated ourselves are comfortably ensconced just below the level of awareness. If we are aware of them, we have made up some intellectual justification for them: "It's my interpretation," or "It's part of my character," or "That's the way I am." When we truly put the patterns to the test, however, we become aware how they block our true energy capabilities and prevent us from doing what we wish to do. Placing extra pressure on those control-interference patterns makes us aware that, in trying to control, we have in fact lost control, and that we must give up predictive control to gain in-process control.

Control-interference is the elephant we try not to think about. But sometimes we find a rose exercise that replaces the elephant and removes the interference. When this happens, it is always a revelation to listeners who become aware in retrospect how much the performer had been interfering with vocal energies. The performer, however, may have feelings of not doing enough because it is too easy or feels very good. In most cases, the removal means not doing something that the performer believes should be done. One way of leading performers into that process is to have them talk to you conversationally and then signal them to go into their speech without making any change in the use of the voice. The same approach can be used on a physical and facial level. The "something" that they ordinarily add to their performance is left behind, and that something is usually the control-interference pattern. When a rose exercise focuses the performer's attention on something else, allowing the not-doing to take place, positive feedback from the group is vital in enforcing the acceptance of that noncontrolling way of feeling.

In both cases—revealing the control-interference by stronger uses of energy or removing it by focusing the attention elsewhere—the goal is to allow more energy to flow more freely. Both approaches should be explored because they interact with each other. The rose approach is an unconscious one (that is, the interference is removed without conscious awareness of the fact), and it often involves a natural, everyday use of energy. When that energy is heightened consciously, the interference wants to return to accompany it. In releasing that elephant, remembrance of the rose state of being can be helpful. That simply means maintaining the unselfconscious state while increasing the output of energy.

Exercise of the hearing/vocal mode is an idea foreign to most young American actors. Having listened to more than a decade's worth of performers trying to exercise language musicality in class, and questioning them about how they work on it outside of class, I am convinced that young actors rarely do it on their own. This is not an accusation, for the omission arises from existing circumstances more than laziness or obstinacy. They do not live in a hearing/vocal mode dominant country and they are seldom asked to exercise their language musicality in either rehearsal or class situations. They may have been asked to speak "louder" or "faster," but beyond such generalities, they are seldom asked to change their language musicality in specified and significant ways. Sometimes, if they are blessed with strong hearing/vocal mode instincts (dominance?), they are led into striking uses of the language by certain kinds of roles. But such accidental collisions of script and natural potential occur so infrequently that no consistent skill in language musicality is developed.

Many inhibiting factors seem to prevent the American actor from dealing directly with hearing/vocal mode energies. Principal among these is the idea that if you actually try to do something with your voice, you will be phony; and its corollary, that if you simply "feel it," the voice will do whatever needs to be done without conscious exercise of technique. The most convincing argument against both ideas is the experience of performer growth when such resistance is overcome. Having heard the significant progress that occurs when students who seemed poor in musicality were given language challenges over time, I am convinced that it is a vital (I would like to say imperative) step to take. Working with language musicality led to a reeducation of my hearing mode and those of my students, and it will do the same for anyone. Before I began making demands on the language musicality of my performers (and therefore of my own perceptions), I was not able to describe the music of the spoken voice with sufficient clarity to help them change it. Each year, with each new group of students, I encounter again the struggle to be specific in describing the musicality of language. It is a triple challenge: first, to describe exactly how one has heard a person deliver a sequence of lines in terms of speed, rhythm, pitch, volume, intensity, tone quality, pauses, and inflections; then to determine what that musicality means; and, finally, how that meaning can be changed or communicated more clearly by modifying the initial musicality. The *how* of the description is one thing and the *what* of the meaning is another. Achieving specificity is often a trying task, but it is essential if one is to help the performer make meaningful, clearly communicated, conscious changes in language musicality. Early attempts at description by the group often involve words suggesting emotional states—"excited," "involved," "committed"—or generalized vocal states of being—"snarling," "grating," "smooth," "round," "open," and the like.

The actor can enhance awareness of this descriptive process by becoming more familiar with musical terminology and by learning to apply it to language. For the singer, learning to connect music they already know with actual actor meanings is equally important. In both cases, the feedback relationship between technique and meaning is strengthened.

We cannot actually describe the complexities of the spoken vocal score, subtleties that are beyond the descriptive capacity of any language or scoring system; but we strive to make a clear-cut, general description of the score within which the subtleties can play. The subtleties must be allowed to emerge of their own accord in response to the intuitive sense of the hearing/vocal mode mind.

Making Sense with Musicality

When beginning such work, one commonly fails to have a firm grasp of how the lines "work" in terms of musical meaning—that is, how they make sense when spoken. How does one say the lines so that they sound right? Every performer must answer that question not with their intellectual resources, but by understanding the lines *with the voice in action*. The in-action, musical meaning of the line is its operative structure, or how the musicality of the language works in making sense of the line. To understand the line, one must first find its operative structure. Although the musical pattern of stresses and inflections that allow it to make sense is too complex to be described in detail, listeners can almost always agree upon the appropriate operative structure when they hear it. Intellectual arguments can go on for hours about every conceivable reading, but the cleverest arguments often produce the most unlistenable rendition. No matter how brilliantly such readings are defended, their lack of actual musical sense becomes clear when they are spoken. In this classic collision between the analytic left brain and the intuitive, synthesizing right brain, the intellect interferes so completely with the speaking-musicality skills that the performer is unable to perceive (and to give) any reading except the one that performer has been arguing for, which may be a faulty one. Once a line-reading pattern is established (which takes only a few repetitions), enormous effort is required to change it, to break through the intellectual mind-set that forms around that reading. The depth of the mental rut that is created by the first line readings given under pressure is astounding.

A common phenomenon that demonstrates the "rut principle" is the progression from the first reading of a play to its production some weeks later. The performer's first line readings are often essentially the same readings one hears on opening night. Rehearsal may allow them to be delivered more confidently and precisely, but the reading itself—the operative structure—remains basically the same. Significantly, those line-reading decisions were made long before the performers had the necessary information and understanding. Decisions would be possible after three weeks of studying the characters, experiencing the lines and situations in action, but not at the first or even the fifth reading.

To the competent actor, this danger may seem obvious; but it is surprising how quickly such line-reading ruts can form, even with highly skilled performers. The ability to avoid these ruts is a vital skill, and one that is developed as a by-product of expanding the musicality skills of the hearing/vocal mode. For these skills to grow, many different line readings must be explored with the voice in action, thinking with the voice (rather than the intellect) so that the lines can be heard and reacted to as part of a live process.

The hearing/vocal mode mind is the first of the three mode minds that we will develop as a concept for the performer. This voice mind practices daily in developing its ability to communicate. It does this with almost no conscious, intellectual awareness or control. It works in-process, and if the intellectual mind attempts to predict and control that process, it interferes with it. The hearing/vocal mode mind must be as free-flowing as possible in its exploration of meaning and music, with no judgment or criticism allowed in early stages. The task of the intellect here is observation and description, not judgment. The same rules that apply to creative brain storming apply here: try as many musicality ideas as possible in searching for potential readings and avoid all criticism until many possibilities have accumulated. Statistics from brainstorming sessions have demonstrated that early ideas are not as creative as later ones. The mind apparently needs convincing that the "no criticism" rule will be honored. Once it is, the ideas flow with increasing freedom. The same thing applies to the individual mind: convince the intuitive imagination that the intellect will not criticize it, and the creative flow of ideas rises dramatically.

Once the lines have been explored in some depth, the many possibilities should be allowed to cook in the unconscious, blending and intermingling, before the final choice of readings is made. Typically, the most appropriate reading emerges of its own energy. It is surprising how a given reading, which made no sense on Tuesday, acquires the most compelling and significant implications on Thursday.

The words I write here can only suggest ways of working that have proved useful in actual practice. The work itself is a process of thinking with the voice. For the teacher-director-coach, this means learning to *hear reality*, that is, hearing the sense of the line that actually emerges from the musicality rather than filtering the spoken words through a preprogrammed intellect; it means hearing with the right brain in cooperation with the left brain, rather than allowing the verbal-analytical screen of the left brain to dictate the total response.

The intellect is very skilled at analyzing the language for such things as operative structure. Once there is an understood structure, the intellect is loathe to give up control, trying to *make* the structure happen and converting it into lifeless, mechanical vocal patterns. Each operative word tends to come out in the same way, with the same kind of stress. In attempts to clarify the perceived intellectual structure, musical rhythms and pitches are slowed down and overcontrolled. Again, the musicality challenge must be turned over to the part of the mental system that can handle it—the hearing/vocal mode mind.

The concept of operative structure can refer to singing as well as speaking. A singer's understanding of what the words say and how the lines would be spoken can and should influence how a song is sung. Sergius Kagen, in his book on vocal technique, recommends that a singer learn an art song in stages, the words first and then a believable, spoken recitation that is gradually extended technically until it approaches the composer's musical setting, merging finally into the song itself.[1] One may not be able to follow that pattern completely, but the need to exercise the relation between musicality and meaning is essential for both singers and actors.

Let us take a short and simple line and examine the possible operative structures. We will only deal with obvious stress patterns, picking out the operative words that create the structure. But even that will establish a basis from which to begin musicality explorations. The line "I love you," for example, can be stressed in several ways. The change in meaning suggested by each operative structure appears in parentheses.

"I love you."	(Unstressed, the basic verbal meaning is that the speaker has a deep feeling about the person being addressed.)
"I love you."	(Even if someone else doesn't.)
"I love you."	(As opposed to simply loving you in the ordinary sense of that word.)
"I love you."	(I love you too, responding to a person who has just said, "I love you.")
"I love you."	(But I don't think you love me.)
"I love you."	(And someone else just likes you.)

With one of those readings chosen, the operative structure of the line has been decided upon. We are now ready to exercise the musicality of language with that operative structure, communicating the line in many different ways. The exploration process begins all over again, but now the underlying meaning has been decided upon and remains constant. This is often a point of confusion. Performers exercise musicality by changing the operative structure. Underlying meaning changes as well as musicality, and chaos ensues. Musicality and meaning become hopelessly entangled.

A useful way to approach this problem is as follows. Take the specific operative structure, "I *love* you." In exercising the musicality of language, that structure would not change. However, the line could be spoken without changing that operative structure in the following ways:

Fast or slow

Soft or loud

Legato or staccato

In the upper or lower register of the voice

With the inflected "love" higher or lower than the surrounding inflections—or as a pop or a bump

With a pause between "I" and "love" (a pause between "love" and "you," given the operative structure, is a greater meaning stretch, but it could be tried)

With "love" as a sensual word

With various nonverbals before, between, or after words

With a sudden change of process in one of the in-time categories.

Although the basic meaning of the line remains the same, each use of a different musicality enriches and enlarges upon the implications of the line. As the line is explored, both the performer's capabilities and the subtext potentials of the line are expanded.

The next step in the exercise process is to extend the musicality of the reading so that each meaning is unmistakably clear. One should not have to *think* about what has been said to understand it, but simply *know* it. Every line has a whole series of potential musicalities that make the line clear on both intellectual and emotional levels. Finding and choosing one of these musicalities is the function of the search. To do so, one must genuinely explore each of the in-time and out-of-time categories in speaking the lines. Each category should be exercised separately and in combinations until one is using them all intuitively. It is not unlike the way we exercise the modes system as a whole: we isolate each individual component to build strength in that component (for example, in the hearing/vocal mode we learn to use our upper register with skill, ease, and believability); we then combine the components to build a flexible relation between them (we use our high register in combination with staccato and legato patterns); and, finally, we turn our newly acquired strengths and skills over to the mode minds to use as freely and unselfconsciously as possible in the service of the performance (we simply speak the lines as they make sense to us, allowing our new upper register and rhythm skills to function intuitively).

One can begin with any musical category, but the goals are the same: first, to create change in the way the performer uses the language; second, to find the meaning in that change; and third, through the interplay of one and two, to exercise the feedback process between music and meaning. Every change in the musicality of language has a potential meaning contained within it. This does not assure that the meaning will be found. It is possible to make a change in the musicality without making sense of the change, producing a reading that sounds affected, phony, or simply "techniquey." For many performers, however, simply making the technical change is challenging enough and should be encouraged regardless of their ability to make sense of it. But the second step must also be dealt with eventually, and it should be kept in mind as a goal. That second step is taken by answering the question, "What needs to be added to what we have just heard to allow the reading to make sense?" (Or sound believable, or sound as though there was thought behind it.) Again, however, that question must be answered with the voice in action, not merely with the intellect. In almost every case, the technique will have overcontrolled the musicality so that the speaker can make the technique "do" the assignment. Such overcontrol produces precisely the "techniquey" reading referred to above.

Moving from Technique to Meaning

To achieve a greater sense of naturalism and believability, the technique must be retained but released. This may seem paradoxical, but it is not difficult in actual practice. The technique must be *allowed* to happen, rather than being *made* to happen. When this is done, a natural language complexity is added to the bare bones technique. And this must be the case if the line is to make sense. If "fast" was the assignment, and the speaker did nothing but speak rapidly in achieving the first step, the second step involves changes in the speed (there are many kinds of "fast"): the addition of pitch, inflections, rhythm, and volume changes of energy as well as progressions that add the complexity necessary for sense. Whatever the technique asked for, it will at first tend to distort and flatten the meaning as the speaker tries to make it happen. At those times I repeat a little Zen koan doggerel (if there is such a form):

> Fast is not Fast
> Slow is not Slow
> High is not High
> Low is not Low.

In other words, to make sense out of going fast, it is not enough merely to go fast; other ingredients must be added, and the speed itself must be varied. One can ask for seasonings from the other musical categories—a dash of pitch, a pinch of tone color, a dollop of speed, a soupçon of intensity, all of which make the meaning recipe more palatable.

As the performer tries the second step, the move from pure technique to technique-plus-meaning, one can almost hear the wheels turning, the gears creaking and groaning as the feedback process between the external music and the internal meaning starts to come alive. Every technique, every kind of language musicality, can relate to a whole cluster of possible meanings. For example, "fast" can relate to anger, joy, passion, fear, or exuberance, depending upon the character and situation and verbal context. In more complex combinations, to speak a line rapidly or staccato or intensely or legato in one's low register has a meaning cluster connected with each choice. Low, rapid intensity has a cluster around anger; low, slow, and relaxed has a sexy-soothing-sensual cluster; low, slow, and staccato has a sarcastic, biting cluster, and so on. For one of those potential meanings to emerge clearly, however, requires an intuitive mixture of seasonings from the other categories. One can and should suggest these possibilities in helping the performer bring out the meaning flavor more clearly. For example, one might ask for more intensity, more staccato, or a slowing down to make a sudden change in the volume work; or for more relaxation, more low register, or greater pitch variety to help the performer use more natural vocal capacity. But it finally becomes a matter of the performer allowing intuition to come into play, thinking with the voice, with the energies of the performer's own vocal musicality, rather than with the intellect alone. The hearing/vocal mode energies must become equal partners with the intellectual-verbal thought process.

Although this is the goal, many hours are passed in process exercise and play with vocal musicality before a oneness of mind, meaning, and music is realized. But this unity of intent, technique, and execution often happens surprisingly early in the exercise process, even if only for brief moments. I have heard and felt astonishing changes in performance capability long before I had expected to. Even more surprisingly, these changes occurred most often when the musicality techniques were assigned in a totally arbitrary way. The process works like this. After performers have delivered their soliloquies several times over a period of weeks, they are given language musicality assignments. A typical assignment might be as follows: make a progression from fast to slow to fast and accompany it with another progression from staccato to legato; include two sensual words, a tactical pause, a nonverbal, a pop and a bump, and a sudden change of process in pitch. This assignment is then taken home overnight, although it can also be given and performed with only fifteen minutes or so to work it out. In either case, the results are often startling in their power, and almost always superior as performances to the previous "natural" versions with which the rest of the group has become familiar. This is true despite the fact that the assignments are totally arbitrary and are given with no thought as to their relationship with the soliloquy in question. In fact, I sometimes simply write out several dozen arbitrary combinations on slips of paper and hand them out without even looking at them. Yet the same surprising power emerges from the performances.

Achieving a better product, however, is not the major purpose of the exercise, which is intended to stretch the imaginative, sense-making capacity of the voice-in-action. It also exercises the external-internal feedback system by supplying an external statement that the internal sense-making capacity can make sense of through appropriate nuance and modification. Surprisingly (or perhaps logically), the exercise also creates a product that is almost always superior to the performer's habitual performance.

ANECDOTE: As one young performer said about his performance of a soliloquy with arbitrary musicality assignments, "I have used that soliloquy for years in classes, in auditions, and for exercise, but the reading I gave with the arbitrary language assignment was by far the best version I have ever given." His friends, who had often seen him perform the soliloquy, agreed. That reaction echoes dozens of similar comments from performers who have worked with the arbitrary musicality exercise.

The fact that an arbitrary assignment is this successful suggests that any assignment forcing a change in the habitual leads to a better performance. Why? Perhaps because the performer must think anew about what he or she is doing; new thought—whether correct or otherwise—does more than old thought for the performing process. Genuine thought processes are always more vital than habitual, nonthinking processes. Note, of course, that we are speaking of mode thinking in action, not intellectual thinking, even though the intellect is cooperating in allowing the alternative thought processes to function freely. The process also suggests that dozens, even hundreds of different performances are available to performers. Many are more exciting than those that are actually given. Unfortunately, these potential performances are rarely given because the stimulus is not there. If such a stimulus were an automatic part of the actor's rehearsal process, if the actor's internal-external feedback sensitivity were developed to the point of trust in the ability to make fresh external choices, incredible performances would result.

Let us renew our awareness of the two-step format: the first step is to do the technique, the second step is to modify that technique to make sense of it. As performers change their language musicality they take step 1, actually using greater pitch variation, more volume, different rhythm patterns, or whatever the assignment may be. They are dependent upon the listener for assurance that they have actually taken the step and for encouragement to take that step further. Until performers have actually made a change in their musicality, there is no way of exercising the external-internal feedback process. One can only add meaning to a statement that already exists; until the performer has made the change, taken step 1, there is nothing with which to exercise.

As performers change the musicality, tension holds in the voice may prevent the subtle musical changes necessary for the move to step 2. These tension holds are sometimes difficult to recognize, particularly in skilled actors who have been cleverly disguising their problems for years. The more experienced the actor, the better are the holds disguised, and the more difficult it is for the actor to release them. Anything that holds the voice in a fixed relationship to pitch, rhythm, speed, volume, or tone quality keeps the performer's natural musicality from emerging.

Performers are not only their own instrument; they are also their own score. Each performer is a compendium of scores containing an enormous range of musicalities based on years of practice in using the voice, years of absorbing other people's language musicalities, and years of exercising a personal imaginative sense of language musicality. The instrument and the score that are the performer are interconnected in a manner unique in the performing arts.

From the moment he or she begins to talk, the performing individual is exercising two things: compositional skills, through the creation of language musicality scores; and voice, the instrument used to create and play the score. During the years before the move from being a performing person to being a performing performer, the individual has been exercising both capacities in everyday life. The instrument (the voice itself) and the scores it can play (the actual language musicality that the voice chooses to use in communicating) become closely identified. In fact, the idiosyncrasies of the instrument and the scores created with it often seem to be the same thing. The nasal voice, for instance, and the musical style of speaking with that voice become identified. If the performer is then challenged to play a new score (one created by someone else), say a Shakespearean role, there is a sudden vocal identity crisis. The score is different, but the performer's instrument is the same — or is it? Since the score and the instrument have become identified, the performer may feel the need for a new instrument to play the new score, a new kind of voice to deal with the demands of the score. Our nasal friend may try to change the old sound and create a "Shakespearean voice" to play the new score. Adoption of a new voice instrument may entail loss of the musical capabilities with which the performer played the accustomed instrument. The vocal hold required for the new voice also places a hold on the musicality that the performer is able to play.

ANECDOTE: I sometimes tell my classes the story of the young clarinet virtuoso who, by the age of eight, had become so skilled on his instrument that he was given a Carnegie Hall recital opportunity. But on the night of the performance, the boy unaccountably decided to play a different concerto than the one he had practiced. This would have been fine, for he was a superb sight reader, but he also chose to play it with an oboe rather than a clarinet, feeling perhaps that the concerto was more suited to the oboe, that it would sound better and make more sense. Such an auspicious occasion, after all, demanded something special. The inevitable happened: he could not play the oboe nearly as well as the clarinet, and the recital was not a great success. The boy had discarded the instrument (and the musicality skills) he had developed over a long period of time in order to play a new score. Although the concert was not a disaster — the boy after all was a great musician and could play any reed instrument with some skill — he was coping with two challenges (a new score and a new instrument), and the audience was disappointed because he was not the sensation they had been promised.

The story was created for a specific teaching occasion, but the moral is apt: anyone who discards the instrument musicality he has developed over a long period of time for one that he has not practiced in order to play a new score is taking on a double burden. He cannot be expected under those circumstances to do justice to his capabilities. It is sometimes difficult to detect this change in the use of the performer's instrument musicality, but the simple device mentioned above of engaging in normal conversation with a performer and then asking for a move into the performer's soliloquy will reveal it clearly.

This use of instrument musicalities is not to be confused with the expansion of the performer's ability to play other characterization scores. The performer's own instrument musicality must be used while practicing other character "tunes" having wider ranges of pitch, rhythm, volume, speed, intensity, and tone color, as well as learning to use all the out-of-time musical techniques (nonverbals, tactical pauses, sensual words, pops, bumps, and noncadencing). The performer should also be able to change diction or accent without betraying the sense of a living instrument musicality.

Vocal technique, as taught by a singing teacher or in a voice class, is a separate concern. Whatever the technique, it should expand the student's ability to exercise language musicality. If it does not—except for those times when the voice teacher wants the student to avoid certain practices to break a habit or heal a damaged voice—it is not a useful vocal technique.

Singers, as well as actors, develop holding patterns in their voices and often fail to use their own instrument. This situation, however, is considerably more complex because singers are using a vocal technique that is already stylistically removed from their speaking voice. But the holding, the attempt to make a "special" sound that is not their own natural sound, occurs with great frequency. One way to release this hold in singers is the tension check exercise, in which other performers manipulate the singer's body during the singing and help release areas of tension in the physical being that are inevitably connected with the vocal hold. A vocal hold of any kind is almost always created by some sort of kinesthetic interference with the hearing/vocal mode; the physical hold and the vocal hold go together, and releasing the physical hold tends to release the vocal hold as well. The tension check exercise also helps the speaking actor. Holds in the speaking voice may seem easier to release than those in the singing voice, but because they are more easily disguised they can be equally difficult to remove. (Tension checks and related physical techniques are covered in greater detail in chapter 6.)

As performers exercise in one category of musicality, control takes over and interferes with meaning in other categories. For example, when speed is being exercised — fast or slow — rhythm, pitch, and volume are often held or maintained unnaturally. Sometimes the category being exercised is itself overcontrolled in an attempt to make it work. When pitch is exercised — either in using a higher or lower tessitura, or in trying to employ a greater pitch range — the pitch itself may be held at one general level or the changing pitch may be repeated over and over in an attempt to force a greater pitch range. In both cases, the attempt sounds artificial because any hold or constant repetition is unnatural. If volume is being exercised — especially when trying to project more loudly — the overcontrol is perceived by the volume remaining at one level; the person sounds as if he or she were shouting.

ANECDOTE: One young woman who, trying to be natural and "feel it," did not project enough to be heard, decided to change her average volume level. At first she sounded as though she were shouting: volume, pitch, speed, rhythms, and tone quality all remained on one level, but at least we could hear her. It was a matter of allowing those factors to have the variety they do in natural speech. We were able to describe what made it sound unnatural, and with that awareness, she was able to begin sounding more natural on the spot without losing her projection. She was also able to work on the problem outside of class, and the growth from class to class was discernible and exciting.

Most of the time, one encourages the use of more energy by the performers. Less energy is seldom a problem — less tension, perhaps, because tension is often difficult to release, but not less energy. While encouraging greater energy, one listens for believability and a sense of the natural. This point is where the conflict occurs. There is a deceptive equation between use of energy and naturalism, in which naturalism tends to be equated with low energy. I often ask my classes to deliver their Shakespearean soliloquies as naturalistically as possible. Inevitably, their hearing/vocal mode energies drop dramatically from their previous readings. In decreasing the energy, the actors are expressing the unverbalized belief that the idea of naturalism is directly related to low vocal energy. Although this is clearly nonsense in reality, actors who express the belief in intuitive action are responding to the fact that it is difficult to increase one's vocal energy and continue to sound natural, believable, and authentic. Anyone can whisper and sound believable in doing so: it takes real effort to make a whisper sound phony. There are directors who ask their Shakespearean casts to whisper their lines as a rehearsal technique to get them to sound more natural. The exercise is a surefire bet to work while the cast is whispering, but it will do nothing to ensure the authenticity of the lines once more energy is used. To learn to work with energy, one must work with energy. Obvious, perhaps, but not so to teachers-directors-coaches who cry "relax," "take it easy," or "cool it," diminishing energy in order to achieve believability. A reduced-energy prescription may be helpful for the purpose of achieving immediate product believability, but for the purpose of singer-actor development it only eliminates the essential exercise of using greater energy without tension.

Having said that, we must also acknowledge the opposite: persuading performers to use their own instrument musicality (or, more simply, to use themselves) often means making them relax, work with less effort, avoid pushing. It was undoubtedly this reduction in vocal energy to achieve a more natural sound that gave rise to the mumbling caricatures of method acting. A mumble, like a whisper, tends to sound natural if nothing else. If being authentic and believable is more important than being interesting and vital, energy will always have to be reduced for the young performer in production-oriented situations. If that reduction becomes a habit (and lower energy is habit forming because it is more comfortable), it becomes a creed for the mature performer. Films and television have heightened this tendency. The use of strong vocal energy in those media can be disastrous unless accompanied by the kind of technique that we have noted in the work of BBC performers. If a performer is able to use large-scale energies effectively, it is a relatively simple matter to reduce the scale and retain the believability—the anyone-can-whisper rule. But the reverse is not true. As Peter Brook (among many others) has pointed out, "A good stage actor can act in films, but not necessarily the reverse."[2]

Our goal is to enable the performer to use maximum energies in all three modes and to use these energies skillfully and meaningfully without unnecessary tension. If we accomplish this, we can be certain that the performer will also be able to modify the energies as necessary for more intimate work, moving from stage to films to television regardless of which mode is the primary communicator.

The greatest obstacle we encounter in helping performers acquire greater hearing/vocal mode energy skills is the product demand. We encounter the competition between product and process at every turn. When performers try to use an unfamiliar musicality, they may not give as good a performance the first time as they would in relying on their old habits. That gives rise to another bit of doggerel that I repeat during the early weeks of exercise:

> It may feel worse doing something new
> Than doing what you're already able to do.

I must say it to myself as well because the pressure is always on the teacher-director-coach to come up with instant performer salvation, to find the trick that will create a better performer product on the spot. That pressure must be applied to the real issue: what can the performer do to make those "worse" energies—the unaccustomed energies—sound more believable? What adjustments can be made in the use of energy without giving up the energy challenge itself?

Performers are always excited to realize that their new language awareness gives them a specific tool to deal with mind-reading requests from their teachers or directors. The use of the language communicates independently of the thought process that accompanies it—an obvious point, yet one that is sometimes denied by implication when mind-reading instructions are given.

ANECDOTE: One of my students related the following experience. An acting teacher (and a very good one) had asked him to use some internal tactics in a scene for the class. The performer decided that instead of worrying about the internalization, he would choose appropriate language musicalities that would convey it. He chose a high-fast-staccato beginning musicality, which he would suddenly change to a low-legato at a crucial point in the soliloquy. He felt totally technical about the performance, but at the same time it was easy and fun to do. The scene was highly emotional, and when he made the sudden change of process the audience gasped. As the performer put it, "The moments I was least involved and the most technically aware were the moments of greatest power for the audience—and they were wonderful moments for me as well, although very different than I was used to."

The teacher complimented him warmly on the success of his internalization. Needless to say, he did not share the means he used to fulfill the assignment, although it would have been gratifying had he felt the permission to do so.

The theme returns: the need for process thinking, for descriptive thinking, for nonjudgmental, nonproduct thinking when attempting to develop new capabilities. The teacher-director-coach can encourage this greatly by demonstrating the kind of attitude being asked for from the performer. It is the teacher's job to give honest, descriptive, but nonjudgmental and supportive analyses of the performer's work, thus nurturing growth whatever the performer's skill level. What is needed is the teacher-director-coach who can explore along with the performer, who can say, "I don't know the answer," who can respond to what has actually happened rather than what was supposed to happen, and who admits mistakes openly. We need teachers who are not only unafraid of genuine process, but who welcome it; who are not only willing to give up control when appropriate, but who actively seek ways of releasing themselves and their performers from useless control of all kinds.

Exercises in Language Musicality

When exercising the hearing/vocal mode, any capability can be challenged by combining the various categories of language musicality. We can create an almost unlimited series of exercises for performers by using progressions within each category. The simplest progressions are single combinations.

Single Progressions
Fast to slow to fast to slow, etc.
Slow to fast to slow to fast
High to low to high to low
Low to high to low to high
Loud to soft to loud to soft
Soft to loud to soft to loud
Intense to relaxed
Relaxed to intense
Staccato to legato
Legato to staccato
Continuous to discontinuous
Discontinuous to continuous

Each progression can be made more complex by assigning a different rate of change, from gradual to sudden.

Combining any two of the preceding progressions further increases the exercise potential.

Double Progressions
Fast to slow to fast to slow

plus

Staccato to legato to staccato to legato

Intense to relaxed to intense to relaxed

                                        plus
Low to high to low to high
and all other possible combinations.

These double progressions can be further complicated by having the
progressions overlap in various ways.

Double Overlapping Progressions
Fast to slow to fast
                                        plus
Intense to relaxed
and all other possible combinations.

One can also create triple progressions.

Triple Progressions
Continuous to discontinuous
                                        plus
Legato to staccato
                                        plus
Low to high
and all other possible combinations.

These triple progressions can also overlap.

Triple Overlapping Progressions
Slow to fast
                                        plus
Relaxed to intense
                                        plus
Continuous to discontinuous
and all other possible combinations.

No performer is likely to take a triple overlapping progression, execute it technically, and make sense of it the first time it is attempted any
more than one can play perfect tennis after only having watched it for
years. But when step 1 has been accomplished and the technique has
been executed, one can make repeated attempts at step 2 until the meaning and the music are joined. The very scale of the challenge is the fun

of it: the most accomplished actors can devise hearing/vocal mode exercises that challenge and develop their capacities. There are no failures in such exercises. In truth, the only exercises worth doing are those one can't do already, for they are the only kind that allow one to grow. As Marilyn Ferguson puts it in *The Aquarian Conspiracy*, "If we take the artist-scientist's point of view toward life, *there is no failure*. An experiment has results: we learn from it. Since it adds to our understanding and expertise, however it comes out we have not lost. Finding out is an experiment."[3] It is not so much a matter of coming to enjoy failure (although that is better than remaining in the judgmental trap) but of redefining the term as it relates to performer growth. From that perspective, one could define performance success as failure if it was simply a nongrowth repetition of something one could already accomplish. Even without going that far, it is vital that we arrive at a new and positive understanding of the concept of failure as it relates to the exercise process.

The progressions given above are designed to exercise the in-time categories. In exercising the out-of-time categories, we must attend to several diagnostic factors.

Nonverbals

In listening to the execution of the laughs, grunts, sighs, moans, and all the other sounds that make up the nonverbal category, one should be particularly aware of glottal tension. The tension is necessary in some cases to create the sound, but the same tension can easily become a part of the nonverbals. For example, one cannot laugh or grunt without glottal tension and release. Both sounds are made by creating a flow of air by abdominal pressure, stopping the flow of air with the glottis, and then releasing it explosively. The glottal tension that is used in vocal indicating is often revealed by periodic or continuous laughing or gasping during performance, which is a way of justifying the necessary release of the sustained glottal tension. That tension originates in the need to indicate emotion with the voice. Pressure is built up between abdomen and glottis: it is uncomfortable, it must be released, and the result is a nervous laugh. But that release does not take care of the problem, for the tension immediately returns and builds up the pressure all over again to another laugh release, and so on to the end of the performance.

Once the performer and listeners are aware of the tension interference, there are two methods of eliminating it. One is to take the risk of not doing the tension in question — speaking or singing the passage without the tension and without trying to figure out why the tension is there in the first place. This is a great psychological challenge, of course, because it means not doing something that one believes (intuitively and habitually) to be necessary to make sense (or to be believable, good, loved, respected, natural). Nonetheless, if the tension has been raised to the level of awareness, one may be able to take charge of it, to become the master of one's energies in that specific area.

This "don't think about elephants" method can sometimes be aided by what I call the psychoanalytic approach: one can try to understand why the tension is there. Because there is no good reason in the present to maintain a tension habit that is only justified by the past, it should be possible ("Would that it were so!" cries the intellect) to release the tension through the new understanding. The desired change of behavior should be aided by awareness of its origin, by recognition of the fact that it is a useless interference in the present that has a totally erroneous basis in the past. Unfortunately, understanding the causal past seldom alters the behavioral present. The kinds of behavior we are talking about — performance tensions — are no longer accessible to the verbal-intellectual mind. They have become body-voice-emotion habits with wills of their own.

This leads us to the second, or "think about roses instead" method. We can ask the performer to concentrate on another task, using one of the other modes, and the tension in the hearing/vocal mode may be released. Within the mode itself, habitual tensions are so interconnected with musical meaning that concentrating on a different language musicality seldom provides the release desired. For the rose to work, the performer must give up the meaning connection of the musicality in the hearing/vocal mode mind, which may result in a feeling of not "doing" anything. The group must then reinforce the performer's efforts as strongly as possible with assurances that not only is something being done, it is being done with greater energy and freedom than ever before — that it is *wonderful* to hear the release of interference.

And it will be. One of the most gratifying events in achieving release from mode interference and entanglements is the response of the group to the new feeling of freedom in the performer. The group's awareness is usually a bit ahead of the performer: they are aching, literally, to experience the release of the performer's tension. When it happens, the response is nothing one could have programmed; it is genuinely *visceral*—a nonverbal, nonintellectual energy flow in all the observers who have become attuned to the performer's struggle to achieve freedom. Cheers and applause burst out spontaneously at the simplest breakthrough because our own body-voice-emotion minds participate in the joy and warmth of the energy release. That sounds mystical, but it is simply the creation of high synergy in the performer-audience system. The performer has been capable of releasing energy freely to the observer-audience, and that audience responds. The performer has initiated a synergistic relationship with those observing by demonstrating his or her freedom of energy flow vulnerability; this vulnerability is in turn protected and supported by the energies of both the observers and the performer.

We also confront the judgment issue when exercising nonverbals. Words can be judged as right or wrong, as true or false; because we know their meaning in advance, they give us the security and comfort of predictive control. They are intellectually definable, providing the left brain with a sense of knowing where it is going and why. But nonverbals are by definition difficult to define. If they could be defined, it would be better to use a word to fill the function of the non-verbal. Even though *felt sense*[4] is usually very clear, nonverbals inhabit the realm of pure music as imaginative, musical, creative utterances of the right brain. They range all the way from "err" and "uhh" (hesitations of fumbling speech) to "Ah!" and "Oh!" (exclamations), to laughs, to growls, to purrs, to explosive, spitting, barking sounds, and to sounds that are virtually abstract. The more abstract the nonverbal sound, the greater pressure it places on the left-brain intellectual control system to determine its "meaning" and its acceptability as part of hearing/vocal mode communication. In the words of modern technology, nonverbals often do not compute; that is, they are not accessible to the verbal system. As such they are superb exercises for developing the imaginative, sense-making capacity of the right brain (by asking it to add musical seasoning to the nonverbal) and for encouraging the releasing capacity of the left brain. This double challenge recapitulates the two primary themes of our work: developing the sense-making capacity of the three mode minds as they cope with new communication techniques and promoting the willingness of the intellect to allow the new techniques to emerge without interference or overcontrol.

Tactical Pauses

Performers who have been trained in the mind-reading school (think the right thoughts and your acting will work) are often more concerned with showing that they are really thinking than with whether their acting is really working. Being engaged in thought process becomes more important than being interesting, compelling, and unpredictable. Either goal can lead one astray, but mind readers begin doing things externally that presumably show that they are thinking. They often develop what I call the Stanislavsky Stammer, a hesitating, groping pattern that says, "I'm really thinking, searching for alternative word choices." Just listen: "I . . . er . . . never thought you'd . . . er, ah . . . act the way . . . uh . . . you are." For certain inarticulate characters of whom the contemporary theater is fond, this approach is appropriate. But applied, albeit unconsciously, to all playwrights and all characters, it reveals itself as a technical trick to convey naturalism; in fact, it is merely a surface indication having little to do with the actual relationship between speech and thought. Even in those characters for whom the technique is justified, it soon becomes pointlessly predictable as it conveys the same message over and over: "I hesitate and speak slowly because I'm inarticulate." Or, "I'm careful about choosing my words because I'm concerned about how I will be judged when I say them. I run them through in my mind, and if I don't like the effect I'll try another sequence." These are messages that don't need repeating.

Most of the time when we are communicating verbally, we are *thinking with our voice* in the very act of using it. Using the concept of the hearing/vocal mode mind, we are thinking with *that* mind and not with our judgmental, intellectual-verbal mind. Whatever aspect of mind we are using, that mind is able to move infinitely faster than our voice can speak. The major challenge in communicating the text of most play-wrights is training our hearing/vocal mode capacities to function on the more highly energized level of stage life. As Hegel put it, actors must be able to "live at unimaginable speed"—must be able to think and keep pace vocally with a thought process that is far more complex, compressed, and energized than most segments of naturalistic life.[5] A character speak-ing the lines of Shakespeare or singing the words and music of Mozart is living, thinking, and communicating at an intensity and depth far beyond the capacity of the ordinary human being. To pull these extraor-dinary characters back to the level of everyday life (which Mozart's score—*dank sei Gott*—does not permit) is to deny them their very essence.

We have erred in even referring back to everyday life for our example. We do not think, then speak in life: we think and speak virtu-ally simultaneously, and our mind is so magnificently complex that it can observe what is happening vocally, what is going on with the listener, and where the line of thought is going at the same time that it thinks about what is being said at the moment. These awarenesses are only the intellec-tual-verbal part of the total mental system. Nonverbal awareness includes all sorts of other body-mind knowings. To imply that the voice must slow down or hesitate to allow the intellectual mind to keep up is simply a denial of the truth for all but the dullest among us; even for them, it is usually a matter of verbal skill or habit rather than the mind being slower than the voice. There may be occasions when a slow vocal rate, a momen-tary hesitation, or even stammering are appropriate; but it must not be a generalizing trick of naturalistic persuasion.

Continual, predictable hesitations and pauses make the effective use of intentional, tactical pauses difficult. A great many meanings can be associated with a tactical pause. A pause can say "I don't like what I'm going to say" or "I *relish* what I am going to say," or "Listen very carefully to what I say next," or "Did you hear what I just said? I'm going to give you time to assimilate it," or "I just had an idea that stopped my previous train of thought and launched me on a new one." The most important message, however, is the one that accompanies all the preceding ex-amples: "I haven't finished. Continue to pay attention, in fact pay *closer* attention!" During a tactical pause, the thought process must seem to continue so that the listener remains tuned to the thinking of the character. (Unless, of course, the characters and situation call for a succession of empty, Pinter pauses, and the like.)[6]

A related issue is the language musicality issue of noncadencing. A cadence is simply a descending pitch on a word at the end of a sentence, indicating the conclusion of a thought-phrase or the end of communication. For the singer, this factor is handled by the composer. A singer can also sing "through" rests, making them rests that connect phrases rather than separate them. But for the spoken hearing/vocal mode, the ability to control the cadence becomes a way of sustaining the thought. Many performers have a habit of what I call "kitchen-sink cadencing," which breaks up long speeches into short, musically disconnected sequences by continual cadencing. This automatically stops the thought process over and over for the listener, negating the potential cumulative power of the speech and undercutting the significance of a tactical pause. If we think the speaker has concluded, we do not fill the pause that follows with the energy of our attention to the speaker's ongoing thought process. In a lengthy soliloquy or monologue, the whole can be greater than the sum of its parts if we allow the energies of delivery and audience attention to accumulate through noncadencing. Cadencing, on the other hand, robs both energy processes of their true potential.

When noncadencing is combined with the tactical pause, the performer has a great resource for connecting and energizing long speeches and sustaining theatrical time. A long speech can seem repetitive and wordy if it is broken by cadencing; sustained by noncadencing, that same speech develops a mounting sense of involvement that makes it seem shorter than it actually is.

For one who is accustomed to cadencing, it can be remarkably difficult to avoid. Yet the ability to do so—to sustain by musical means the thought process that overarches the spoken text—is essential in working with language that is richer and more extended than everyday speech. Not just the poetic language of the Shakespearean variety, but even a Chekhovian monologue (along with its contemporary descendants) can profit immensely from noncadencing, which signals the audience clearly that the thought process, the strand upon which an assorted variety of verbal pearls is hung, is continuing to sustain the spoken process.

When exercising the noncadencing capacity, the performer should be asked to go beyond the ordinary uses of the technique and to deliver a complete soliloquy or monologue without cadencing. Besides testing the sense-making capacity of the performer, this exercise compels both performer and teacher-director to seek out the many varieties of non-cadencing. The simple grocery list sequence: "milk, eggs, carrots, butter," etc., etc., uses a simple and similar rising inflection on each word until the end of the list, when a cadence tells the listener that the list is complete. The rising inflection is the most common kind of noncadencing, but the effect can also be achieved by simply maintaining the pitch level at the end of a phrase, signaling the listener that the thought is continuing.

We always return to the two-step growth pattern: doing the technique itself, regardless of meaning; and making sense of that technique through more complex uses of energy. Although one might assume that anyone can execute the techniques we have been discussing, a surprising number of performers find it almost impossible to contradict their felt sense of the musical meaning of a line. If the musical meaning they have learned (in trying out the line and rehearsing it) involves a cadence, for example, they have a terrible time trying *not* to cadence. A simple thing like maintaining the pitch level of a word or giving it a rising inflection also seems easy, for the actual output of energy is small. But once the music and the meaning have become entwined, the rut principle mentioned above takes over. A rut is created in the speech road, and each time that road is traveled the rut becomes deeper until it is the only path that can be taken. Enormous energy is needed to break out of that rut.

Part of the blame for the rut lies with the one-way, internal-to-external process. The performer *thinks* the meaning of the line, then *says* it in that way; most performers cannot change the way the line is said without finding a new way to think about it. It is remarkably simple, however, to find different ways of saying the line without worrying about the sense of any of those musicalities. But if one has not traveled the route from external to internal—deferring the sense-making until one has actually said the line in a different way—it feels like a blocked road.

Once a performer breaks out of the rut created by traveling the one-way route, the return route—from external to internal—may be developed.[7] When both directions are free, the performer can begin to deal with the challenge of making sense out of the new external techniques, both personally and for the audience. Sometimes a new nuance of meaning becomes clear the moment the musicality is changed; in other cases, more musical adjustments and seasonings must be added. But once the two-way route is open, many meaning-music interchanges are possible and one is unlikely to get permanently stuck in ruts.

The more challenging the problem, the more fun it can be to solve it. Fun is essential when working with the intersection of new techniques and meanings. The fun and excitement of exercising sense-making skills only happens, however, if one gives up a product-oriented, judgmental approach to the process. Treated as a process, as a game and as play, sense-making exercises can be exhilarating experiences. If an immediate product is demanded by the teacher-director-coach or by the performers themselves, if they insist on something that works the first time, the results will be the same: a fearful, control-oriented, nongrowth situation. That often happens when the hearing/vocal mode is exercised in a theatrical context.[8] If we can release the energies of the performer from the crippling effects of judgment, all the rest falls into place; a climate for genuine growth, creatively based and process oriented, is created.

Pops and Bumps

Noncadencing, with its concern for control of the inflective process, leads directly to the idea of pops and bumps. As defined above, the pop is an upward gliding inflection that rises freely in response to a strong energy emphasis and may even glide lightly off the upper scale. The bump is simply the use of the lowest possible note in one's register on a given word. As with all other techniques, pops cannot be forced but must be allowed to happen. Men often tend to increase volume or intensity as the pitch rises, to make it relate to the strength or timbre of the voice in lower registers. Or a performer may try to hold the pitch in place as the volume or intensity increases. In both cases, the performer must develop other, more flexible capabilities. The voice must be allowed to thin out freely as the pitch rises in response to increased energy. A pop cannot occur with a tense or held vocal production; only if the voice is freely functioning can the upward glide occur flexibly. Thus the attempt to pop is also a

useful diagnostic tool for vocal tension; if accomplished, it often releases
residual vocal tension.

The bump, on the other hand, is the most relaxed use of the vocal
folds, for to sound their lowest note they must be as relaxed, loose, and
long as possible. The only difficulty here may be the psychological inhibition of exploring an unfamiliar area or the challenge of making sense of
such a low note.

The bump often becomes a version of the sensual word exercise.
Sensual words are specific words in a spoken line that are given a special
color, a descriptive nuance or onomatopoeic quality. Sensual words can
growl, purr, snarl, caress, be breathy, hollow, gargled, oozed, and so on.
The bump, by descending to the lowest possible pitch, often gives a
growling or grunting quality to the word. Although there are no limits
in exercising sensual words during training, their use in performance is
only occasional.

The same is true of the other out-of-time techniques. Overuse of any
of them, with the possible exception of skillful noncadencing, quickly
becomes mannered. As such, they are useful for broad characterizations
or caricatures. When exercising the technical capacity, however, no holds
should be barred. Find a technique you have never used, try it out, then
make sense of it. To *play* is the point, to treat the voice as an instrument
capable of playing freely with and making sense of new musicalities and
new energies, creating thereby new meanings and new potentials for
personal expression.

Much of what we do to grow feels strange and unaccustomed: it feels
wrong even when it is right. Much of what feels customary and comfortable needs to be discarded or altered: it feels right even when it is wrong.
To risk feeling wrong with the mode minds, even though the intellectual
mind knows it is right, is a huge psychological challenge demanding new
awarenesses, courage, and support. The person who has never used strong
vocal energy consistently is faced with another kind of inhibition problem. The other two modes try to come into play to help out, and that
attempt needs to be inhibited. Before that point, however, they may
need to participate, to be slowly weaned away as the hearing/vocal mode
develops its own muscle and independence. The muscle, of course, is the

performer's trust that the mode is not only adequate to the task but an equally favored means of communication.

When exercising "baby modes," those that haven't functioned alone enough to develop their full musculature, the performer must remove any responsibility those beginner modes may feel for being as skilled and powerful as "solo modes." One way is to impersonate people who use strong, free-wheeling vocal energies—a revivalist preacher, a political tub-thumper, or a high-pressure street salesman. The performer's vocal energies can be used with greater than ordinary freedom because somebody else is responsible for the musicality in question, and imitating them can be an enjoyable game. The exercise pattern is the same: first get the energy going in the hearing/vocal mode, not worrying about whether the impersonation is accurate or appropriate to the character being portrayed; second, try to make sense of it for the actual characterization in question. In the case of the southern revivalist preacher, that might mean dropping the accent and the stylized vocal characteristics but retaining the higher energy. Finally, blend the actual meaning of the speech and the character by using the energy provided by the impersona-

tion, and modifying that energy in various ways. This process, like the others, should be fun: it should be play, it should be free of performance responsibility, it should be described and not judged, and it should be treated as what it is—a process and not a product.

Any device that allows the hearing/vocal mode to free itself from the stern overcontrol of intellectual judgment is useful. It may be only a technique at first, but work with it long enough and one will be able to do what must be done with all technique: forget it and allow it to function as a useful, flexible tool of the hearing/vocal mode mind. Exercising the mode means working with hearing/vocal energies in actual practice, not just intellectualizing about them. The hearing/vocal mind must develop its power and flexibility as a free, intuitive entity. To do this the performer must work with as many language musicality techniques as possible while exercising the sense-making feedback process. Any overcontrol by tension will be signaled by lagging rhythms, overregularity of rhythm, lack of pitch variety, hitting the same pitch level consistently, the subtle and edgy feeling of the glottal hold, and the rise and fall of volume as the performer forces the voice over the glottal interference and then lowers the volume to ease the pressure before tackling it again.

It is those who listen who must help performers become aware of what they are doing (as opposed to what they *think* they are doing.) Listeners should also endorse the positive effects of tension release. To revert to our culinary metaphor, the feedback should include suggestions for seasoning to make the performance recipe taste better. But unless the unpalatable tension spices are removed, any seasoning techniques to improve the taste of the performance may make it taste even worse. Sugar in an oversalty recipe may not give the taste desired, even though the goal is sweetness.

The teacher-director-coach must help those who are listening to develop perceptual awareness along with the projective awareness of those who are performing. Awareness precedes growth, and the teacher must point out to both listeners and performers what is happening before awareness can begin. The teacher serves as a leader, but in my own classes I have been delighted when observers have mentioned factors I had missed. Our different mode makeups lead us to varying perceptions, regardless of our so-called expertise. That is the true beauty of the modes concept: it is both enlightening and equalizing. It reveals new ways of perceiving the performer and places everyone on an equal footing in this respect. We may have done little intellectualizing about psychological motivations, but we have all seen human beings projecting energy all our lives. We have seen, heard, and felt the energies of the projective modes regardless of our cleverness at mind reading. If a premium is placed on what is actually seen, heard, and felt, then we can all contribute, for we have all practiced those skills in special, individual ways as long as we have lived.

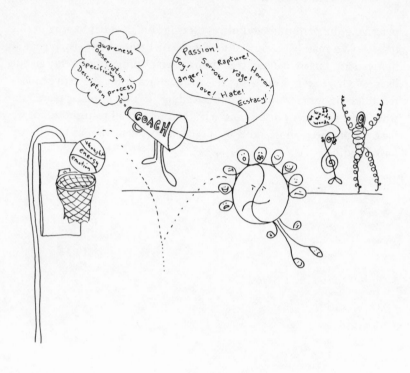

Chapter 5
The Facial/Emotional Mode

The controversial facial/emotional mode, the most difficult to define, continues to require intensive discussion whenever I introduce it to a new group of performers. The resistance that surrounds the facial/emotional system relates directly to those things with which the American actor is most deeply concerned. It is the most personal mode—the "windows of the soul" mode—through which we send open and vulnerable messages that can be threatening if the sender has been guarded in habitual communication. Working directly with the face raises the awful possibility of indicating or mugging, the cardinal sin of Stanislavski-based acting methods.

Nonetheless, it is intriguing that American acting in general is based on the facial/emotional mode.[1] For that reason, acting teachers in this country are cautious about any overt technical approach to the use of the mode. The idea of making faces, grimacing to convey emotions, or even working with facially oriented techniques is anathema to those who have studied and worked in American theater traditions. It took considerable psychological effort on my part to ask students to exercise in the facial/emotional area. At first they resisted the attempt to define this area, although they had no difficulty in doing so with the kinesthetic and hearing modes. Actors were more resistant than singers because they brought to the concept the kinds of preconceived notions we have been discussing. Singers, being involved in a highly technical act to begin with, accepted the concept more readily.

With every group, the irrational nature of the resistance is recognized and eventually overcome. It becomes clear that we can always return to our previous approaches, whatever they are because we are not committing an irrevocable sin by exploring facial technique. We then begin working with the concept, and though our fears make us hypersensitive to the problem of mugging or indicating, I have yet to see a case where that violation is made. More important, the change and growth made available through the exercise and development of the facial/emotional mode have been genuinely astonishing.

ANECDOTE: *Over a period of two years, I have gradually shed all inhibitions about dealing directly with the facial/emotional mode. I am rewriting this chapter during a training institute (June 1983) in which the facial/emotional mode and its relationship to the release of energies in freeing both the kinesthetic and the hearing/vocal modes have become crucial. Because it has been the most sacrosanct mode, it has the greatest potential for exploration and discovery. It is virgin territory that has never been adequately examined from the performing point of view. As a result, new findings continue to emerge. There are still unrecognized inhibitions about working with the face; as they are slowly released, new understandings continue to surface. As a result, this discussion is necessarily open-ended in its conclusions. It will reflect most clearly the process orientation of the search.*

The Message of the Mode

What makes the facial/emotional mode difficult to define is the fact that both the kinesthetic and facial/emotional statements are seen with the eyes. Their respective messages are sometimes difficult to untangle. For example, it is particularly difficult to separate facial/emotional statements from kinesthetic statements when the latter involve the head. Shaking the head, nodding the head, tilting the head are all kinesthetic statements; but the message communicated by the face that is within that shaking, nodding, or tilting action are facial/emotional statements. The two modes are communicating simultaneously, cooperating in sending messages, with a part of the kinesthetic system that is very closely related to the total facial/emotional system. The kinesthetic mode can also interfere with the facial/emotional mode. Indicating or mugging, for example, is the kinesthetic mode in a state of tension forcing its overly active messages through the facial/emotional mode. In spite of these interconnecting relationships, the two modes are demonstrably different communicating channels.

Here are some examples of the precise ways in which the two modes are distinct and separate message delivery systems:

A woman is sitting with her body relaxed and unmoving, but her face is a grief-stricken mask with tears streaming down her cheeks.

An orator is gesticulating wildly, his body a veritable contortionist's dream of communication, but his face and eyes are coolly observing the audience to learn the effect of what he is doing.

A man is smiling at you, in a seemingly friendly way, but suddenly he slaps you in the face hard, and his smile never wavers.

A woman is sitting in front of you with an impassive face, seemingly indifferent to what is happening, but you notice that her body is racked with tension.

In these examples, which could easily be multiplied, the kinesthetic system is sending one message and the facial/emotional system is sending another. The messages in the examples were opposites for purposes of clarity; that is, they were incongruent. One can easily imagine instances, however, in which the messages would be different but not opposites, or congruent patterns in which the two modes deliver messages in agreement. For example, the smiling, happy face could be accompanied by a large variety of kinesthetic messages, from static relaxation to a frenetic burst of gesticulation. Some of those messages would be different, some congruent, but none of them in disagreement or incongruent. The unhappy face can be accompanied by either a minimum or maximum of kinesthetic energy, with none of the statements incongruent with the facial messages.

We thus see that the facial/emotional mode is a communication system distinct and separate from the kinesthetic. Although the two modes interact in both negative and positive ways, our immediate concern is how to exercise and develop the facial/emotional mode independently from the kinesthetic. The question is whether the facial/emotional mode, as we have defined it, can actually be exercised and usefully developed, or whether we are tampering with a delicate, personal factor that will lose its essential intuitive innocence and become a playground for phony and mannered technique.

One of the most difficult things to accept in working with the facial/emotional mode is the fact that it can and does send messages that have nothing to do with what is going on in the mind. But because we want to know *why* the face expresses what it does regardless of how believably it may be expressing it, that *why* will often take precedence over the *how*.

ANECDOTE: At a demonstration for the National Association of Teachers of Singing, I asked a group of young singer-actors to work with the facial/emotional mode, sending messages while the pianist played background music. The six performers all looked believable and natural in their communication of mental and emotional processes. Yet there was an expressed concern with "what the singers were really thinking" as they did the exercise, what was really going on in their minds. The answer, I said, is that we can't know what is going on in their minds (unless they tell us — and they might be hard pressed to do that). We can only go by what we actually see. Although we aren't mind readers, we are all excellent face readers. As it turned out, none of the young singer-actors had any sort of internal scenario to match what they were overtly communicating. In the face of this potentially judgmental situation (a singer in

*front of an audience of voice teachers!), it was refresh-
ing to see their sense of satisfaction as they acknowledged the lack of internal-external correspondence.
They were free of the judgment that would have been
implied by* having *to project their actual mental-
emotional state. And they were pleased with having
communicated clearly and specifically with their
facial/emotional mode, and having done so believably
and naturally.*

This sort of event confirms the law of internal-external noncorrespondence, which states that on stage there is never a one-to-one relationship
between what is actually occurring in a singer-actor's mind and what the
audience is supposed to believe is going on in there. This law also operates in life, and when it does it is called the law of tactical advantage.
As a tactic in life, we communicate to people what we think will be of
greatest advantage to us, not what is really going on in our minds. I made
up both of those laws, of course, with a little help from Robert Cohen's
Acting Power for the second law.[2] Both laws are true, however, and both
deal specifically with the facial/emotional mode and the messages it
communicates, which are often independent of the inner feeling or
thought process.

This bothers people—including actors. It doesn't seem organic, it
lacks integrity. Facial/emotional communication is not truly "real" unless
it is real all the way; never mind that it is convincing. *Seeming* is not
sufficient, it must *be*. Enormous amounts of energy are spent in ferreting
out clues to the contrary that are only perceptible to the informed. The
feeling seems to be that if there is not a one-to-one correspondence
between the inner and the outer, the communication is not honest. Yet
the cool teenager who most despises role-playing would be horrified if his
external facial communicators revealed his internal thoughts and feelings
in a truly organic, one-to-one manner. The one-to-oneness of the internal-external relationship has nothing to do with the believability or
naturalness of what is actually communicated by the external facial communicators. Once that fact is accepted, the facial/emotional communicators become a tool to develop and use, rather than a mysterious capacity

that does what it wishes in spite of our needs. I have seen people begin to transform themselves and their performing power in a matter of days and to experience radical and positive change over a period of months and weeks with consistent exercise of the facial/emotional mode.

ANECDOTE: An actress in one of my classes seemed to be a hearing/vocal mode dominant. She had a good instrument potential and a strong, intuitive grasp of how to use it in speaking, which suggested the dominance; she had no vocal training, but her singing voice also had a wonderful potential. Her facial/emotional mode, however, was consistently neutral and inexpressive both as a performer and as a person. Although her vocal gifts did much to compensate, I suggested that she should concentrate on exercising and developing her facial/emotional mode.

After class, she told me that she had not been accepted into the graduate acting program. I was stunned, especially given her powerful hearing/vocal talent, which was much stronger than that of actresses who had been accepted. But then I realized that she had been rejected on the basis of the prevailing facial/emotional dominance of American acting. Whatever her vocal gifts, she simply "didn't have the guts," she didn't "feel it," she didn't seem to be "involved" on the facial/emotional level. In a hearing/vocal dominant culture like Great Britain, she would have been accepted. But that didn't solve her problem, because she was an American actress.

I advised her to begin working on her facial/emotional skills through exercises to be discussed below. In days she had made discernible progress, in weeks she was a different performer. She had always appeared middle-aged and somber (and was generally cast in those kinds of roles). Now she seemed years younger, more vital and happier. And, in fact, she was

*all those things. The progress was evident to all of us,
and it was a particular inspiration to the other members
of the class who needed facial/emotional mode development.*

One of the logical fears of working with the facial/emotional mode
is felt by film and television actors who are deeply concerned that their
intuitive communicating gifts may become self-conscious mannerisms.
Many film stars are what they are because of a personal quality that is
neither trained nor trainable. That is the reason for film tests—some
people photograph well, others do not. Those who photograph well are
not responsible for doing anything to achieve that state of being. In fact,
one of the things film actors must learn to do, especially those who have
had any theater training, is to trust doing less than seems necessary. The
face either says a great deal and communicates many different messages
without effort—for example, I am highly intelligent, I have deep feelings, I am very complex, I have ideas you wouldn't guess in a thousand
years, I am mysterious, sexy, overpowering, cool, hot, wise, calculat-
ing—or it does not. Whether these messages reflect the truth is unimpor-
tant; they communicate something compelling with great clarity, and
they do so believably. Any interference with an already natural process
that communicates in this manner or any attempt to train or develop it
may render the process unnatural, unusable, and unsalable.

There is enough truth in the risk, that a generation and more of film
actors have lived by the Miesian formula adapted to read, "Less may be
more, but nothing at all is better yet." Things have begun to change,
however, as good actors from the British school (who are far more willing
to risk the use of technique in all areas because they have succeeded so
well in one) make films in which the facial/emotional mode is not dependent upon a six-inch close-up to convey emotion.

*ANECDOTE: A television transmission of a stage play—an
adaptation of James Agee's novel,* A Death in the
Family—*was presented as performed by film, television, and stage performers. It was astonishing to see the*

erratic quality of performances as film-trained per-
formers demonstrated total incompetence in fulfilling
the hearing/vocal mode demands of live theater. Some
of them revealed a remarkable amount of interference
with their facial/emotional mode as they attempted the
unfamiliar task of projecting with greater vocal energy.
Others, without the advantage of close-up camera
shots, came off with extraordinary blandness of char-
acter. Those with theater training as well as film train-
ing, like Ned Beatty, performed magnificently. There
was, in short, almost no ensemble whatsoever. All in
all, it showed the mode limitations in film and televi-
sion training, as well as the disastrous effect a mode
limitation can have in the wrong media.

Part of the repression approach to film acting may stem from the
American Gothic aspects of our national experience, in which showing
nothing with the face is safer than showing anything. Emotions have
been safely locked up behind neutral masks, and people who actually
allow the face to show emotion are not to be trusted. Neutrality of fa-
cial/emotional projection is passed from one generation to the next.

ANECDOTE: A young performer in one of my institutes was
almost impossible to "read" facially. As we were discus-
sing the problem of facial communication, she men-
tioned her father (whom she had acknowledged admir-
ing very deeply) and then said, "You can never tell
what he is thinking." The rest of the group said, "Ah
ha!" and we suggested that although it was useful for
her father not to show what he was thinking or feeling
overtly—he was a businessman—it was definitely not
useful for a performer. It would be no reflection on his
worth if she were to exercise or allow the showing of
thought and emotion freely. She agreed and made
rapid progress in that area almost immediately.

For whatever reason, the facial/emotional mode is the most sensitive and entangled mode to deal with from a technical point of view. There are a multitude of dance and movement instructors for the kinesthetic mode and thousands of voice teachers for the hearing/vocal mode, but how many facial/emotional instructors does one encounter? They are called acting teachers, but their work is so intertwined with the other two modes and with concepts of the internal thought process that the facial/emotional resources are never given an opportunity to develop independently.

Once the process of disentanglement is begun, once the situation is clarified, the misconceptions begin to disappear. One realizes that the facial/emotional mode is simply another communication system and that it need not be an untouchable, sacrosanct area. We use it every day in highly technical and manipulative ways that are totally sincere, unaffected, and believable. To do so as a theater exercise is simply art imitating life in yet another way. As Robert Cohen has demonstrated so brilliantly in his book *Acting Power*, we spend our lives playing roles with great integrity and sincerity; we act constantly, and we err greatly if we fail to draw upon these experiences in creating life on the stage.

Everything we can do, we learned as a technique while we were still children. We learned to walk, gesture, communicate facially, talk, and sing through imitation, practice, and persistence. That is how we acquired all the ways of being that we regard as "natural" and "the way we are." Those natural ways are no more natural than the chairs we sit on, the paintings we look at, or the words we speak and sing. It would be an immense error to deny ourselves access to the continued growth offered by the range of technique available in real life all around us because of a "naturalistic" credo. The facial/emotional mode is an integral part of the technical system that life exercises so effectively for some people. We can and should expand our resources in the facial/emotional area just as we do in the other two modes.

In exercising this mode, we should perceive the difference between the process of growth and the performance product, for they will often seem to be in opposition. Because of the insecurity involved in being one's own instrument, the actor or singer-actor is unable to make objective evaluations of the effect of the art. In contrast, a clarinet player, sculptor, or painter can perceive and judge the art they are creating.

Actors and singer-actors thus gravitate toward what feels natural or comfortable in performance. This tendency is often artistically productive, but the security and comfort are usually based on the actor doing what he or she can already do. As soon as we move into unfamiliar areas of action, as soon as we change our patterns of behavior, some discomfort is inevitable. To grow, however, we must exercise those new patterns, we must wear those new shoes until they become comfortable. At that point the techniques become available for use. We are able to make choices based on artistic necessity rather than comfort, discomfort, or habit.

This general principle of going outside the comfort zone to grow applies to the development of all three modes. Except for those who are extraordinary communicators in each of the modes, performers must venture outside the comfort zone to increase communicative power. The understandable reluctance to venture into the risky area of discomfort — not wanting to appear foolish, phony, awkward, unsophisticated, or uncool — is intensified when one is dealing with the facial/emotional mode. It is the most personal mode, and it is also the mode that conveys the greatest vulnerability; conversely, it is the greatest weapon for hiding one's vulnerability. We have less awareness of how and what our own facial/emotional mode is communicating than we have with our kinesthetic and hearing/vocal modes. We cannot see it nor hear it ourselves, and it is felt with far greater subtlety than we feel our physical or vocal efforts. In fact, the only time we feel it strongly is when it is being interfered with by the kinesthetic mode and is being held in a fixed position — for example, the tension of the held smile.

It is also the mode that brings into clearest focus the disparity possible between internal feeling and external communication. If, for example, a person is feeling either happy or unhappy, that performer has three basic choices: the inner state may be communicated by the facial/emotional mode, it may be denied (smiling when unhappy or scowling when happy), or the communication may be neutral. We have all had the experience in life of not realizing that a person was feeling something very strongly until that person burst into tears, rushed from the room, or blew up in anger. Positive emotions are less threatening and more likely to be reflected openly through the facial/emotional communicators. But even with positive emotions, there is no necessary parallel between what is felt inside and what is projected externally. This is a fact in life, it is a fact in stage life, and it gives the lie to the assumption that if one is thinking or feeling the proper thought or emotion it will be automatically communicated with one's external projective capacities. This idea is perhaps the most significant fallacy in contemporary actor training. We have called it the one-to-one fallacy, and it is a corollary of the law of internal-external noncorrespondence. Together they affirm that, in performance, there is no model for how the internal and the external must relate. They may contradict, agree, or be different in their content; the only important thing is the relationship between what is communicated and what the performer wishes to communicate.

We can speak with some objectivity about the external signals we receive from a person's face, and we can make rational deductions about the meaning of those projective communications. But the nature of the internal emotional state that created that communication, as well as the kinds of inhibition or interference that may have stood between the emotion felt and the emotion perceived, is not available to precise analysis. We are on much firmer ground, I think, if we make the following assumptions:

1. All people feel the same basic range of emotions, whatever they may seem to actually express. Everyone feels joy, anger, sadness, fear, hurt, happiness, and the rest, even though none of these emotions may be externally evident in any given individual. The feeling of a full range of emotions is a constant in human beings.

2. Because emotions are a constant in human experience, they do not need to be exercised as such; that is, they are already felt by everyone and are internally accessible and understandable to everyone. Summoning them up is not the problem.

3. The external means of expression, in this case the facial/emotional communicators, are the variable factor in human beings. Although all people feel the same emotions, they externalize or express them in infinitely varied ways.

4. The singer-actor who wants to be able to portray a wide range of characterizations should exercise and extend the range of the variable factors as much as possible. In this case, the variable factor is the facial/emotional mode.

5. Anyone aspiring to be a performer should try to make external expressive capabilities as responsive to and reflective of the internal state of emotion as possible. Although a one-to-one relationship between internal emotions and external expression is rarely the case in life and is virtually never the case on stage, the performer must strive for as clear as possible a channel and connection between the two.

6. The performer should learn to accept the validity of the external means of expression regardless of how accurately or truthfully they reflect the actual internal state of being. The more the performer trusts the accuracy of that communication, the more he or she will use it freely without forcing, allowing the feedback process between internal and external to function freely.

7. Finally, there is no real duality between the internal and external states. They form a unity, or a unified system, that is not experienced as such because of interference within the system. But the ultimate goal is to achieve a freedom of flow between the two so that unity and clarity can be experienced and shared in the performance situation. The external choice in a performance situation will often involve a nonunified relationship to the internal, but it can be made with a freedom which reflects that state of unification.

The first set of exercises in this mode relate to the flexibility and malleability of the facial/emotional communicators. The concept of body-armoring is well-known as a means of blocking emotional expression or feeling. We stop ourselves from expressing an emotion and even from actually feeling that emotion by blocking it with physical tension. The commonest example of this phenomenon is the involuntary and often painful contraction of the throat muscles to keep from crying. A similar action occurs with the facial muscles. We tighten the jaw, keep a stiff upper lip, stare with unblinking eyes, and generally keep the face impassive when we do not want to show emotions. By doing so we also prevent ourselves from feeling the emotions fully. We feel the repression, but not the expression; whether a repressed emotion is actually felt is a moot question. Certainly the emotional energy does not disappear but is simply converted into something less expressive and usually more destructive than the expression of the initial emotion.

Beginning, then, with the external means only, we can use exercises that break down inhibitions immediately: face-making, mask-making, facial isometrics, anything that allows a freedom of external expression. It is a commonplace technique in all forms of therapy to release internal emotional blocks by bringing their external manifestations into play. As with those hearing/vocal mode exercises that were devised to unleash monotonous vocal patterns, we must devise exercises for those who have deadpan faces, the equivalent in the facial/emotional mode. The deadpan face is precisely what the ice-breakers or rather face-breakers are planned to get at. Those who already have mobile, communicative faces handle the exercise with ease. Students who are strongly product oriented easily justify sustained mask-making or attitude-holding by reference to commedia dell'arte masks, mime masks, or, for some singers, the need to maintain attitudes without tension while singing. The exercise of creating a strong emotional or character mask and maintaining it with the least possible tension for as long as possible is an extremely useful music-theater exercise.

It is important to keep the body in a state of readiness while these facial/emotional isolations are being exercised: no unnecessary tension and no sloppy relaxation, just poised readiness. There is an almost universal tendency for full-body tension to come into play along with the facial/emotional energies. We must encourage the performer to isolate the facial/emotional energies from full-body tension as a vital step, especially for singers.

If the mask-making is done in conjunction with a spoken or sung text, one should listen for an equivalent state of hearing/vocal mode readiness: the voice being used as it would be regardless of what the mask may be doing. Like the body, the voice should have no unnecessary tension and not be monotonously relaxed; rather, it should be vital and always ready to move. The facial/emotional mode itself should also be in a state of readiness, ready to send any kind of mental or emotional message. This readiness is like hearing/vocal mode readiness in that one can detect the state of readiness only after the fact, in its ability to move, to change process. Lack of readiness indicates tension somewhere in the facial/emotional or kinesthetic modes, and it is clearly signaled by the inability of the face or eyes to make a sudden change of process. One would think the eyes would always be capable of moving rapidly at will, but I have seen dozens of singers whose eyes were "hard to move." When the tension that caused the sluggish eyes is removed, the eyes and the whole face come alive in obvious ways.

Even the nuance of the voice is affected by the readiness of the mask. The facial/emotional and hearing/vocal modes are physically in very close proximity, and in exercising incongruency (see chap. 7), it is almost impossible to isolate the two completely at first. The same difficulty holds true for all exercises with the two modes. Nonetheless, the isolating capacity is a vital one that must be developed from the very beginning, even as one is strengthening the modes individually.

This concept is particularly important for the singer-actor. Beginning singers characteristically demonstrate a parallel entanglement of the facial/emotional and hearing/vocal modes. When they try to sing high the forehead arches upward, the head pushes toward the heavens, and the expression becomes agonized; when they try to sing low, the reverse is true. The face reflects the vocal process as a visual metaphor. When young singers decide to pursue singing as a career, they find voice teachers who, if sufficiently aware, help them eliminate the parallel relationship with the facial/emotional mode while teaching them a secure hearing/vocal technique. This is the first step in a necessary process, but the fact that it is not pursued beyond that step helps account for the many singers whose faces seem trained to a passive neutrality. But if the first step is properly accomplished, the skilled singer at least demonstrates none of the more common facial/emotional tics that are a sure sign of the badly trained, amateur performer: the screwed-up mouth, the agonized forehead, the bobbing, popping eyebrows, the tortured eyes, and other tension masks. Neutral passivity of the face is preferable to such contortions.

The next, vital step is to bring the facial/emotional communicators back into play. This time, however, they are to serve the communication of specifically chosen emotional states rather than being an unconscious parallel reflection of the hearing/vocal mode. The facial/emotional mode must learn (or relearn) to express whatever emotional state may be required for the scene or the characterization, independent of the efforts of the singing process. The parallel face-making of the beginning singer is simply the kinesthetic mode's inappropriate attempt to aid the singing process by muscular contortion of the mode closest to the hearing/vocal mode, which happens to be the facial/emotional mode. The kinesthetic mode also continues its efforts to assist the singing process by engaging the rest of the body: shoulder tension, upper back tension, finger-hand-leg tension. Tensions originating in both modes are equally inhibiting, and both interfere with the vocal process in damaging ways (see chap. 8).

Held tension effectively blocks the natural flow of energies in both the facial/emotional and kinesthetic modes, thereby preventing clear communication of natural reality. In the facial/emotional mode, those singing-related facial tensions block believable emotional expression, a fact I have seen demonstrated time and again in exercise and performance situations. Persuade the singer to give up the facial tension holds and the face literally floods with communication. Those who have tension-repression of the facial/emotional mode built into their personal life and who naturally bring that habit to the stage have a more difficult challenge. They must first activate and bring into play the dormant musculature of facial expression, but they too must release the singing-related tensions.

Facial/emotional communication is a two-way process: to the audience and to the performer. Front-row audiences clearly perceive it, but it is amazing how much more power is felt in the overall communication, even at a distance, when facial/emotional and kinesthetic tension-repression is released. Perhaps more important, however, is how the performer perceives and responds to the freedom of the communication. The performer is a unity, a holistic system made up of external and internal subsystems: change the quality of the external and the quality of the total performance also changes in remarkable ways. One would never have guessed how much overall energy was being blocked by the interference. I am constantly surprised at the subtlety of interference, how difficult it is to tell precisely how a performer is interfering with the performance, but the difference is striking when that almost imperceptible tension hold is removed.

ANECDOTE: *A singer who also played the cello found facial/ emotional mode release to be one of the most important breakthroughs for her singing-acting performance. She decided to apply it to her cello playing as well, although that is an activity one would not ordinarily relate to the use of the mode. She was astonished, and so were her musician friends, to hear a tangible, qualitative change in the tone and musicality of her cello playing when she exercised the same freedom of facial/emotional energy flow that she had found so useful to her singing. Somehow, the slight tension hold in the mode restricted not only her singing but any musical activity involving the kinesthetic mode. Releasing the hold allowed all the energies of musical performance to express their intent with greater freedom and clarity.*

Our goal with this (and with each) mode is a special state of being that we have described elsewhere as readiness, but which cannot be truly and accurately described in words. One can make up language that seems to do so, but actually achieving it is the challenge of the athlete: the face in a state of physical and psychological preparedness to act, a readiness to express and to sustain without unnecessary tension whatever is appropriate to the dramatic moment. Facial/emotional mode readiness is a state of external emotional vulnerability—no tension, no eye-glazed deadpan relaxation (although that may be a necessary part of the first step in removing tension); but an alert, vital, open responsiveness to internal and external stimuli. And all while the hearing/vocal mode is performing in a highly stylized, time-extending manner.

One difficult understanding to develop is that an emotion can be reflected totally as a mental process through the facial/emotional mode without any kinesthetic participation at all, beyond a state of readiness to act upon that emotion. Those who do not trust their facial/emotional mode as a projective mechanism (which probably includes those whose perceptual seeing mode is also not their favored mode) often feel compelled to call upon their kinesthetic mode to actually express the emotion they are feeling. I have noticed that performers whose eyes are weak, who need glasses to see at all, tend to be less sensitive to the use of the facial/emotional mode as a projective mode. They are often deadpan, with little feeling for the use of eye-mind focus as a means of communicating thought process. Because their eyes are inadequate as perceptual mechanisms, it is as though the total facial/emotional mode is not trusted as a projective mechanism. A blind person, for example, tends to have very little facial expression. A lack of projective sensitivity in the facial/emotional mode can be seen in the expressionless, emotionless face whose eye movements are random and unstructured. That blank or neutral face can be retrained to expressivity in both emotional projection and in communication of thought process even if it is not naturally so. I will describe exercises that do this.

ANECDOTE: During a three-week institute in 1983, I saw faces that had been trained to long-term immobility or neutrality begin to come alive. Friends from outside the institute began to remark on how the students were changing and how positive the change was. The change was also a positive experience for their fellow performers in the institute, for the immobile, neutral face tends to carry judgmental connotations that are often negative even though no such judgment is part of the mental process behind that neutral mask. When the face begins to come alive, it tends to send a greater proportion of positive messages in life situations. But in releasing sufficiently to send positive messages, it also acquires the flexibility to send negative messages in performance when that is appropriate.

Another interrelationship that creates problems between modes is the fact that, for singers with a strong kinesthetic urge, the facial/emotional mode acts as a trigger that incites the rest of the being into action. It seems to be a natural sequence in real life as well, which may explain the almost compulsive nature of the trigger effect. The sequence operates as follows: When we reach a point in life when we express a strong emotion facially—an ecstatic smile, a distorted mask preceding tears, a twisted scowl of intense anger—the next step is to express ourselves physically or vocally. We cry out in joy or sorrow, we raise our arms in exuberance, we bury our face in our hands, or we run away or attack or shake our fists. But in music theater, powerful emotions must often be expressed without the possibility of acting upon them physically or vocally in a realistic way. We may shake a fist, move rapidly for a moment, attack a person briefly, or cry out, but the action in each case takes place in a very short time; we are left with immense amounts of music-theater time to fill, time that is still in the grip of the original emotion, which must be sustained. Thus, for most performers, the natural course of action is contradicted by the necessary music-theater course of action.

This is an enormous challenge for the singer-actor, possibly the most crucial technique to be mastered in the total art of singing-acting. Acting in America is largely based on the facial/emotional mode. The hearing/vocal mode is not accepted as the primary acting mode, and for the singer the operatic hearing/vocal mode is too stylized to feel natural. The kinesthetic mode is not appropriate for the singer-actor in opera because extreme or excessive physical movement is usually counterproductive and often impossible. That leaves the facial/emotional mode. But once it is released from its tension masks and neutral masks, attaining the readiness between those two opposites that makes free facial expression possible, the trigger effect is brought into play. As soon as the facial/emotional mode begins to express the intense emotions found in many music-theater situations, the voice and the body, *unless trained and coordinated to do otherwise*, try to follow the body-mind's natural, real-life progression. The end result of this trigger effect is discussed in chapter 8, but at this point we will examine ways of exercising the capacity to deal with the challenge.

One way to deal with the trigger effect is to translate the action to be triggered into the hearing/vocal singing process itself. For some hearing/vocal dominants, this process may be automatic; but for those dominant in other modes, the translation requires understanding and practice. The action that would be triggered by the facial/emotional involvement is to be thought of metaphorically as being expressed through the musical action of the score as vocalized by the singer. Rise and fall of the melodic line, pulsing of the rhythms, crescendos and decrescendos, volume changes, speed, timbre and tone color of the orchestral sound can all be conceived of as a mental process. They are the mental energies of the performer as translated into musical terms, and the voice in turn translates those mental-musical energies into the act of singing. The crucial step, of course, is the willingness of the singer-actor's modes system to accept the translation as being sufficient without the addition of extra kinesthetic energies. This willingness can be developed with proper feedback, but it is dependent upon proper coordination with the facial/emotional mode. There is a close relationship between the facial/emotional and hearing/vocal modes, and the translation of the musical energies into acting energies involves the coordination of the two. For example, a burst of musically conceived joy, translated and understood as such by the hearing/vocal mode, wants to be reflected on the face as well, without the full-body tension of the kinesthetic mode.

The extension of time inherent in music theater is largely responsible for the difficulty, but the facial/emotional mode can be trained to carry the burden of the time extension. An emotional state can exist in the mind for an indefinite period of time without calling any physical action into play. One way of persuading the performer to accept this possibility is to simply *do* it—to let the emotion be a thought, not to try to show it but simply to let it be there in the mind. This is the flicker, the inner impulse that needs to work its way out. As we develop the strength of the facial/emotional mode in responding to that flicker, it is important to allow only facial/emotional energies into play, independent of the kinesthetic mode, until they are ready to interact with kinesthetic energies.

Singers commonly fear that in expressing emotion through the facial/emotional mode they will lose control of their emotions and not be able to sing. But it is precisely the control they are afraid of losing that will prevent them from singing. They have mistaken the expression of emotion for the repression of it, a common fallacy that is the primary source of tension-control in performers. The expression of emotion does not interfere with the singing; rather, the blocking of that emotional expression blocks the act of singing as well. In life, we quickly learn to use physical tension to stop emotions we don't care or dare to express, as in the grab of throat muscles that stops the crying impulse. In many cases, the feeling of the emotion and its physical repression become virtually simultaneous events. We come to equate expression with repression. When we are called upon to show the expression of emotion in a performance, we may have difficulty summoning up the inner emotion itself. But we are saved, or so we think, by the equation: we substitute emotion's simultaneous partner, the tension that represses, and we are in immediate trouble. Even if we were able to arouse the genuine emotion, the inhibitions of the performance situation plus our long-practiced repression habits would still create the old repression-of-expression dance. The academic, judgmental, right-wrong approach that so easily becomes part of the training situation gives additional power to the control-repression mechanism.

Thus we hear singers—great singers and teachers of singing—saying, "You can't cry and sing at the same time," and "Our job is to make the audience cry, not to cry ourselves." What is truly the case, however, is that one cannot *stop* one's self from crying and sing at the same time; one cannot *repress* the crying urge and continue to sing. Stopping one stops the other.

ANECDOTE: This was only a personal theory until I had several remarkable experiences that indicate its accurate view of emotional energy processes. In one of my summer institutes at the Minnesota Opera Company, a talented young singer said that she had great difficulty with an aria by Bellini, but not for musical reasons. She so identified with the character and her tragic plight that she wanted to cry, making it difficult if not impossible to sing. I suggested that since we were in a class, she treat it as an exercise and allow herself to cry while singing the aria. If she sang badly or couldn't continue

*singing because of the crying, there was nothing to be
lost because it was not a performance and there was
much to be gained because she would learn something
from the experience that she could learn in no other
way. She agreed to try it.*

*It was a stunning experience. She sang with greater
freedom and power than any of us had experienced
from her in previous class performances. The emotional
impact of the performance was overwhelming: tears
running down her cheeks, singing better than she ever
had, and performing magnificently. She finally stopped
and said, "The only problem I have is that I keep trying
to stop my crying and that stops my singing." It was a
classic demonstration of the principle that stopping the
flow of energy in any aspect of our being tends to interfere with the flow in other areas. Freeing the flow of
energy in any energy area frees it in others.*

*ANECDOTE: In a studio class at the Minnesota Opera Com-
pany, a young singer who had previously demonstrated
a great deal of overcontrol, both emotionally and physically, was performing Pamina's aria from Mozart's* The
Magic Flute. *It is one of the most devastating yet
sublimely ethereal expressions of grief in operative literature. She sang it well, but with little trace of the kind
of feeling that Pamina is undergoing either musically or
facially.*

*After discussing the problems of technical control
and emotional commitment, I suggested that she think
back to the most devastating emotional experience she
could recall. She was to tell us nothing about it — it was
to remain her private experience — but she was to relate
to it as she sang the aria. After further discussion and
a certain amount of persuasion (including a recounting
of the crying-while-singing anecdote above), she agreed
to try it.*

> *Once again, the singing was greatly improved and*
> *the total impact of the performance was immeasurably*
> *more powerful than it had been. In this case, I sensed*
> *that she was losing control and side-coached between*
> *phrases: "It's O.K., you can get back in control without*
> *giving up the emotional involvement completely." And*
> *she did. I continued, "Now you can move easily be-*
> *tween the two—control as you need to, allow as you are*
> *able." She never broke into crying beyond the tears in*
> *her eyes, but she gave up enough control in that area*
> *to release wonderful amounts of performance energy*
> *along with a sound that was more free and compelling.*

Singers should not go around weeping as they sing, although it would be exciting to see it happen occasionally. But we should recognize that repression and overcontrol of any aspect of our being limit all the others. That is far more to be feared than the potential damage of allowing the flow to take place. We are often afraid of our personal emotional energies in performance, but we do more damage to ourselves and our performances in the long run by blocking and repressing them than we ever would through their free expression in the service of the characters we play. The same is doubtless true of life itself, but that is another issue—although a possible serendipitous by-product of performing freedom (see chap. 9).

In exercising the communicating power of the facial/emotional mode, it is useful to differentiate between thought structure and emotional content. The structure of thought, the change from thought to thought and the clearly communicated definition of the movement of thought, can be understood separately from the feelings one has about that structure. One can search for a point of view, find the idea one is in search of, concentrate on it, have a sudden change of thought or flash of a new idea, get involved with the actual environment—looking at mountains, clouds, or buildings—suddenly get a new idea, wander from thought to thought for a moment, and so on, all without considering the feelings one has about any of the thoughts. That structural process can be communicated independently of the emotional involvement, just as the emotional content can also be communicated without a clear structure of thought to define it. The energies of anger, joy, depression, shame, rage, and bliss can be felt and perceived without a specifically communicated thought structure to contain them. Although it is clearly desirable to have form and content—the internal and the external—in synchronized unity with each other, it is always possible to exercise the two separately. Like the isolating exercises we have been suggesting for the modes themselves, the isolating of thought structure and emotional content within the facial/emotional mode gives the performer an important measure of control, flexibility, and power in using that mode.

Before working with the action of communicating thought process, let us examine the concept of facial/emotional mode readiness in greater detail. Our concern is with that state of being that underlies all facial/emotional messages and continues to communicate between them. If the state lacks vitality, it can become a transitional state that is the facial/emotional equivalent of cadencing for the hearing/vocal mode. It will fragment the thought process and lose energy rather than accumulating it. How can we create a vitality of thought process independent of specific emotional statements? Perhaps the projection of a permanent attitude of "interest," "concern," "involvement," or "expectancy" would be a useful exercise in establishing such a state. Let the singer-actor stand in front of the group and communicate those attitudes with the facial/emotional mode alone, not with the full body. The goal is to cultivate awareness in the performer of the nature of those transitional states: if they are not alive, ready, and vital, they should be described as such so the performer can begin changing them.

The Use of Focus Techniques

Let us turn to the action itself—the focus process. I discussed the idea of focus and its relationship to mental process in *The Complete Singer-Actor*. The concept of focus and thought process communication, like all the techniques and exercises I have devised for training the singer-actor, stems directly from actual human behavior. Observation and intuition make it clear that there is a parallel between the movement of the eyes and the movement of the mind behind those eyes. When the eyes are focused on a point, the mind is also focused on a single idea; when the eyes wander, the mind is wandering; when the eyes search, the mind is searching; when the eyes make a sudden shift of focus, the mind has made a sudden shift of thought or attention. From observing and working with the focus process, I have identified a few basic eye-action possibilities:

The Moving Focus: The eyes move from point to point, stopping briefly at each point then moving on as though trying to find the thought. If the search is not intense but wanders casually, it conveys boredom—a wandering mind. If the search is rapid and intense, it suggests anxiety or fear.

The Fixed Focus: The eyes fix on a point but in such a way that it is evident that one is not looking at an actual object—one is simply thinking about something with great concentration. (I believe that we do this when trying to concentrate to eliminate the additional sensory input provided by a wandering gaze.) If one *is* looking at an actual physical object, one often moves the head slightly as though to see it better. The kinesthetic dominant, for example, often does precisely that when thought-focusing (as opposed to object-focusing). Perhaps the action creates a spatial relationship between the focuser and the object, whereas thought focus is simply a mental relationship. (We are speaking here of performance focus, in which the performer is looking out toward the audience and creating an imaginary thought space, even when that space is made "real" as in the environmental focus below.) A thought focus can be maintained for as long as desirable, and it is the principal weapon in conquering time in music theater. And that, as we have suggested, is the primary challenge of the form for both singer-actor and actor. Thought focus can be used to sustain musical phrasing and thought phrasing; with the best composers, of course, these two go hand in hand. Although one sometimes speaks of focus as though one were seeing the experience or idea or person being thought about, one should be careful not to imply

THE FACIAL/EMOTIONAL MODE

that the performer should actually "see" things, although some do. When used properly, the performer may appear to see a vision or to be singing or speaking to the image of someone, but in training the focus technique one must be certain that the performer does not try to show that he or she is focusing (as opposed to going through the eye-mind thought process that creates the focus). The "showing" syndrome is a counterproductive tendency for singer-actors generally, and it should be watched for here and elsewhere in the training process.

The eye shutter: When one closes one's eyes, one is pulling inside the self either to concentrate or to deal with something strongly emotional (apart from relaxing or sleeping, of course). When the emotional situation is happy, it communicates a sense of intense joy that can be relished better by shutting out the world. Similarly with an unhappy situation: the person must either pull inside to control the situation or cry out in anguish. Whenever I introduce this concept there is at least one student who has been told that shutting the eyes shuts out the audience. This is wrong on several counts: first, the audience is not present for the character in a dramatic situation except for those rare moments of direct audience address; second, the communication between performer and audience is not based on the kind of eye contact found in everyday life. The audience is observing a character go through an emotional experience, and the strength of the emotional experience is what is important, not whether one can see the performer's eyeballs. Because shutting our eyes under emotional stress suggests a character undergoing a heightened emotional experience, the communication becomes more powerful rather than less so.

Because of the intensity suggested by the eye shutter, it is a technique that must be used judiciously. If used too often, it can become an affectation. Just as an evening of nothing but high C's would become meaningless and boring, one can only undergo the depth of emotion suggested by the eye shutter with relative infrequency. Opera, however, is a form with a remarkable number of emotional peaks; if popular singers can use the technique as often as they do, generally to good effect, the young singer-actor could well risk erring on the side of overfrequency, especially while developing the technique.

The timing of the eyeshutter—the length of time it is sustained and the way it is released—are matters that must be dealt with in process. Initiation of the eye shutter is the easiest step, and how long it is sustained depends upon the length of the musical-dramatic phrase in question. The quality of the phrase ending also determines how one emerges from the inner experience. In most cases one does not suddenly shift from a profound emotional experience to the everyday world, nor does a musical-dramatic phrase often make a sudden shift from a statement of great emotional depth. It follows that the eyes should not simply pop open in a matter-of-fact way, except in those cases where there is a sudden change of process musically or dramatically.

The light bulb: The name comes from the well-known cartoon technique in which a character has a sudden bright idea that is shown by a light bulb glowing in the thought balloon over the character's head. The sudden change of process suggested by the light bulb concept is created by a sudden shift of focus by the eyes or, more rarely, the whole head as well. It is like seeing a new piece of information or hearing a sudden sound: the eyes (and sometimes the head) shift suddenly to another point of focus.

The performer should be watched carefully for the tendency to bring a startle-tension into play in the attempt to "show" the reaction with additional and unnecessary tension. The light bulb is an excellent diagnostic tool for detecting unnecessary tension in the performer. Superfluous kinesthetic tension strongly limits any attempt at a sudden change of process in any mode. The performer in a state of tension is unable to execute the light bulb concept freely and flexibly.

Just as with the eye shutter, the number of light bulbs in a performance is limited by the relative rarity of the occurrence in human behavior; but the very rarity of that kind of mental event is what makes it special and useful.

Environmental focus: On many occasions, the vast imaginary space between the performer and the audience can be transformed into an actual environment. The performer can focus on actual elements of the imaginary environment, looking at trees, mountains, moon, clouds, armies, etc. Two prototypical environmental arias occur in Carlisle Floyd's *Susannah*: "Ain't it a pretty night" and "The Trees on the Mountain", both involving a character focusing on various aspects of the mountain environment. This kind of focus is similar in structure to the search, but the search is mental whereas the environmental focus intends to create the sense of seeing actual objects and landscapes.

The vision: While all focus techniques tend to create a sense of the performer seeing things, events, and experiences, the heightened fantasy focus becomes literally visionary. It is one thing to think about a series of ideas and another to envision the face of one's beloved, a field of skulls, one's deadliest enemy astride the world, or any powerful fantasy. Such visions can become panoramic, filling the entire proscenium frame.

If performers attempt to show that they are focusing, especially in the case of the visionary focus, the showing attempt is generally manifested in the body as the head juts forward or full-body tension takes over. It is useful to suggest that performers allow the focus image to come to them to let it be implosively oriented rather than being explosively projected by the performer.

A simple and effective way of exercising the focus idea is to set up a sequence of focus ideas and then have the singer use the sequence regardless of its seeming inappropriateness. The sequence could be: moving focus search, fixed focus, eye shutter, environment, light bulb, moving focus search, fixed focus. Surprisingly, this or any sequence will make total sense with any aria even though it is totally arbitrary. This suggests, again, that anything specific communicated from the facial/emotional mode tends to make sense for the observer—a gestalt, a whole is put together from the independent meanings of text, music, and facial/emotional messages. The messages delivered by the focus process are remarkably easy to recognize, both when they are clear and specific and when they are not. Observers new to the concept quickly become skilled at recognizing the clarity of the thought process (or lack of it) and can identify the factors that interfere with that clarity. The concept is based on the way the eye-mind system functions in life—it is simply a matter of describing that functioning and making use of it.

The performer also benefits from the clarity of the process. Making the process specific relates it to the performer's own mind as well as communicating specifically to others. The fixed focus helps the performer concentrate on the idea at hand better, for example, than a wandering focus; the searching focus helps in understanding the search process that is going on in the character's mind as well as communicating that to the audience. The same is true with the other focus techniques.

ANECDOTE: *A young woman who sang her aria with an arbitrary focus sequence exclaimed as she finished, "That's the first time I really knew what the character was thinking about! And the only thing I did differently was to get specific with my focus." For many singers, the facial/emotional mode is often incongruent with the thought process implied by the aria; that is, the mode is sending generalized messages that don't relate to the potential meaning of the text and music. Anything specific crystallizes the inner-outer relationship. The important thing is that the singer realize that she can do that, that she can make specific focus choices that give the meaning a channel through which to flow and communicate.*

It is relatively easy to prepare a focus scenario that relates specifically to the thought process of an aria. The arbitrary focus exercise prepares the technique for use and the analysis of the aria by the performer creates the specific meaning structure that the technique can then communicate. We should remember, however, that the arbitrary sequences also worked.

Possibilities are far wider than our rational analysis perceives. A little use of arbitrary sequences reveals these other possibilities and keeps our analytic mind from excluding the creative potentials that are there.

This is particularly true in the area of emotional choices. The capacity to fill the thought process structure with emotional energy can be exercised at the same time as the focus sequences. The two exercises are very similar. In the arbitrary attitude exercise, the performer picks several cards from a deck on which are written various emotionally oriented suggestions—angry, rhapsodic, frightened, amazed, ashamed, and the like. Regardless of their seeming appropriateness to the aria in question, the performer than sings the aria using the attitudes drawn. The arbitrary attitudes almost always seem appropriate in action, despite how one might judge them intellectually. Any attitude can be made to work if the performer blends it with the existing attitudes implied by the aria. There is no such thing as a pure attitude; that is, there is no such thing as pure anger—it is always anger with a mix of other elements. The same is true of attitudes in general—they are all blends of various combinations. One can almost always blend a combination of attitudes to make sense out of any aria situation. In this way, the exercise becomes a challenge to the imagination, compelling the performer to think about the character and the situation in different ways.

Here again, performers have the opportunity to keep their creative processes fresh. The intellect analyzes characters and situations and comes up with an eminently logical set of attitudes. But have a performer draw four attitudes from a pack, and the choice (although seemingly irrational) make as much sense as the logical ones. What is more important, those arbitrary choices are often more interesting, compelling, and theatrical. They are sometimes more believable. They also keep the performer's mode minds alive with the challenge of new ideas and keep the intellectual mind off the vocal process. A little practice with arbitrary attitudes helps the performing process to become easier and more flexible.

ANECDOTE: *Several young singers with whom I had worked in a summer training program auditioned for me some years later. I was pleasantly surprised by their perfor-*

mances. Their emotional choices were particularly inter-
esting, showing a mental vitality and spontaneity that
was very attractive. Only after the auditions did I dis-
cover that each of them had been using arbitrary atti-
tudes drawn just before the audition from packs of
cards they had made for themselves. Needless to say, I
was delighted; but I was even more pleased by how
much they enjoyed the process of auditioning as a result
of giving themselves arbitrary creative challenges to
work with. "It gives us something fresh to think about
and keeps our minds off all the judgment going on."

The arbitrary attitude exercise also helps to free the facial/emotional mode from the kinesthetic mode. The more extreme the emotion, the more useful the exercise. The singer-actor can inhibit the kinesthetic response by translating the energy into the hearing/vocal mode as well, but the principal weapon is the ability to trust the facial/emotional mode to carry the major burden of communication while the kinesthetic mode remains in readiness. A person who is powerless to act, who would lose his life if he did act, may project amazing amounts of emotional energy with the face and without the body doing a thing. He is ready to act but must wait for the best opportunity to do so, or he must find another outlet for the energy. The singer-actor waits in readiness for the right opportunity to act, and meanwhile pours the emotional energy through appropriate channels—specifically the facial/emotional and hearing/vocal modes.

Because this response to high-intensity situations is not natural, it becomes a matter of exercise. The habits and natural impulses of the performer are often inappropriate for music theater. New habits come by changing one's patterns, being patient with discomfort while exercising the new patterns and persisting in the exercise until the new patterns are comfortable and available for use in performance. The old patterns may be useful tools for some occasions, but one simply wants to acquire new capabilities, to expand one's potential choices in performance, to break in new performance shoes.

Taking the next step

After overcoming one's inhibitions in working with the facial/emotional mode, there are many exercises to make it more responsive to the communication of internal impulse, to allow the flicker to come through.

ANECDOTE: *A young singer with whom I had discussed the problem at length began demonstrating a distinctly stronger and more believable facial/emotional communication in rehearsal. When I complimented her on it after rehearsal, she said she had watched herself in a mirror while singing. Now this is anathema to those who fear tampering with the facial/emotional mode. For this singer, however, it provided an important awareness: "I saw that I really am a deadpan singer, and I don't want to be. So I started doing some exercises on my own, and I think it is helping, at least it feels like it is." (Note the twin opinions: the intellect thinking and the mode minds feeling.) I was delighted to be able to assure her that it* was *helping and that the released energies in the mode seemed to have softened her kinesthetic tensions as well. She had been a very controlled performer when she began work, and it was gratifying to see another demonstration of the interconnectedness of the modes—as the face and body released, so did the voice.*

The armoring of the face, like the armoring of the body, is something we can become aware of and release even though it began as an unconscious process. The first step is awareness, but that is not as easy to acquire as one might think. Our friends are much more aware of our facial/emotional communicating power than we are, but they are hesitant about sharing that awareness with us. We simply don't talk to each other about the strength of our facial communication. We could ask, of course, but sometimes we are afraid of the answer, so we don't. But if we do, or if we are given the information in a class situation, the next step is acceptance of that fact. Acceptance may be aided by corroboration on our own: the use of a mirror or a videotape to see our face in action while performing. After awareness and acceptance of the need to do something, the action is taken: simply getting those facial/emotional communicators in action.

ANECDOTE: *A performer who had strong facial/emotional mode inhibition was working on the external mask release — "cultivating the external garden so the internal seeds can grow." She made a series of grief-terror masks (the role she was exercising for was Baba, the title role from Menotti's* The Medium*). I was side-coaching, and when she created one particularly strong mask I said, "Let it release into reality," by which I meant to sustain the mask but release the tension hold that created it.*

She did so, and the group watching her gasped in shock. Her face sent extraordinarily powerful messages of anguish and horror, with no question of their reality. Our gasp was a response to the total believability of the moment.

Later, in discussing the scene with the performer, I pointer out that her believability had been a result of pure technique. She replied, "But the instant I released the tension hold, I felt the power inside—when you gasped, I felt my own gasp inside at the effect my face had on my emotions." It was a striking validation of the power in the feedback process between the external and internal once the tension block between them is removed.[3]

Besides simply exercising the musculature of the face and allowing more communication to flow through it, there are some useful exercises that singers should do every day, as routinely as brushing their teeth. One of these is the facial mirror, in which one person gives the singer a series of facial masks to mirror while singing. The singer should continue to sing as well as possible, but allowing the new masks to change the sound rather than trying to maintain the same tone. If the performer does attempt to maintain the same tone, tension will be needed to do so. The changes are almost always vocally positive because the release of facial tension in order to make the new mask releases voice-regulated tensions as well. The important thing is for the singer-actor to continue to sing while the facial/emotional mode does something totally disconnected.

As part of regular class warm-ups, I ask performers to do at least five minutes of "face-brushing." This exercise, which is done to music (either improvised by the pianist or from existing literature), is in three phases: facial musculature warm-ups, mask-making, and real emotional states. In phase 1, the performers simply work the facial muscles in as many ways as possible to warm them up, stretch them, and get the blood flowing. In phase 2, they create exaggerated masks with their faces and sustain them with as little tension as possible for phrases lasting 10–15 seconds. They are encouraged to explore as many different kinds of masks as possible, releasing within each of them. In phase 3, they allow real and natural emotional expressions to be projected with the facial/emotional mode, and they sustain those expressions for 10–15 seconds with a minimum of tension. An important extra step is to extend the natural mask, to take it further so that it begins to move into the extremity of phase 2. The natural is thus slowly expanded, just as the mask-making phase is allowed to release into naturalism.

The importance of isolating the vocal technique from the unconscious play of the facial musculature cannot be overemphasized. Deadpanning while singing may be a necessary first step in releasing the parallel relationship between the facial/emotional and hearing/vocal modes, but the facial mirror promotes the next and equally important step—the ability of the facial/emotional mode to express any appropriate message independently of the highly technical efforts of the voice. I have worked with many of the finest young singer-actors in the country in the past decade. Well over half of them (twelve of the twenty-one I am working with at this writing) have significant problems of interference between these modes. All need greater freedom and expressivity in the facial/emotional mode while singing.

If this is true of performers on that level, what of the rest of the young singer-actors? Voice teachers everywhere should be required to look at silent videotapes of their students as they sing their most difficult literature, with close-ups of the face as well as views of the entire body. Teachers who continue to ignore what singers do to establish almost ineradicable performance habits should have their viewing time multiplied until they learn to watch the face and the body as attentively as they listen to the voice. Voice lessons, along with vocal coaching and singer warm-up time, are the prime breeding ground for singer-actor problems. Too many of us in one-on-one voice teaching and coaching positions are like untrained mechanics who have only one special skill—for example, cleaning carburetors. But to get at the carburetor, we have to take apart the entire engine—in this case, a Rolls Royce. Knowing nothing but carburetors, we blithely dismantle the motor to clean what may arguably be one of the most important parts of the engine. The carburetor may emerge in splendid shape, but the fate of the rest of the motor is unpredictable. Some teachers have developed enough understanding to get the complete engine back in running order, but others reassemble an engine that is doomed to falter or to fail completely.

Coaches and teachers who throw about Stanislavskian clichés or who ask for physical tension products from performers to achieve performance excitement deserve a special circle of puninshment in Dante's Inferno— perhaps a permanent seat at a performance by singer-actors whose voices have been ruined by unnoticed mode interference. Seated alongside them should be those who simply ignore all those facial and physical things that are going wrong as the singer tries to become a singer-actor. Joining them both will be my directorial colleagues who ask the performers for complete singing-acting performances and for deeply felt, emotion-packed products, demands that create obvious vocal difficulties for the performer. All three of these latter-day Inferno inhabitants can be called mode-deficient so far as working with the singer-actor is concerned.

To become a singer-actor is not to become a physical acrobat, nor an emotional sobber and gasper; it is simply to place the resources of the human being totally in the service of the music and drama of music theater, and to make certain that those resources are used with a minimum of interference and a maximum of support from each other. This level of skill is far more complicated than the knowledge needed to obtain a medical degree. It demands a knowledge of one's self and one's communicating capabilities; it requires technical and emotional skill and the performance flexibility to use that knowledge effectively. We who are responsible for training these advanced technocrats of the body-voice-mind art must also possess perceptive capabilities far beyound what we can be paid to attain, beyond what anyone can teach us. We must be dedicated to a kind of humanness, a surpassing artistic vision of what the human being is capable of doing that will only rarely be rewarded in proportion to the energy expended.

Such a piece of preaching deserves a measure of honesty to prove the need for continued observation and growth. Earlier I said that I had never encountered indicating and mugging when working with my acting classes. In the course of writing this chapter, however I did encounter it when working with singer-actors. Opera singer-actors, in particular, are so accustomed to the residual effects of facial tension in connection with their singing that the only way they can break through it is with facial effort amounting to mugging. The cure is a matter of first releasing the residual, singing-induced tension; then allowing the newly softened and vulnerable facial musculature to reveal the underlying emotional statement. Nothing need be done once the facial tension is released except to allow the natural process to occur. However, the natural may be insufficiently projective as it is, and the development of sufficient performance projection may require exercise outside of performance. The process is the same for each mode: First, release the tension-interference that prevents the mode from communicating with all of its natural power; next, develop the communicating capacity of the mode independently of the assistance of the other modes; finally, reintegrate the working relationship of the three modes.

The process begins again as new challenges are presented to the newly integrated modes. Each sequence of isolation-strengthening-reintegration carries the performer to a higher level on the upward spiral of growth—returning on each circuit to the same challenges, but each time from a point of greater awareness and power.

ANECDOTE: *When a professional actress, who had developed an operatic singing capability, began working with facial/emotional communication it took months to undo the contitioning of her acting training. She had to give up the "feeling-it-internally-first" pattern, the accompanying physical tension that she induced in order to "feel it," and then allow the facial/emotional mode to express a whole range of emotions that it had never experienced projectively because of the tension-repression. The emotional power that emerged when she gave up the tensions, and the enhanced vocal power that accompanied them, was stunning. As another singer who observed her said, "I understand the power of that music for the first time." (It was turn-of-the-century verismo.) "Usually the singer's face is expressionless while the voice is impassioned, and the contradiction is annoying. But get the two together and it's overwhelming." The singer herself said that she didn't feel as if she was doing anything but that it was exhilarating to feel the power pouring through her without the usual effort. Performance had become fun instead of hard work, yet it had many times the power of the "hard work" performances. It was one of those experiences that made sense out of the term* performer enlightenment.

The exercise of the facial/emotional mode, the most personally vulnerable of them all, must take place in as safe a psychological environment as possible. The exercise arena must feel like a protective space where the right to fail is more than merely a catch phrase. The subtle but almost impervious guarding of the mode in tension situations can only be released effectively with openness, caring and honesty, in an environment where all three factors are in play. Neither the blankly passive nor the tension-mugging facial/emotional mode can be accepted, but the human sensitivities of the performer who may not be aware of either condition must be respected. We must encourage the release of the factors that stand in the way and nurture the factors that communicate more clearly. The need for confidence in one's self, of belief in one's personal validity, is nowhere reflected more clearly than in the facial/emotional mode. And nowhere is the anxiety of singing and performance insecurity reflected more clearly.

In opera, the facial/emotional mode might seem to be the least significant one. In absolute terms, it probably is. Granted that the first dozen rows or so in a large opera house are an important portion of the audience in terms of ticket prices, they are nonetheless a small portion of the total audience. But there are three significant points that argue for the importance of the mode in opera.

The first has to do with the increasing number of live television broadcasts of opera. The facial/emotional mode is the fundamental one for films and television. Its projective power and freedom from entanglement with the hearing/vocal and kinesthetic modes are essential to believable television performance. Opera singers like Teresa Stratas and Placido Domingo are already able to do their own performing in filmed opera (albeit with dubbing, in Zefirelli's *La Traviata*), and this will become an increasingly important issue in coming decades.

A second point is the interrelationship of the modes. What happens to one part of the system affects the total system: the facial/emotional mode both reflects what is happening in the other modes and affects them by its state of being. It sends messages via the other modes that would be indiscernible without the systems effect.

Third, the messages the performer sends the self by healthy use of any of the modes are at least as important as the messages sent to the audience. If any part of the being is used in an anxious manner, the performer will *feel* the anxiety, which is the last thing any performer needs to feel more of. All performers say that they can use all the positive messages they can get, but they don't always realize that they can send positive messages to themselves. The facial/emotional mode is primary in the feedback messages it sends to the performer. For this reason alone, it deserves to rank as an equal partner with the other two modes, even though it has received less attention as an independent entity. Perhaps we can begin to rectify that situation.

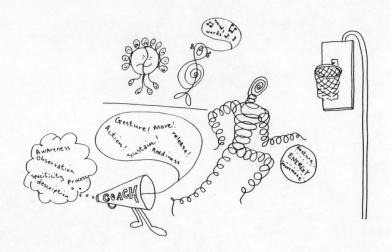

Chapter 6
The Kinesthetic Mode

In the past two decades, the kinesthetic has been America's favorite mode. It is the action mode, the do-it mode, the dance mode, the jogging mode, the running-exercising-swimming-playing mode; it is the celebrities-jumping-in-the-air mode, the slam-dunk mode, the touchdown-spike mode, the high-five mode, the dance-is-the-ultimate-art mode, the body language mode, and the mode psychotherapists encourage us to use in letting our "true feelings" show. In theater, the culmination of the kinesthetic came in *Chorus Line*, a musical comedy by, about, and for kinesthetic dominants (dancers) in show business. Few pieces have captured the American imagination in quite the same way. And *Chorus Line* is kinesthetic not only in its characters, direction, use of stage space, and story: by placing a principal male character (a nonsinging, hearing mode role) behind the audience, where he remains with brief exceptions for the entire performance, a kinesthetic spatial relationship is created between the stage and the house.

Apart from the kinesthetic mode's obvious place in musical theater, can its use as a dominant mode be applied to the art of acting? As I write, I have in front of me a newspaper interview with a young director who is trying to make the kinesthetic mode the focus of his acting system: "We don't have a tradition of movement in this country. Our background with the Method, Strasberg's Actor's Studio, Stanislavski and all, has been internal and word-oriented. Yet in communication, what do they say? That 80 percent is nonverbal. If words say one thing and actions another, the audience perceives the words as dishonest and goes with the action." This director, a true kinesthetic dominant, is speaking from his dominant mode in propagandizing for it. The observation that actions speak louder than words is ancient folk wisdom, however, not a new insight from "communications." And that ancient wisdom adds nothing about how to act roles in which the actions do not contradict the words, nor about roles in which they do. It only leads us to conclusions about the effect of such acting.

But the director's principal point is unarguable: there is no tradition of kinesthetic training for acting in this country. The most conscpicuous and successful attempts to create a kinesthetic acting craft were Meyerhold's work with Bio-mechanics in the first two decades of the twentieth century and Grotowski's strenuous and exciting Poor Theater in the 1960s and 1970s. Grotowski's work was the impetus for a great deal of the kinesthetic interest in acting in the United States during that time, along with the sprouting of mime troupes throughout the country. Although attempts were made during the past decade to make physical training more integral to the acting process, none has led to a consistent and organic theory of acting based on the kinesthetic mode. In some cases, kinesthetics were overemphasized as a means to train another mode. It was made so much a part of spoken vocal training in those decades that many voice classes came to resemble movement classes rather than classes in the training of the hearing/vocal mode; at the least, they were voice classes with a heavy emphasis on physical relaxation and guided imagery. But no movement training has actually made a difference in either the acting or the vocal work of actors.

My own experience as a student in drama school demonstrated this clearly. Actors in the training program received an intense movement class three days a week for three years. Yet three years later, having observed actors before, during, and after all that kinesthetic work, I could not see (feel) any significant difference in the acting performance as it related to the kinesthetic means. The failure may have resulted from the specific nature of the dramatic material, or from the faulty perceptions of those making the observations. If the material was to blame it reflects upon the narrow range of dramatic material to which the kinesthetic mode can make a significant contribution. The observers were unlikely to be in error, because we watched intently for whatever might contribute to a more effective acting performance—whether physical, vocal, or emotional. We were concerned precisely because some of the actors did not move well, did not use their kinesthetic means effectively, and showed no improvement in that respect in the three-year period.

Whatever the cause, there was a gap between work expended and results achieved, between the kinesthetic training of the actor and significant change in the actor's performance. The actors were no doubt better conditioned than they would have been without the movement class, but there was no real connection between their performance and what they had learned about the relationship of the kinesthetic mode to the other two modes. Since that time, I have seen singers and singer-actors taking movement classes on every hand; but I see little evidence of substantive difference in the total acting performance before and after the kinesthetic training.[1]

I do not deny the excellent kinesthetic training being offered in movement classes throughout the country, nor do I expect movement or acting teachers to accept responsibility for the performances of their students once they leave the classroom. (Some of my own teaching comments and ideas have returned to me in distorted fashion, either through performance or quotation. The result is sometimes a virtual parody of what I had intended.) Nonetheless, our individual teaching efforts desperately need integration with one another. And if we do not take responsibility for the integrating process, who will? Our training programs are like superb supermarkets, in which a great many excellent products are offered. But when students come to the checkout counter with all those good things, we expect them to go forth with no further advice and prepare a gourmet meal. No cookbook is provided, just "go home and do it by instinct." Although there are instinctive cooks among our trainees, the other 98 percent need all the integrating help they can get in learning to combine the excellent ingredients they have purchased. One ingredient is their kinesthetic training and what is needed—among other integrations—is a deeper understanding of how the kinesthetic mode can aid or interfere with the acting and singing-acting process.

Kinesthetics and the Breath Support System

The modes form a holistic system in which each part interacts with and affects the others. Any change in the functioning of one part alters in some way the functioning of the others. This interaction is also true within the separate mode systems, but only the kinesthetic mode is of sufficient scale to make intramode relationships easy to discern.

One of the most significant kinesthetic mode relationships within its own system is the breath support given to the rest of the body. There is a great deal of confusion about how much of the body needs to be directly involved in providing breath support for the voice. Some voice teachers tell their students to grip the floor with their feet, or to squeeze their buttocks together (like French Foreign Legionnaires, holding coins with their buttocks as they march), or to clench their thighs, or other kinesthetic suggestions designed to promote a better relationship between the body and the voice by concentrating on parts of the body that seem to have little to do with the voice itself. Because each of these newly induced physical tensions sometimes releases a tension elsewhere in the body or distracts the student from thinking so much about the voice (thinking instead about feet, buttocks, or thighs), an immediate improvement may be created. But the long-term result is simply another bad habit (tense feet, buttocks, or thighs) that is rapidly locked into place forever (unless someone spots it later and helps the performer to release it). No kind of held tension can be justified in the dynamic ebb and flow of singing and acting, however striking the immediate improvement when a new tension is first induced. So long as breath goes in and out, so long as the heart beats, so long as all life is a system of effort and release, expansion and contraction, no part of that life or its art can be healthily based on held tension. Muscular work, yes; moving tension to produce support, yes; strong dynamic action in process, yes; but held, static tension, no.

From this point of view, we arrive at the first specific isolation problem for the singer-actor. The vocal breath support system must be a finely tuned and powerfully capable organization of muscular interplay. Few performance processes are more exciting to observe than that of a well-coordinated singer working with the body to produce sound in the healthiest way possible. The effort is massive, dynamic, and flowing, and the sound that is produced rides on a beautifully controlled fountain of air that maintains its precise relationship to vocal need through the effort of the body. Any superfluous tension—tension that does not contribute directly to that process—robs it of energy. Any held tension is a drain on the total system, both psychologically and physically. Unless the young singer's first voice teacher is as concerned about inappropriate muscular tensions as about the vital function of breathing and breath support, a set of interlocked and entangled physical habits can be set up that will plague the singer forever. The cure may be to unlearn it all and start over with breathing in isolation from the rest of the kinesthetic system.

ANECDOTE: Early in my work with performers, I encountered a young professional who had just such an entangle-ment; i.e., an effective breath support system inter-woven with an energy-robbing and destructive set of superfluous tensions. It was easy to spot the inappropri-ate tensions because they were of the lifted-shoulder variety that could be perceived by anyone who was aware.

When we asked the performer to eliminate the seemingly unnecessary tensions, he was glad to do so. his overall performance improved noticeably. It was exhilarating to see him enjoying his new freedom, and it was strongly reflected in the vitality of his total per-formance. Back-patting all around seemed in order for the next few days. Then the voice began to send out trouble signals. At first we thought that they were the usual midrehearsal vocal fatigue problems that disap-pear with a little rest. But rest did no good. To my chagrin, the problems intensified and there seemed to be no good solution because none of us understood the origin. In all such cases, as the voice goes, so goes the total performance.

What had happened was simple: the performer had released his breath support system along with the superfluous tensions. At that time, I was not as aware of the potential danger in eliminating superfluous physical tensions when they are in close proximity to the breath support system. When tension originates in the shoulder or upper chest, it is often intricately entangled with the breath support system. It takes a total reeduca-

tion of the body to allow the support system to be iso-
lated and function independently of the missing ten-
sions.

In retrospect, I have no idea whether a return to the
sustained tension would have solved the vocal problem.
I doubt it very much, for once a singer is in vocal
trouble during rehearsal for an actual performance, it is
extraordinarily difficult to reverse the process.

That experience was the first of a series of lessons related to this entanglement problem — or rather, the first of which I was aware. Since then, whenever beginning work on physical tension performance problems, I repeat the lesson over and over: it is easy (sometimes sophomorically so) to spot unnecessary tension in a performance, but it is an extremely complex and sophisticated process to remove that tension without jeopardizing the integrity of the vocal support system. This fundamental isolation for the singer-actor deserves more attention than any other physical factor.

Whenever one tells a person to relax, the tendency is the same: everything, even the useful body vitality, is released. The singer who "shakes out" before an exercise, then comes right back to a situation of tension to perform, is an example of the holistic nature of the relaxation problem. It tends to be all or nothing — tension or relaxation. Isolated relaxation is a difficult but vital skill for the singer-actor to master.

The relationship of the kinesthetic mode to the breathing and singing process is not unlike the relationship of the facial/emotional mode and the singing process discussed previously. In that relationship, we want to see a face that looks natural and is responsive to the emotional impulse of the music and to the psychology of the character. We do not want to see vocal effort reflected in the face, but we want a vocal effort that conveys the size and splendor of the operatic experience. We want a free, natural face and a technically skilled, operatic voice — the ability of the facial/emotional and the hearing/vocal modes to work in interdependent isolation. The problem for the actor who is attempting to use the language with great musicality without facial distortion is the same as for the opera singer, only slightly less demanding.

With the kinesthetic mode and the breath support system, we are dealing with an isolation within the mode itself. The process of breathing is an integral part of kinesthetic functioning. We want to experience the natural body, alert and responsive, ready to act on any impulse: the body, in short, in a state of athletic readiness. At the same time, we want the breath support system within that overall kinesthetic system to be functioning at maximum energy and efficiency, working enthusiastically to create the necessary conditions for the joy of singing. We want the appearance of the ready-to-act body along with the sound of the technically skilled breath support system. I say *sound*, because that is the ultimate test of the use of the breath support system—how it allows the voice to function.

It is a coordination problem of immense complication, one that is partially intuitive to some performers (but never completely so) and a daunting challenge to others. But it means the difference between a long and a short career, or even between being hired or not being hired at an audition. Faulty coordination of the support system within the kinesthetic mode can undermine the vocal process, shorten vocal life, and prevent the realization of the potential quality of the voice. If these hearing/vocal mode aspects of the problem were not sufficient motivation, the appearance of the singer-actor who is in a state of physical maladjustment because of faulty coordination between the two can bar the door to employment or, at least, create an obstacle where none is needed.

Together, the two isolation problems—natural face and operatic voice, natural body and operatic support system—are the fundamental challenge for the training of what is blithely called the complete singer-actor. The sense of what "complete" means in that context needs revision. It does not mean how many things a singer-actor can do, but rather how well the singer-actor can coordinate and integrate the things that he or she can do. One does not need to be able to play every character in the world (that is, to use any mode makeup with complete freedom) to play one character. One can be *free* to do without being able to do, simply not making the choice to do what one is unable to do (like hitting a high A above high C). But that does not alter the state of freedom that allows any choice.

In the same way, "complete" should never be taken to imply the attainment of a finished product, for if one element of the three-part holistic system is altered, everything must be altered. Any time a new characterization is learned, there must be adjustments in all three modes. New physical, emotional, and vocal ways of being must be mastered and coordinated with already existing capabilities. It is always a process, always a becoming, for even if all preparatory ideas seem defined and specific, the performance itself, new colleagues, a new conductor, and a new director (not to mention new costumes, setting, props, lighting) are accidents of the moment that combine to create new circumstances that necessitate process adjustments. But the state of freedom into which all new elements can be incorporated, worked with, or altered remains the same.

Whatever point of view is brought to performance, the learning process is precisely that — a process. Successful careers may have been built on the unhealthiest, product-oriented, rigid kinds of thinking; one can only speculate about the scope of such talent were it free of the crippling effects of judgmental fear. But the capacity of unhealthy performers to survive despite energy-robbing, ensemble-destructive, process-crippling states of being does not prevent us from sensing and working toward what can be accomplished through healthy functioning.

This challenges the teacher-director-coach who is present at the working out of the process. If teachers request a change in any aspect of the performer's process, that implies a responsibility for the effect of that change upon the total system. The teachers must be aware of changes in any of the modes as well as in their interrelationship. Even when lacking the answers to the untangling of the complications created, they must develop a sensitivity to them and begin the search for the means of achieving an integration. They may not know how to help a singer-actor develop a better support system, but they must know that if the singer-actor asks for a change in the physical organization of the body, that person is also tampering with the support system. If they are asking for more emotional expression, they must be aware of all the hazards a young singer-actor can face in achieving greater emotional expression, help the performer become aware of those things, and overcome or eliminate them.

Teachers should go to colleagues in the art and find out what they are asking their students to do, or how they deal with related problems. Interpretation, singing, and acting should be discussed with other coaches, conductors, voice teachers, and dance or movement teachers to find the basis for some of the problems encountered. All of us should investigate each other's methods of dealing with the singing-acting problem to discover how we can help young performers achieve some measure of coordination and integration in the midst of our often conflicting and sometimes confused demands.

Most of all, we must become fanatic observers of the total singing-acting process; we must become scholars of the mysteries of integrated operatic performance — the most demanding and complex artistic act known to the human being — so that we may help our students find their way, healthily and happily, to the essence and humanity of its expression. It is a task for which written material, such as this book, is essentially worthless, except as a stimulus, guide, and warning. As with any good performance, "You had to be there." No rules can be set down for the observation process beyond the general one that any held tension is counterproductive, but that its removal is complex and creates unpredictable changes in the total system. That, in fact, is the only predictable thing: once you have begun the process of observation and change, the results are always unpredictable. And that is why teacher-observer awareness of the total system is imperative: the complete singer-actor demands the complete teacher-perceiver. There is no other option, given the prevailing public and directorial climate. Nothing less will do.

Losing Tension and Gaining Power

When we discussed the facial/emotional mode, we differentiated between the communication of the structure of thought process and the emotional content of that structure. In a similar way, we can think of the structuring of the kinesthetic energies to communicate potential states of being. The next step would be defining the content of that structure, but at that point the parallel breaks down; the body seldom makes specific the emotonal content of its gestures and states of being. That definition is accomplished by the hearing/vocal mode, the facial/emotional mode, and the situational context of the kinesthetic statement.

Let us examine a few cases. The energy of a fist in the air is strong, but it is undefined until we see the smiling face or the angry face, hear the "hurrah!" or the scream of anger. The intensely poised body contains a strong energy statement, but until we see the beloved waiting to be embraced or the enemy waiting for the attack, hear the "darling!" or "you bastard," we do not know what that intensity means. Physical and gestural statements by themselves are much like music: a form of pure, undefined energy waiting to be defined by the human circumstances— the face, the voice, and the situation.

What does that mean to the kinesthetic mode mind? Simply that it need not, cannot, and should not take total responsibility for the meaning of its statements. It must interrelate and cooperate with the other two modes. But does the kinesthetic mode allow that relationship to develop? The answer to both questions is often no. The body seems to insist upon taking responsibility for performance beyond its capability to do so. In taking this responsibility it interferes with the message-sending ability of the modes that should be responsible, damaging one (the hearing/vocal mode) and robbing the other of its true performance capabilities.

Chapter 8 describes the damage done to a whole generation of young singers by a lack of awareness of how the modes system operates. At this point, our concern is with the proper territory of the kinesthetic mode: what it can and should do, and what it should allow the other modes to do. All three modes must deal with the challenge of expressing emotion. The kinesthetic mode has a particularly significant role in this challenge. In the last decade, it became one of the most popular ways of releasing pent-up frustrations and negative emotions. Self-help books would be lost without a chapter or two on release through physical expression; body language manuals, physical therapy books, and kinesthetic methodologies abound. There are many useful efforts in this area of physical expression, but the physical release of emotions in therapy does not mean that those emotions are specified as communication as they are released. The person pounding a pillow, or running with great intensity, or shoveling sand with gusto may be releasing years of frustration, anger, shame, or fear; but the release is a generalized phenomenon unless the person engages the facial/emotional or hearing/vocal energies to specify the nature of the emotion released. Specificity is often encouraged by therapists because it is helpful in the therapeutic process, but it is outside the communicating range of the kinesthetic mode. Let us examine the same demand for specificity of emotional communication as it occurs in the singing-acting performance and how it is dealt with by the kinesthetic mode.

Perhaps the most fundamental information we have in this crucial area is that human beings commonly repress and suppress emotions through physical tension. We have mentioned the example of this phenomenon in the involuntary grabbing of the throat muscles when one feels the urge to weep; that tension effectively stops the weeping unless the pressure is great enough to break through it. Certain schools of psychophysical therapy work specifically with the long-term physical tensions that suppress painful emotions. Rolfing and Reichian therapy are concepts based on the idea that there are muscular tensions on a deep physical level that were brought into play early in life at the time of a traumatic emotional experience, or as a means of doing something physically that the body-mind believed needed doing. At that point in the past, the physical tensions blocked the free and natural expression of emotion; because of the continuing fear of that expression, the tensions had to be maintained and became locked into place. There they remain, blocking not only the original emotional statement but also interfering with emotional expression throughout life. If these physical tensions are released, so goes the theory, the emotions blocked by the tensions will also be released and the channels of emotional expression will be cleared for a freer expression of emotion. Many clients tell of reliving long-forgotten emotional experiences at the moment certain physical tensions are released. The blocked expression had been forgotten, but the body release allowed it to be remembered and experienced. Once that tension twig is removed, the logjam of suppressed emotion is allowed to flow, along with any new emotional logs that come floating down the experiential river.

Whether we agree or not with these therapies, the basic point is clear and easily demonstrated: we do not *express* emotion through tension, we *repress* it. The repression-tension may communicate the fact that there is a strong emotion being contained or held in check, but it is not the expression of that emotion, anymore than a singer who wants desperately to sing but is afraid to do so would be taken for one who is actually singing. Why, then, do we so often mistake repression for expression? Because our society frowns upon the free expression of emotion, most of us

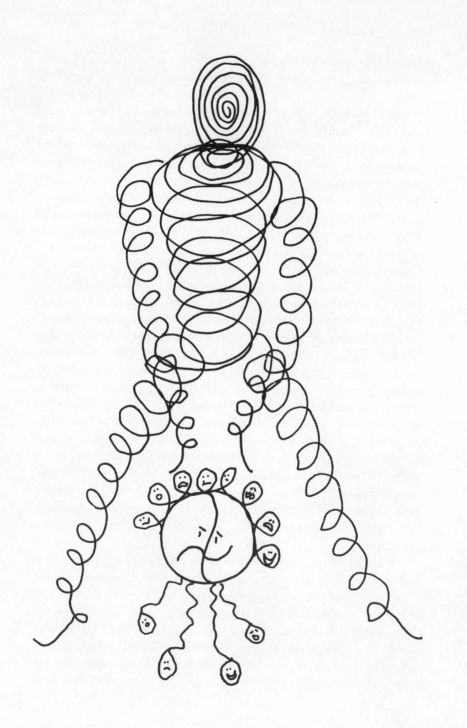

have learned to repress emotion at the instant we feel the urge to express it. The two occur as virtually the same event in time, and we have come to equate them. When we are asked to express anger we hunch our shoulders, knot our fists, and hold ourselves in a state of tension; but what we are communicating is the repression of the expression of anger.

Actors in theater may get away with this fallacious habit, although enormously increased power emerges when the repression is eliminated. But music theater isolates and clarifies the dangers of repression-tension because of the fundamental convention of the form: alteration of time. Ordinary time is often extended to twice, three times, ten times its natural duration during the course of a music-theater performance. An experience that lasts ten seconds in life—for example, a young woman saying "I am so unhappy that Jack has left"—can last the length of a song or an aria during a music-theater piece. Within that new space of time, the singer-actor must seem to live believably. If an emotion is initiated at the beginning of an extended sequence, that emotion must be sustained as well. But if the expression is equated with repression-tension, the performer must also hold on to that tension for the same length of time or feel that she has denied the very thing being expressed in the first place. Although this is not true—the release of tension need not deny the ongoing emotion, and it is invariably felt with relief by the audience—it is an intellectual double-bind for the performer. She may realize that she is in a state of tension in order to express the emotion, but if she drops the tension she seems to be admitting to herself that she was wrong in using that means to express it. This she cannot do. Yet if she holds onto it, she also knows—assuming she is aware—that she is in a continuing state of relative nonfreedom, unreadiness, and impotence. To make it even more complex, the tension is almost always initiated on a nonintellectual, nonverbal level. The rational awareness comes later. One of our exercises will be to show performers that they can safely release tension in midperformance without making it evident that they made a mistake initially, and, further, that doing so is the strongest positive step they can take.

A useful example of the distinction between expression and repression that also suggests the loss of power in repression concerns potent or impotent schoolteachers. The impotent teacher stands in front of the class angered to tears, physically tense, shoulders hunched and fists knotted, saying in a tight voice: "You kids stop it!" The kids respond by yawning and continuing to do whatever they wish to do, knowing that there is nothing to fear. The potent teacher, on the other hand, stands in the same place, equally angry but physically poised, eyes alert, ready to move quickly after any offender, and saying in a quiet but threatening tone: "Not another word." This time the kids respond by holding their breath and not moving a muscle. One teacher has power and is capable of acting with swiftness and strength; the other is powerless, fighting tension, incapable of doing anything except wasting personal energy, the picture of futility.[2]

The performer who is in a state of tension is similarly powerless except to convey the sense of being powerless, which is a possible kind of characterization. But even that characterization can be portrayed from a state of power. And power is our goal, the power of the performer to do whatever he or she wants or is asked to do, to make any kind of kinesthetic, emotional, or vocal statements in any kind of combination. The greatest single obstacle to that power is tension. No matter why or how it occurs, it is a power drain on the singer-actor's communication system. The powerless, tension-locked teacher *feels* the communication of some sort of intense emotion. But the actual communication is the futile struggle of that emotion to escape the physical bonds that prevent its expression. Again, repression is being mistaken for expression.

Unfortunately, that self-convincing repression struggle is addictive. The more tension exerted in the cause of expressing emotion, the more the actual emotional possibilities are bottled up; the more they are bottled up and frustrated, the more they demand expression; the more they demand expression, the more physical tension is necessary to repress them—a classic vicious circle. Furthermore, the repression technique is not thought out, not an intellectual process; it is a right-brain, culturally conditioned error that has no intellectual-verbal reason behind it.[3] That may explain why the tension addicts with whom I have worked, whether actors or singer-actors, have been extremely defensive about their habits and often skilled intellectual defenders of whatever they are doing. There is no intellectual rationale for the pattern, only intuitive reasons. But the only way to communicate about it, to discuss and defend it, is to use words; the verbal-intellectual mode must defend what has no verbal-intellectual reason for being.

One could be silent, of course, but that is very difficult for a kinesthetic dominant who is driven to *do* something. The only thing to do is to talk, and so they talk and talk seeking an answer that cannot be found by talk. Most tension addicts, already in the grip of doing, talk endlessly and often brilliantly from long practice. Because the talk never gets at the real reason, however, the defensiveness simply intensifies with the frustration of trying to justify what they feel. Their body has made up their mind for them, and there is no reason — only feelings, body feelings that say, "We are our own reason" and cannot be denied.

What does one do in cases like that? One approach is to use those very intellectual weapons in return in persuading tension addicts to try releasing the tensions as they perform. Feedback from the class and from their own bodies is usually enough to persuade them to continue the process. The inevitable reaction of the group observing is, "How much *better* it is without the tension!" The reaction of the performer is a pleased but puzzled, "But I wasn't *doing* anything!" The kinesthetic mode is the "do, do, do" mode, the mode that wants to feel itself doing something, which resists sustaining a single action, which demands physical expression with one action after another. If kinesthetic dominants are not physically expressing themselves, then they believe they are not really expressing anything. It matters not that they are speaking or singing, and that their face may be filled with passion; there is only one mode that truly communicates and that is the kinesthetic mode. But problems arise when the situation is not appropriate for physical expression. The kinesthetic dominant may then try to find a way to feel the physical expression without actually moving: by the mode's struggling with itself, fighting against itself, muscle against muscle. This "Charles Atlas School of Acting" is the dynamic tension method of one muscle against the other. Once the habit of inducing that feeling is developed, it goes the way of all habits and lives below the level of awareness. The habit becomes the true addiction with no rational basis; it simply feels good (or correct or necessary), and it demands feeding on a regular basis. To overcome the addiction, the performer must learn a new relationship between the physical being and the expression of emotion. This takes time, great patience, and liberal amounts of positive feedback. The response of other members of the group is as important as any other factor, for they are the neutral audience. The instructor or director may be seen as having a special ax to grind (which is often true) and who cannot be trusted to give honest feedback. But the class as a whole is usually trusted, and their feedback is needed to convince the performer that he or she is in fact communicating better when not "doing" anything.

The drive for continual doing is also fed by the uncomfortable state of tension in which many kinesthetic dominants find themselves. Something has to be done to release it, and the logical thing to do is to move. If the tension were not present, there might be little pressure to do anything. We have been calling performers who do things continually kinesthetic dominants, but they may be hearing/vocal or facial/emotional dominants who have got themselves into a state of tension that drives their movement. To relieve the pressure, they move their head or their hands or their body in small, possibly expressive but excessive ways. The question of dominance, therefore, is not as significant as the tension itself.

Another approach is to give tension addict performers a tension check while they are performing. This technique simply massages, pushes, and pulls the tension out of them without their volition. Two or more members of the class manipulate the body of the singer while he is singing. He should not resist nor collapse physically but cooperate with whatever the others do, even while continuing to sing. The head may be gently rocked about, moved forward and back, the arms lifted, the shoulders massaged; he may be bent over at the waist, legs moved, knees bent, and so forth. Any resistance encountered is usually a sign of held tension. A singer who is overprotective of a certain kind of sound resists head and neck movement. And yet, if the head is allowed to be moved freely and to release, there almost inevitably will be an improvement in the quality of the sound.

The tension check takes the decision to release the tension away from the performer, who is freed from the responsibility for either maintaining or releasing it. Tensions are often below the awareness threshhold, and efforts to deal with them consciously lead either to more tension or to excessive and superfluous relaxation. Because neither state feels right, the performer moves back and forth between them, creating a pendulum effect. The tension check is the first exercise I introduce to new groups of singer-actors once they have had the opportunity of singing for the whole group in their normal performance style.[4] It makes several impor-

tant points immediately. First, physical tension interferes with the singing process; most performers sound noticeably better during the tension
check than they did during their initial performance. Second, singers
become aware of tensions they had not known existed and find that they
can perform without them. Third, singers often discover what one young
soprano expressed following a tension check rendition: "It was so much
easier to sing!" (without all that tension). Of course, a typical performance does not include someone to massage and manipulate the tension
out of one's body: the performer must eventually find the means to release the tension alone. But awareness always precedes growth, and that
is the purpose of the tension check (and of all exercises).

Other positive by-products come from the tension check. Some
singers have a "don't touch me" attitude, probably fearing that physical
contact might disturb the voice. They learn, to the contrary, that they can
sing and often sing better under the most extraordinary physical circumstances. Sometimes a whole group lifts the singer into the air or puts her
down on the floor, and the singer learns that she knows how to sing under
almost any condition *so long as she doesn't resist*. That important piece
of body-mind knowledge opens the gates for other kinds of freedom on
all levels.

The tension check is usually a revelation both to performers and
observers. But it is not one of those exercises that is to be touched once
and then abandoned; it should be practiced every day—another "tooth-
brushing" exercise. The kinesthetic and facial/emotional modes should
be exercised with the same commitment given to the hearing/vocal
mode. The performer cannot be too alert in the search for residual physical tension, particularly if it has become an habitual part of performance
behavior.

In dealing with tension problems, the great law of opposites comes
up regularly. The opposite of tension, which is relaxation, inevitably
seems to the performer to be an appropriate goal with which to replace
the tension. The importance of that issue and the fallacy it embodies was
stressed in our discussion of breath support. That system must be in a
state of dynamic ebb and flow, neither relaxed nor in a static state of
tension. Similarly for the physical being that surrounds the support
system. The encompassing kinesthetic being must be in a state of dynamic readiness rather than one of relaxation or tension. The body sur-

rounding the vocal support system can undercut that system if it is either tense or too relaxed. Relaxation can create as much interference with the support system as tension, as we learned with the singer who collapsed his breath support system along with the rest of the tension. Although we have discussed the concept of isolation at length, it too is an opposite: the vocal support system cannot be completely isolated from the rest of the body because they are inextricably interdependent. The interrelationship is truly positive only when the rest of the body is also in a state of readiness, a readiness to work in harmony with the support system with as little unnecessary tension as possible. To find and maintain this state of interrelating physical readiness is a lifelong process for the singer-actor. As one aspect of the physical being is altered, the total kinesthetic system must make new adjustments to achieve and maintain that ideal state of readiness.

The first changes to be made are obvious. Tense performers must learn to release tensions that are evident to all observers. The means are conscious relaxation, a tension check, or some other exercise that allows the energy to flow in another way and thus to release the tension in question — thinking about roses as opposed to not thinking about elephants. Performers with no sense of physical vitality, who appear to be too laid back, must risk generating tension to find that place of poised readiness between relaxation and tension. For the tense performer, the release of tension leads at first to overrelaxation; for the overrelaxed performer, the attempt to achieve a state of apparent vitality leads at first to unnecessary tension. Many performers afflicted with excessive physical tension got that way by trying to achieve a state of vitality. Many young singer-actors are filled with false tensions that they have adopted to appear "noble," "royal," "bigger than life," "impressive," or "strong." The singers themselves have used these terms in telling me what they wanted to achieve through their postural tensions. When they are persuaded to release these poses, they feel naked, or inactive in front of others. But once they have taken the risk of just being there as themselves without the tension masks and are given some positive feedback, they can accept the new comfort and capability.

At that point, performers often go through a phase in which they may not appear sufficiently vital for a given role. They have overrelaxed and must find their way to a vital, as opposed to tense, use of kinesthetic energies. Releasing the tensions in the first place is a fundamental step, but vitalizing the overrelaxed phase must be handled with equal care. Observers who have seen the performer's "noble" or "bigger than life" tension poses find the overrelaxation less acceptable, and sometimes they encourage the performer to return to the "exciting" state of being. Some of the vocal coaches with whom I have worked bring to the observational process what I call the lay person's eye. Although they are highly trained experts in hearing/vocal mode work, their sense of how the body and face should work in coordination with the voice is often on the lay person's level: "You don't use your face enough," "You should use more gestures," or "You aren't as exciting as you should be." All these are actual quotes from expert coaches, and the quotes were accurate so far as evaluation of the product at that point in the process was concerned. But specific advice on how to achieve a stronger use of the face, more gestures, or greater excitement in their performance is not forthcoming. As a result, the performer inevitably induces tensions that are not only counterproductive to good performance (although they may be perceived otherwise) but can lead to disastrous long-term consequences if they are not corrected. It is as though an acting coach were to say to a young singer whose vocal technique was not under control, "You should sing better, with more excitement, with more intensity." This advice would be absurd, particularly if the acting coach expected anything to happen as a result of the comment. Singing-acting on the level we are discussing is a far more complex process than it is perceived to be. Certain aspects of the process can be achieved intuitively, but no part can be treated with lay generalizations.

Using Gestures in Music Theater

The gestural process, because it is so little understood, is also treated in the generalized style of the lay person. How to handle the problem of gesture is perhaps the most neglected and poorly comprehended of the kinesthetic skills in singing-acting. Whenever the topic comes up in my classes, I refer to it as the greatest single unsolved problem for the singer-actor. The response is vigorous nodding and a unanimous rolling of eyes to the heavens. Why is this the case? Why should such a clear-cut problem remain unsolved for so long?

Let us approach that issue with another question: what is the primary communicating function of the kinesthetic mode in singing-acting? One answer might be that the mode acts as a mediator between human reality and musical abstraction. It exists as a tangible, physical reality that relates to the normal time-flow of events. It is the "do-do-do" mode, the one that feels the need to keep a normal flow of time going. The musical flow, on the other hand, alters and extends time, placing a concrete obstacle in the path of the kinesthetic time flow. The singer-actor is caught between two possibilities: use gestures and movements that flow with the musical time structure, and that tend as a result to be slow motion, nonbelievable, and operatic (the kind that are parodied by honest observers of operatic performance); or use gestures and movements that follow a "real" time flow, but that must then be repeated to fill the extended time, to the point of repetition and boredom. The third possibility—doing nothing at all—can be ignored for our purposes. To do nothing effectively demands a high state of performance being, depending as it does upon sustaining an ideal state of physical readiness. Voice teachers often tell their students to do nothing but sing because the student can't deal effectively with gesture and the teacher has neither the time, interest, nor skill to help. But that is a challenge that we will confront directly. To do so, let us return to the other two possibilities.

The kinesthetic mode must act as negotiator or mediator between extremes. How can it do this? Is there a way of viewing the gestural process that will blend the two worlds? After testing various approaches to gesture over a period of years, I have found that one pattern continues to be effective.[5] We will call it the sequential approach. In any gesture sequence, there are three segments: the initiatory or impulse phase, the sustaining or time-extension phase, and the release or reinitiation phase. The first two phases can also be thought of as the naturalistic and music-theater phases, respectively. Let us examine them in order.

No matter how dignified or stately the character or the music, the first phase of gesture can and should be initiated freely and with impulse, just as gestures are initiated in life. This does not mean jerkily or staccato, but with that swift softness with which we begin gestures in everyday communication. To seem to be real or believable, a gesture must get to the point, to the statement that actually communicates its intention. When the thought occurs, the gesture moves immediately to communicate it — from no statement to statement — and the transition between the two is usually not significant. The transition only becomes significant if, because of its slow-motion quality, it calls so much attention to itself and its lack of meaning that the real meaning of the gesture is lost by the time it gets there. A slow transition may also be used to indicate hesitancy, confusion, or bewilderment. But unless these are part of the communicating intention, the slow-motion transition simply remains unreal and unbelievable. For example, if the hand is moving to the head, the hand on the head is the statement, not the move from hand-at-side to hand-on-head.

A slow-moving gesture can also be used to help describe something, or to accompany a verbal description of a graceful movement or a feeling that is best characterized by graceful, flowing gestures. A gesture describing the slow rising of a balloon rises slowly to characterize that event, and a gesture describing a feeling of bliss or transcendent joy may float in slow motion to communicate the sense of the feeling. But these gestural demands are rare exceptions to the "swift-soft" rule. Descriptive gestures in general make up a very small percentage of the gestural vocabulary.

The believable initiation of a gesture depends upon a nontension state of readiness. Any unnecessary or superfluous tension in the upper body makes a natural, believable gesture impossible. If the voice teachers who advise their students not to work with gestures had been able to solve the readiness problem, the gesture challenge, in some cases, would have been solved as well. I suspect that most slow-motion, reality-denying gestures are caused by general body tension and do not result from an aesthetic decision to underline the extension of musical time. We will pursue this idea below, but let us return to the second phase of gesture.

Whereas the first phase establishes the human reality of the gesture, the second phase assumes the challenge of relating to the musical reality of altered time. This sustaining phase relates to the phrasing of the music and the verbal-dramatic thought process, two interacting energies that often continue for a much longer time than would be logical or natural for a realistic gesture. But even a realistic gesture can be sustained for an

amazing length of time so long as it has been initiated without superfluous tension.

If the initiatory phase comes swiftly and softly from a state of readiness, sustaining the gesture is no problem. It is the combination of these
two opposing impulses—the naturalistic initiation and the stylized sustaining—that allows the gesture to bridge the music-theater continuum.

The third phase of the gesture sequence, the release or reinitiation,
has two possible branches. The existing gesture may either transform itself into a new gesture (initiated again with a naturalistic impulse) or it
may release to the relaxed but ready position from which any gesture can
be initiated. If the new gestural impulse is to move freely, swiftly, and
softly, the new ready position can involve no unnecessary tension. This
ready position can vary from the hands hanging down in totally relaxed
freedom (for naturalistic roles) or to the hands and lower arms held out
slightly to relate to costuming (for more stylized roles). The second kind
of readiness, style readiness, can often be confused with those kinds of
tension holds in which the performer is trying to be noble or grand; but
the difference can be quickly diagnosed by the performer's ability or
inability to initiate a gesture with naturalistic impulse.

The most difficult of the three phases is the initiatory phase, for
many young singer-actors have been told that the gesture must relate to
the full body and the music, or that it should be initiated from the floor,
or the lower back, or the thighs, and so on. Each of these concepts creates
an interference with the natural flow of the gesture. The intellect, as
usual, relates to a verbal concept and tries to fit the free flow of gestural
energies into it. The idea of relating to the music with the gesture is like
those phrasing exercises that grade-school children are asked to perform
in which the arms are moved through space in an arc that lasts as long
as the musical phrase. Unfortunately, a slow-motion gesture does not
characterize or relate to the musical phrase beneath it unless the music
is incredibly boring. All good music, however slow, has infinitely more
interest than does an arm moving in a slow arc from point a to point b.
A swift and soft impulse gesture does not deny the music that it accompanies, no matter how slow the music is. I once worked with a singer who
was performing a very slow Handel aria. Despite some resistance on his
part, I had him initiate his gestures in a naturalistic style, that is, swiftly
and softly. The effect was striking: it did not deny the music at all, and

the singer-actor no longer seemed like a robot in the service of the music. More recently, I worked with a group of singers on arbitrary gestures. In case after case, the strangest gestures seemed natural and made perfect sense, but only when they were initiated with a swift-soft impulse. The sustaining relationship to the music—which is the underlying issue here—is handled by the second phase of gesture, which we call (for that reason) the sustaining phase.

The idea of the gesture originating from some other part of the body, which also leads to "slow-motionitis," may have arisen from a movement-oriented instruction that was designed to get the singer's "dead" body into an alive and involved relationship with the gesture. The result for the singer, however, is often the slow, sustained arm movement of a ballet dancer without the dancer's graceful skill. The physical arc of the gesture becomes more important than the meaning of the gestural statement toward which the arc is moving. We are back to the problem of what I call molasses or mechanical-crane gestures: the gesture moves slowly from a nonstatement position to whatever the point of the gesture is; from there, it moves just as slowly back down to nonstatement again. This is neither real nor musical.

Gesture must be sustained in relationship to the music, and it must obey the laws of human behavior; it must relate to the combined complexity suggested by the music, the drama, and the character. It can only do this if it inhabits both worlds: the world of natural human behavior and the stylized, time-altered world of music theater. And it can only do that if it combines the opposing characteristics of both worlds in some way. Thought is instantaneous, and gesture follows after it as swiftly as possible. Although many rates of initiatory speed exist within that swiftness, very few move as slowly as opera convention seems to suggest.

One of the biggest challenges in the sustaining phase is keeping the gesture alive rather than simply holding it out like a piece of dead wood. As with decay in the sound of a piano tone, there is gestural decay. To keep the gesture alive, one must first understand clearly, on a body-mind level, what the gesture means. This does not mean a verbal definition, but an intuitive, kinesthetic understanding which can only be achieved if there is a state of readiness free of superfluous tension to begin with. In addition, one can keep the gesture alive by minor sculpturing adjustments. If the arm is extended, palm out in a gesture of rejection, one can sustain the life of that gesture with small, punctuating, hand-wrist movements, sculpting the gesture delicately to keep its sense of life.

A gesture is difficult to sustain if it goes outside our personal space, that cylindrical zone that is ours and that extends eighteen to twenty-four inches from us on all sides. If that zone is entered by someone else and a group of observers is asked to clap their hands at the moment the zone is entered, their response will be virtually simultaneous. The zone of personal energy is real and tangible, and if one moves a gesture beyond that space it is more difficult to sustain. In fact overextension of a gesture might be defined by its extension beyond the private space. Anytime the arms are fully extended they reach outside the private space, and it takes a great motivation—quieting a large crowd, holding off potential attackers—to sustain it. Overextension generally results from an overall state of tension. Practicing less extreme extension will also aid in releasing the generalized tension.

In the release of the gesture, speed varies greatly from a naturalistic dropping of the hands to the side, to a gentle floating down. Again, it is seldom necessary to float down in slow motion as though a little mechanical crane were lowering the arms. The release itself can become a gesture, as when "giving up," or "giving in," or "accepting what is," or "preparing for new action" are conveyed in the release of a gesture. Careful attention should be given to the completion of the release. Performers commonly hold onto slight residual tensions, and the tiniest bit of held tension (in the hands, for example) draws the attention of the viewer in a compelling way just when that attention should return to the facial/emotional mode as the primary visual communicator. Wherever superfluous tensions reside in the arms or body, the average audience is remarkably accurate in identifying and being distracted by them rather than concentrating on the true source of power in the performance. Time after time I have pointed out a slight and (I thought) unnoticeable tension in a performer to a lay person in the audience, only to find that the person was not only aware of the tension problem but was disturbed by it. We must watch closely for those tilts in the wrist, stiff fingers, clenched fingers; all are tiny statements, but they indicate an overall tension that will interfere with the next gesture and affect the total modes system as well—voice, face, and body.

The release of a large gesture, one in which both arms are held out at full length, creates the special case of a two-stage release. It is inappropriate to allow the arms simply to plummet to the sides, except as a statement of frustration or annoyance. The large gesture is usually released in two stages, moving first to an intermediate point, perhaps with the arms pulled part way in towards the body; the gesture can then be released or a new one initiated.

Once the three-phase gestural structure pattern is made comfortable for the performer, the whole process of gesturing is eased remarkably. One has the means to obey the logic of both musical and psychological necessities. At first the process must be practiced and observed closely, because like all new shoes it may pinch a bit. But the impulse phase soon becomes convincingly naturalistic, and the sustaining phase (if properly prepared for by a free-flowing initiation) becomes increasingly easy and meaningful. The third phase follows easily so long as some attention is given to exercising the various release possibilities.

Learning to Exercise Gestures

We come next to the issue of content: what kinds of gestures are to be used for exercising the three-phase sequence. Any gesture is appropriate for the purpose, but the larger the variety, the more effectively the three-phase sequence will be exercised. The next step, then, is expansion of the gestural possibilities available to the performer. Several exercises are useful for increasing gestural vocabulary. The most familiar are mirror exercises, the simplest of which is for a person who is not singing to create gestures and body patterns that are mirrored by the singer. The singer's gestural capabilities can be stretched in any way, depending upon the imagination and skill of the initiator. This is also a concentration exercise: the singer must continue to sing while observing and duplicating an action that has nothing to do with the singing. It is also an isolation exercise in that the singer is asked to move in unaccustomed ways without disturbing the breath support system or the vocal process. Finally, it may "clear some brush" in the singer's kinesthetic system by stimulating movements that free the singer of slight but significant muscular inhibitions.

An advanced version of the mirror exercise focuses directly on the expansion of the gestural vocabulary. In this version there is a delayed reaction to the mirror. The initiator gives the singer a single gestural pattern to work with—for example, placing one hand on the back of the head while waving the other hand in the air. After observing the gesture, the singer begins the aria and tries to incorporate it into the context of the aria; that is, the singer tries to make sense of it. Although it may be modified slightly, the singer should try to capture the essential statement no matter how ludicrous it seems. There is a general rule that applies here: the more unusual the gesture, the more useful the exercise tends to be. Challenging gestures stretch the sense-making capacity to the maximum. When the first gesture is completed, the singer continues to sing and the initiator provides another gesture to incorporate. This process may continue for as long as desired. It is often useful for the performer to rework some of the gestures to see how they might have been incorporated even more effectively. Observers should be fully involved in this process of imagining how the gesture might be incorporated, and the mental exercise is as significant as the physical execution.

The person initiating the gesture gets a workout as well. If a performer is having problems with gestures, I often ask them to provide a mirror for someone else. Once the attention is off themselves, they gesture very freely. The same is true of facial/emotional mirror exercises. A performer with a neutral facial/emotional mode often releases facial inhibitions when acting as the initiator in a mirror exercise because the concentration is on communicating specific messages through that channel, not on judging one's self.

Any gesture can be incorporated in *any* context. All it takes is exercise and imagination—practice, play, and persistence—by the performer. Strengthening the performer's imaginative power in making sense of any gesture is a fundamental goal of the exercise. Accomplishing this requires observers who are deeply involved in the process of diagnosis and validation, for it is their feedback that confirms the development of the new creative capacities and nurtures the continuing growth.

Another exercise that expands the gestural vocabulary is the use of arbitrary gesture cards, which function similarly to the arbitrary attitude cards. Although I began using them only recently, they have become indispensable as an exercise tool in providing a creative challenge to the performer's imagination. Their purpose is very simple: to find a stimulating, nonjudgmental way of compelling the performer to expand the gesture vocabulary. One of the greatest values of the exercise is the systematic nature of the brush-clearing that can go on. It is possible to cover the gestural territory completely, which is unlikely to happen with mirror exercises that depend upon an initiator. Arbitrary gesture cards can give the performer a thorough, well-defined, and nonrepetitive workout in a relatively short time.

Each card has a specific gesture suggestion: a hand held to the forehead, a fist held out in front, both hands on the chest, a hand caressing the thigh, a finger pointing in the air, and so on. The number of possible gesture cards is limited only by the imagination of those creating them. The quality of the gesture can be left undefined so that the performer can give each of them the kind of energy that makes sense in context. It is possible, of course, to include quality cards as well that define the movement of the gesture: jabbing, stroking, punching, and the like. The important thing is for the performer to be able to test virtually all possible gestural and quality combinations, allowing them to take on different meanings as dictated by specific situations and characters. If a full range of gestures is included in the list, the performer is able to explore most of the inhibited "wilderness" areas in his or her physical communication system. Having done so, the brush is cleared for the intuitive, impulsive self to work in those areas without inhibition. The accompanying list includes some of the gestural statements that could be included on the cards.

Hand to head	Both hands to head
Hand to shoulder	Both hands to shoulders
Hand to stomach	Both hands to stomach
Hand to chest	Both hands to chest
Hand on hip	Hands on hips
Hand to neck	Hands to neck
Hand touches thigh	Hands touch thighs
Hand to cheek	Hands to cheeks
Hand to forehead	Hands to forehead
Hand caresses body	Hands caress body
Hand touches opposite side of body	Hands touch opposite sides of body
One hand held out, palm down	Both hands held out, palms down

One hand held out, palm up	Both hands held out, palms up
One arm held out to side	Both arms held out to side
One hand finger point	Two hands finger point
Hand slaps chest	Hands slap chest
Fist held out in front	Fists held out in front
Fist hits chest	Fists hit chest
Fist strikes thigh	Fists strike thigh
Hand held over head	Hands held over head
Head turns sharply	Head nods

An interesting phenomenon occurs when working with the arbitrary gesture concept, whether with mirror incorporation or with arbitrary gesture cards. As performers execute the often unusual gestural suggestions, they often find it very difficult, stopping in the middle of the gesture to say, "This doesn't make sense." And the observers respond, "You were doing beautifully!" because it made perfect objective sense to them. The difficulty in allowing growth and development in the use of new kinesthetic ideas is thus perfectly illustrated: it lies within us and our reactions, and not in the objective truth or falsity, sense or nonsense of the statements we are making. *We* create the problem, not the thing we are doing; and the outside observe sees that clearly. Our habitual intellectual mind-set rebels against anything it cannot immediately and conventionally rationalize. But if we simply allow our body-mind to make the statement, it finds the reason-for-being that the observers immediately perceive as a possibility.

As we try to make sense of arbitrary gestures, the modes concept comes into play once again. The kinesthetic mode depends upon either the facial/emotional or the hearing/vocal modes to make clear the specific meaning of its statements. The clenched fist can be a positive or a negative statement depending upon the statements from the other modes that accompany it. This principle applies to all gestures and their relationship to the facial/emotional mode techniques. For gestures to be filled with meaning, they must interrelate with the focus and attitude of the facial/emotional mode. If the face is blank or neutral, gestures seem to lack content and become the empty semaphores of popular parody. The interconnection is vital: gestural exercise must be accompanied by and integrated with facial/emotional statements. Without that involvement, gestures are worse than not useful: they are counterproductive because they establish a habit of neutralizing gestural meaning for both the performer and the observer. The kinesthetic statement is like music — it is suggestive but unspecified energy; the facial/emotional statement (along with the words and the situation) gives that energy specific meaning. An important part of our search is finding the interrelationship between energy and meaning in all the modes.

As a general rule, the performer must be able to isolate the facial/emotional from the kinesthetic mode. The first should be capable of communicating a full gamut of mental-emotional states with no accompaniment from the body beyond the readiness to act, that readiness being a tangible body-music capable of interrelating with any facial/emotional message. But in exercising the kinesthetic mode, there should always be a specifying, sense-making message from the facial/emotional mode.

Performers making new performance choices, whether gestural or emotional, are confronted with responsibility for their choices. The judgment that comes from this responsibility often inhibits the growth process. Both arbitrary gesture and mirror exercises remove responsibility from performers because they are relieved of making the choice. But can we also help performers take the next step? Can we put this creative freedom of the arbitrary assignment in the hands of the performers themselves? Can we allow them to provide their own creative stimuli?

Perhaps we can call upon the intellect as an arbitrary choice-maker. For example, the intellect can say, "I will hold both hands out in front of me and shake them, without deciding whether such a move is good or bad, and without trying to make sense out of it before doing it." (We have suggested the same sort of task for the hearing/vocal mode in choosing language musicalities.) This assignment can then be turned over to the body-mind to play with, practice, and make sense of. Giving the creative responsibility to the mode minds, trusting them and releasing predictive control, is a wonderful exercise for our intellectual minds. It should be practiced consistently until trust develops and the intellect *knows* that the mode minds are capable of doing things that it literally cannot dream of. Developing that trust and the willingness of the intellect to share responsibility for energy decisions may be the most important step for the performer in attaining true power. But the step is challenging and often difficult, and it is helpful to show the intellect the creative potential, the simplicity, and the fun of the process by relieving it of responsibility for the choices.

Opera and music theater deal continually with intense emotions. The kinesthetic mode is often asked to make strong gestures that can create all sorts of tension difficulty. A useful way of exercising this problem is to make sudden, intense gestures and then maintain the gestural statement without tension. This exercise differentiates between the strength of the gestural statement itself and the residual tension that often lingers when the statement is sustained for music-theater purposes. Earlier we referred to the swift-softness of a strong gesture, which may seem contradictory in this instance. But no matter how intense the gesture is, swift-softness is still an accurate description if the body is in a state of readiness and the gesture is created naturally and impulsively. If there is tension, however, and the performer tries to make a powerful statement, it tends to be jerky and spasmodic (or, as I describe it, "glass-shattering"). The last few millimeters of a strong gesture glide into place with a coordination beyond the understanding of the intellectual control mind. Take, for example, the gesture that places the hand on the chest in indignation—a gesture that says, "Me!?" If the gesture is freely and naturally initiated, it does not slap the chest (that is another kind of gesture); it arrives there rapidly, strongly . . . softly.

The Zen of gesture says that we already know how to gesture, that our body has the music of gesture built into its circuits and all we have to do is allow that music to flow without tension-control. The swift, soft strength of gestural power is already ours—we only need to allow it.[6]

Gestures can be as strong and large as desired; maximum challenge develops maximum understanding. Once the gestural statement is made, it should be sustained to make certain that all unnecessary tension has been released. If it is uncomfortable to maintain the statement, too much effort is being used. The sudden startle-tension associated with a strong gesture is often confused with the maintenance of the gesture itself. In life or in realistic theater, where the time flow is normal, this extra tension can be released very soon. The arms drop to the sides or a new gesture is initiated, both of which ease the tension. But the time-altering style of music theater demands both the release of the extra tension and the sustaining of the gesture. The gestural intensity exercise is a useful way to develop both capabilities in the context of maximum challenge.

Sometimes a kinesthetic dominant manages to find a relaxed-readiness state of being, but as soon as a gesture is initiated the overall body tension returns. Gestural tension then comes into play along with it. This is another example of the "justification by tension" factor we encountered in working with the facial/emotional mode. If energy is initiated in either facial or gestural areas, that act seems to demand follow-through by the total kinesthetic being—it demands justification. In life, there is often a follow-through for the initiation of gestural or facial/emotional energy. A specific action—fight, fondle, or flight—relieves the pressure of the energy. But singer-actor must suspend that follow-through: the energies may be translated into music, but on a physical level they must be sustained for longer periods of real time. If the justification by tension has been initiated, it must be maintained as well. The singer-actor thereby comes to develop a performance association of tension and meaning. In life, of course, it is ludicrous to gesture with sustained tension. (Try it while gesturing naturally.) But in performance, the practice can quickly become a habit, and eventually any gesture calls full-body tension into play automatically.

In most cases, more tension energy is expended in a gesture than is needed simply to make the gestural statement. The hands go to the head in a gesture of anguish, but at the same time the shoulders hunch up and the whole body tenses spasmodically. The hands to the head are the meaning of the gesture, but the extra body and shoulder tension attaches itself to that meaning. And if tension attaches itself to the meaning of any gesture, it tends to do the same with all gestures in varying degrees. What can be done about it?

One answer is to find ways of disconnecting the fallacious attachment between meaning and tension. We can usually persuade the mind that it takes less energy to do the gesture simply by making the movements without meaning (and therefore without tension). We then learn to accept on a body-mind level that the gesture is the meaning and that it only needs specification and clarification by the voice, face, and situation—all of which are outside the control of the kinesthetic mode.

An exercise that works with this problem is having the singer perform from a released-readiness position and then, on signal, simply lift the arms (without meaning) and work easily with them, making certain (by means of a simultaneous tension check) that there is no unnecessary tension. The singer is allowed to realize that it is easy to gesture in that way, that there is potential meaning in each gesture despite the lack of sustained tension, and that the meaning can be actualized by the voice or by the facial/emotional energies. Once the singer becomes aware of these facts, the exercise can be performed with his or her own awareness. In a single one-hour coaching session, I have seen a performer make this discovery and begin amazingly rapid progress in the power of gestural communication. It is exhilarating to realize that releasing the tension actually puts power and flexibility back into the gesture. Whole new avenues of gestural communication open up, especially for the kinesthetic dominant whose instincts are suddenly unfettered. The singer not only finds that the gesture alone is the statement, but also that the associated tension actually reduced and interfered with the communication of that statement. Tension addicts, you have nothing to lose but your chains—the interference patterns that rob you of your true performing power.

Another exercise that singer-actors can do on their own is to practice gesturing to music, going through the three-phase structure and actualizing gestural meanings with the facial/emotional mode, without actually singing. A useful way of structuring gesture sequences is what I call the face-space-body exercise. The performer gestures with one or both hands in touching the *face* or head, then creates a gesture that relates to the surrounding *space*, then touches some part of the *body* other than the face. The sequence may be repeated in any order, as often as desired. It is an easy way of creating variety and increasing one's range of possible gestural choices. Surprisingly few performers think of gestures as touching themselves, and this exercise allows the performer to think with the body, to give the kinesthetic mode specific and varied material with which to work.

Performers should develop the habit of daily exercise with the kinesthetic and facial/emotional modes independently of the hearing/vocal mode. We have been comparing this process with brushing one's teeth, and it is as important in many ways as the vocalizing that singers do routinely. But it is important to find ways of exercising that are fun and make sense as developmental tools. Otherwise, they will be discarded like calisthenics. Without the play and the imagination, one finds better things to do. So many aspects of gestural work can be developed on their own — the freedom of impulse, the ability to sustain comfortably, the ability to release at different speeds, the ability to make a broad range of gestural choices and to expand gestural vocabulary — that performers need a rewarding means of doing so. They must begin taking charge of the development of their kinesthetic and facial/emotional modes, not waiting upon outside judgment to force the issue. Their potential power as total performers lies waiting for self-discovery.

I recommend "body-brushing" exercises as a part of the performer's daily schedule and incorporate them into class warm-ups along with the face-brushing exercises described previously. Because all gestural work should interrelate with the facial/emotional mode, body-brushing follows face-brushing and incorporates the focus and attitude aspects of face-brushing into its exercising. The first phase of body-brushing employs large, abstract gestural statements (not unlike physical masks) that are unlimited in their use of the kinesthetic being to make statements. This opens the body-mind to all gestural possibilities, regardless of their meaning to the habit-mind of the intellect. The second phase deals with "real" gestures, those that do seem to mean something; but, as with the second phase of the face-brushing, those gestures are extended in the direction of the first-phase abstractions. Eventually, the abstract becomes as "real" as the real and the "real" is understood as the symbolic abstraction it is. The whole range of kinesthetic statement becomes available to the performer; the opposites of abstraction and reality become what they are in actuality — a unified field of physical communication. In both phases, the various possibilities of initiation, sustaining, and release/reinitiation should also be exercised.

What about the state of readiness that precedes all successful gestural work? Can we exercise it specifically, or is it simply a state of being that one asks for and hopes will be achieved? There are actually two different kinds of readiness: prepared readiness and in-action readiness, which is the difference between potentiality and actuality. From a prepared state of readiness one may do anything or nothing and be effective either way. Prepared readiness does not demand specific gestures or movements. The potential it contains makes the lack of an overt kinesthetic statement more powerful than it would be from a state of tension: witness the potent versus the impotent teacher. In the same way, the potential of a moving, in-action state of readiness lends all its gestures a greater power than they would otherwise have. The potential contains the actual and the actual contains the potential: this is the sense of a continual state of readiness.

To develop this capacity for continual readiness, any sudden change of process exercise is useful. The sudden change can involve the move from one gesture to another, from one position in space to another, or from one kind of body statement to another. In achieving a readiness stance, the instructor or a member of the group may signal the performer to move in any direction — forward, back, or to either side. Eventually the performer adopts a physical stance in which he or she is ready to move in any direction, not locked into any position but poised, free, comfortable, and vital.

When practicing exercises involving sudden change, it is useful at first to have the change signaled by the teacher or by someone else in the group rather than leaving the decision up to the performer. Otherwise the performer invariably anticipates the change and short-circuits the process. Eventually, the performer must assume the burden, learning to trick the intuition into play or trick the intellect out of play. But the performer is helped at first in avoiding anticipation by leaving the decision to others. Having experienced the process in that way, it can then be adapted for the performer's own use.

A more subtle factor is that of mental control. The physical being may be in a reasonable state of readiness with no overtly detectable tension, and yet the gestures continue to move in controlled, slow motion. The mind cannot allow the freedom or the swiftness of gesture because that would feel out of control. For the mind to think about what is to be done, and then monitor what is done, inevitably slows the process down below what we might call the belief threshold. We simply don't initiate gestures slowly in life (with rare and specifically intended exceptions); gesture initiation is an impulse following thought as rapidly as it can, and learning to reallow that impulsive swiftness in the initiatory phase of gesture is essential. If it is allowed, the second, sustaining, music-theater phase will be relatively simple to achieve because no tension will be driving it on. If there is tension in the initiatory phase, the sustaining phase either retreats from its statement (the most common symptom) or repeats it (which may be useful in itself but must be a choice, not a tension-linked necessity). If it neither retreats nor repeats, it concludes without a full release because the tension remains.

For example, if the hand-arm gesture relates in space to an image that implies "There it is," and there is superfluous tension in the gesture, it either begins a slow retreat back to the body, repeats the emphasis of the gesture several times, or returns to tension-readiness (as opposed to relaxed-readiness.) All three actions indicate the presence of held tension in the physical being before the gesture. Getting rid of that tension is another matter, but awareness of it is the first step.

Increasing gestural vocabulary is a function of the ability to describe what gestures look like or mean and the ability to execute those descriptions freely. We have discussed several ways of describing what gestures look like, including arbitrary gesture cards, mirror exercises, and the face-space-body exercise. Techniques that try to describe what gestures mean are far more subjective, but they are useful nonetheless. In *The Complete Singer-Actor* I classified gestures according to the three possible functions they could fulfill: *indicating* (relating to the object of focus), *reacting* (clarifying the reaction of the performer to the object of focus), and *describing* (describing either the character making the gesture — for example, a hand gliding down the body; or the object focused on — for example, a vision of a rising tide being paralleled by a hand lifting slowly but inexorably). In any case, the development of gesture is different for each performer, and whatever can release the process effectively is of value. The eventual goal is to release the intuitive flow of the kinesthetic mode mind from whatever interferes with it, whether that interference is intellect, inexperience, inhibition, or tension.

The kinesthetic mode also involves the use of props and furniture, one of the most stimulating exercise areas for the performer. Let us examine one or two specific exercises from which others can be derived.

A use-of-furniture exercise might function as follows. While performing a song or aria, a performer relates to a piece of furniture in as many ways as possible. If a chair is the object to be used, for example, the performer can do obvious things like sitting in it (how the performer sits in and gets out of the chair becomes significant in telling us about the character) or leaning on it. The chair can also be treated according to the emotions being experienced by the character: it can be caressed, knelt to, gripped, pummeled, or slapped. If so, the singer-actor should stay focused on the imaginary presence of the person he or she would like to caress, pummel, or slap and not on the chair itself. If the focus is on the chair, thus lending it a hallucinatory reality, the character becomes mad or unusually silly (neither of which is atypical of opera, of course). The chair can also be used as a weapon, as a central point around which to dance or strut, or a balance for unusual poses.

Prop exercises demand, or rather allow, even more invention. A few years ago, Jonathan Winters did extended improvisations on television with a single prop suggested by the studio audience. A handkerchief could become anything his extraordinarily fertile imagination wished it to be: a flag, a newspaper, a trapped bird, another person, a full meal, or (more realistically), a veil, a piece of clothing, a hat, or even a handkerchief. The singer's challenge is similar: take any prop and use it in as many ways as possible. The exercise can be divided into two stages, like the two-step approach to technique: first do the technique, then make sense of it. The performer first uses the prop in any way conceivable, with no concern for the meaning of the aria or the character—only for the sheer creative, imaginative play of the exercise. The second time, the performer uses the prop to communicate in terms of the actual aria and situation. A third repetition blends the free-wheeling inventions of the first time with the actual meaning of the aria, much as in the mirror incorporation exercises where arbitrary and unusual gestures are made a part of the meaning of the performance.

Many variations can be created on the use of furniture and props in exercising the kinesthetic mode. Everything we have said previously about readiness and freedom from tension applies with equal force to exercising with props and furniture. One of the advantages of working with actual objects is that they can soak up some of the tension. A chair gripped and held in anger is a real act of energy fed into an actual object; but clenching one's fists and locking one's body directs energy against one's self. It is much easier to keep the actual-object tension from creating vocal interference than it is to isolate the hearing/vocal processes from self-directed tension.

The kinesthetic mode is difficult to verbalize about with clarity, especially when it involves the subtle tensions of singing-acting. Like the facial/emotional mode, the kinesthetic mode is a purely nonverbal one that must be worked with in action to be understood. Both modes have been second-class citizens in the world of opera. As a result, there are few sources of information about the relationship of the kinesthetic mode to music-theater performance and none about the facial/emotional mode.[7] When pure dancing is called for, as in musical comedy, or when the dancing singer-actor becomes a significant figure, there are no problems so long as the skill level is high; the kinesthetic mode is not only being allowed to express itself fully, it is required to do so. But where the balance shifts to the other modes, especially where the hearing/vocal mode must become dominant, problems arise. The kinesthetic mode is a mighty weapon, but it is a two-edged sword that can harm as much as

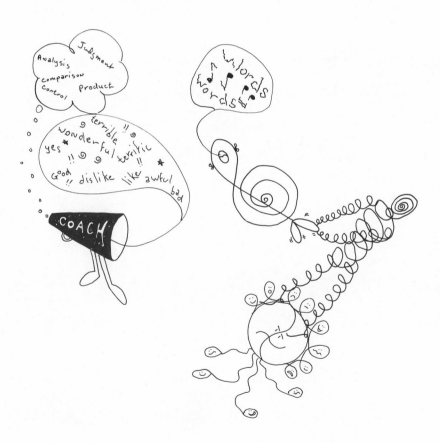

it can help. It is literally the grossest of the modes, the slowest, the most likely to interfere with the others, and it is used by the intellect to control the other two. It has the strength and potential clumsiness of your average giant in relating to more delicate creatures. But we can allow that strength to be potential until needed, flexible and economical when in action, and willing to return to potentiality whenever appropriate. It only takes awareness, followed by practice, play, persistence, and patience.

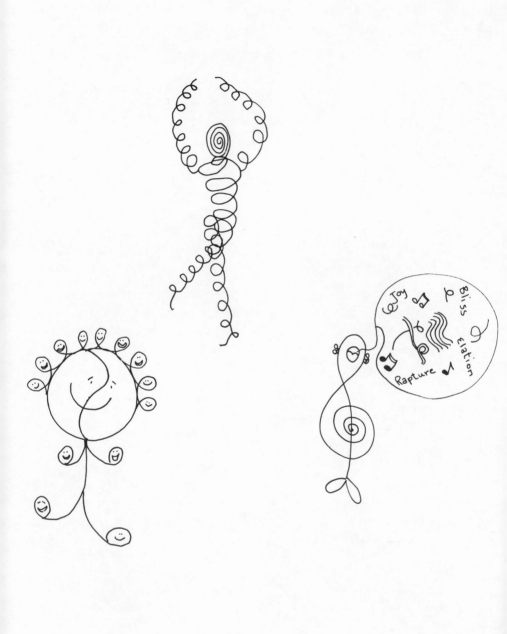

Chapter 7
Mode Combinations

From the beginning, we have been working with the modes in combination. It is impossible to confine our discussion to one in complete isolation from the others because they are inextricably related. To allow the modes to exercise themselves in isolation, we have had to talk about the interference and entanglement of the other modes with those exercises. We have spoken at length about kinesthetic interference with the hearing/vocal and facial/emotional modes, and the entanglements of each mode with the others. But the main thrust of this chapter is the modes in cooperative interplay, developing the capacity to send consciously chosen messages from more than one mode at a time.

Congruency and Incongruency between the Modes

Mode congruency and incongruency refer to the agreement or disagreement between simultaneous messages delivered by the modes. In congruent mode communication, just as with mode cooperation, the messages delivered are in agreement: the voice says something positive in a pleasant tone of voice, the facial/emotional mode smiles, and the body is relaxed and ready. From a therapeutic point of view, congruency is healthy behavior and is a major goal of treatment. The distinction between congruency and cooperation is the difference between *what* the messages say and *how* they are said. For example, the messages sent by all three modes can be congruent (in agreement)—all happy or all sad— but the way they are delivered may create interference or entanglement between modes, and thus they will not be cooperating. In mode congruency, the messages agree but are independent of one another; in mode interference or entanglement, the messages may seem to agree but one mode is interfering with another.

An example might be the expression of joy in the music, joy in the face, and joy in the body. The body can seem to be expressing joy by using one of the familiar held-tension means of doing so—the raised shoulders. But if that shoulder tension is maintained (and it is almost certain to be), that kinesthetic tension begins interfering with the hearing/vocal and possibly the facial/emotional mode as well. The joy could be equally well expressed by any number of other kinesthetic readiness states because the *meaning* of a kinesthetic statement is clarified by the messages of the other modes or the situation itself. Whatever the kinesthetic statement, it takes on the meaning of the facial/emotional and hearing/vocal modes combined. And so the joy could be expressed by a kinesthetic readiness to act, to run, to embrace someone, or to leap in the air, without any superfluous tension. In those ways, it would be congruent but not entangled. Thus it is vital to add cooperation to congruency for the healthiest performance behavior.

Incongruency, on the other hand, is sending messages that are not in agreement: the voice says something threatening but in a pleasant way, with a smiling face and a poised, relaxed body. From the therapist's perspective, incongruency is regarded as unhealthy, and correctly so; for it indicates division, strife, or imbalance within the person. Each mode may be saying something different, and neither the person perceiving nor the person projecting is sure which meaning is true.

To this complicated state of affairs we add the idea of cooperation or interference. The modes can be sending nonagreeing messages, but they can cooperate in doing so, as in the incongruency example above. But the modes can also interfere with each other in sending nonagreeing messages. In the example above, a tension-filled body would interfere with either the voice or the smile. It is more likely that mode incongruency will also be in a state of interference than in a state of cooperation. This is an important distinction for the performer who, ideally, should be in a state of mode cooperation at all times.

In theater and music theater, performers often portray characters who are neither healthy nor balanced and are incongruent in their behavior. Congruency, being a healthy state of being, is more centered and well adjusted and, therefore, less dramatically interesting to observe. Healthy, balanced characters do not compel our attention in the theater the way the Iagos, the Violettas, the Hamlets, the Manons, the Stanley Kowalskis, the Don Giovannis, and the Sweeney Todds do. Performers portraying characters who communicate incongruently must be capable of making incongruent choices. The modes may be incongruent, but they need not interfere with one another.

Developing the capacity to perceive and work with these mode complications requires special efforts on the part of teachers-directors-coaches. As we help performers heighten their isolating capacity, we heighten our ability to perceive those isolations and to discern the interferences and entanglements that prevent maximum development of the modes as they

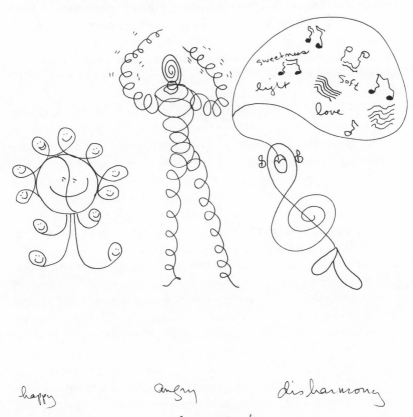

Incongruent modes

are exercised. Each stage in projective mode development requires a corresponding development in our perceptual capabilities. As we work with projective mode combinations—exploring the interrelationships of interference, cooperation, congruency, and incongruency—the challenge is perceptual as well. To help performers move from being Entangled Singer-Actors to being Complete Singer-Actors, we must also move from our state of perceptual dominance to a state approaching perceptual completeness. We have already strengthened our weaker perceptual modes by giving concentrated attention to their projective parallels. Now, like the performers with whom we work, we must develop their ability to discern the interaction of the combined projective messages.

Sir Tyrone Guthrie called the director "an audience of one." As teachers-directors-coaches, we must become the complete music theater audience, capable of responding to all the mode messages that an actual mode-mingled audience perceives. From that perceptual vantage point, we can help the performer to orchestrate projective mode messages to reach the audience as clearly, comprehensively, and convincingly as possible.

Singing-acting is the only performing art in which there is no single person who can tell the performer how to perform the total act correctly. At least two experts, usually more, are needed just to help the performer achieve the basic supporting skills, let alone learn how to put them all together. In other arts, one teacher can usually teach the total skill for that art; one may move from teacher to teacher and from style to style within that art, but the concern is always with the same basic skill projected in varying ways. But for the singer-actor, it is a matter of acquiring vocal skills, musical skills, physical skills, and emotional-projective skills, and then learning how to combine them into the magnificent system that we call singing-acting.

Possessing the separate skills in no way assures the ability to integrate them. In music theater, as in no other performing art, there are two levels of training: one level is the acquisition of all the separate skills and information; the second level is the integration of all those separate skills into the system of singing-acting. That larger system becomes a new and separate skill composed of many subskills. Putting all those subskills together requires highly developed integrating capacities, and there are very few integrating teachers in this business. Many experts teach the individual skills—voice teachers, musical coaches, movement teachers, acting coaches—but these experts often bring a lay person's sensitivities to areas outside their own. Hearing/vocal mode dominants bring lay kinesthetic and facial/emotional mode sensitivities and understandings to their teaching; and facial/emotional and kinesthetic mode dominants have only lay competence in the other modes. But this competence can be elevated by observation and cultivation of awareness, just as they can be in the singer-actor. We who work with performers from whatever skill perspective need desperately to spend more time together in training the singer-actor. We need to learn from one another and to heighten our perceptual skills in those modes that are on a lay person's level for each of us. Admitting this lower level of competence in any area that impinges upon our sense of expertise is threatening, of course, but it can also be a joy to acknowledge our incomplete mastery and continue our own learning process.

ANECDOTE: A coach whom I respect greatly made an agreement with me: we would sit by each other during auditions, and she would tell me what she heard while I told her what I saw. We had several opportunities to practice this perceptual mode interplay, and it was a remarkable education for both of us. It led to long discussions from which each of us received numerous insights. We also shared those joint insights with our mutual students, thus expanding their awareness. In some instances, that kind of interplay is initially threatening; but that threat quickly fades, and the results are more than worthwhile so long as both persons are open and committed to their own growth.

Another difficulty facing teachers, directors, and coaches as well as performers is the relation of the intellect to the modes. We want to have the right words to say, we want to be the sleuths of the singing-acting problem. But no matter how intuitive our perceptions may be, they must be translated into words. The words of the intellect are still our primary communicating tool; but they can create all sorts of problems if they try to control the functioning of the nonverbal mode minds. For the performer, we have suggested ways of creating a true partnership between the intellectual-verbal mind and the mode minds. As perceivers and describers of performance, we must do the same. Unfortunately, that creative partnership is too often a hierarchy in which the intellect reigns as king, sneering at the nonverbal capacities of the mode minds. The intellectual capacities have achieved a position of control, but once they have it they are not competent to deal with the very energies they are trying to manipulate. It is the Peter Principle operating on a larger scale: the intellectual-verbal capacity, an invention that is only a few thousand years old, has worked its way up the responsibility hierarchy of the brain, succeeding with increasing brilliance on each level. But finally it has reached the level of its incompetence: the inevitable path of the Peter Principle has been fulfilled. Operating on the principle of control-by-verbal-analysis, it now tries to control those aspects of performance that are beyond its control. Using one mode, the kinesthetic, as its principle control tool, it tries to bring the other two modes under its predictive jurisdiction; but it only succeeds in messing up the total system. Much of our discussion has suggested ways in which the intellectual fourth mode might be enlisted in a true partnership with the other modes.

It is time to make job descriptions for all concerned modes, the intellectual-verbal as well as the intuitive modes. The amount of territorial encroachment that currently goes on is wasteful, energy robbing, and inefficient. From each mode according to its capabilities, to each mode according to its needs. The first mode combination we should be concerned with both as teachers-directors-coaches and as performers is the relationship of the intellectual fourth mode to the three projective modes. We have seen the negative entanglements that are possible in that relationship and have become intellectually sensitive to them. We must now develop positive interrelationships between the intellect and the intuitive projective modes. The problem is that the intellect has no projective equivalent—outside of the words themselves—and must rely upon the three projective modes to deliver its message.

We have discussed projective mode congruency. Let us also consider congruency between the intellect and the intuition. We want those two resources to be in agreement both as to the nature of the message sent and the specific choice of resources with which to send them. This does not mean that the mental state is accurately reflected through the modes: as we have seen, there is no one-to-one correspondence between the internal reality and the external messages in performance. However, the external messages by themselves may be in a state of congruency.

As a performer, I may be very concerned about what is happening onstage and backstage, the orchestra may be out of tune, an accident may just have happened on stage, my costume may have developed a rip, the audience may be coughing—all these and many other thoughts may be part of my internal processes. Yet I will convey through my projective modes the sense of a man blissfully in love: my face will be filled with joy, my voice will be warm and happy, and my body will be free and vital. None of the thoughts in my mind that contradict that state will be allowed access to the projective resources. That is performing congruency at its best, even though there is little relationship between the actual thought process and what is communicated to the audience as the thought process. But that situation reflects true intellectual-intuitive congruency as well. The intellect and the intuition are in total agreement as to the messages they wish to send to the audience, and they are able to allow those messages to be sent through the appropriate channels even while editing out nonuseful messages.

As an example of intellectual-intuitive incongruency, consider a performer who is singing a passionate aria but is in a state of held physical tension. He is in a state of projective mode incongruency; expressing joy in one mode (the hearing / vocal) and repressing in another (the kinesthetic). In addition, the facial / emotional mode may be in a state of incongruency with either of the other modes: if it appears anxious or neutral, it is incongruent with the hearing / vocal mode; if it appears joyful or neutral, it is incongruent with the kinesthetic mode. All this sends the audience anxiety messages that are not the intention of the intellect. Thus, the intellect is also in a state of incongruency with respect to the choices being made by the intuitive resources. The job of the intellect and the intuition in that instance is to choose from among all possibilities one that allows the modes to communicate congruently.

From a larger view, we want our performers to be able to choose, intellectually, to allow the projective modes to be in a state of congruency at all times in performance. When they have achieved that kind of freedom, they may also be able to create appropriate incongruent combinations for purposes of characterization. An obvious example of characterization incongruency would be the physically enfeebled person who sings with power, whose hearing/vocal mode expresses extraordinary vitality while the kinesthetic mode is next to death; for example, the dying Gilda or the crippled Rigoletto. The facial/emotional mode would need to be in agreement with the kinesthetic rather than the hearing/vocal mode.

Combining the Modes: Readiness and Cooperation

Let us begin by listing those combinations of mode interplay that we have discussed in previous chapters, including interrelationships not yet covered. Since each combination of two modes requires readiness in the mode not in action, let us summarize the concept of readiness for each mode.

We have defined mode readiness as a state of being that allows a projective mode to use energy flexibly and freely at all times regardless of the scale of that energy. If the communication involves maximum energy, it also tests the flexibility and freedom of the mode to the maximum. In the kinesthetic and facial/emotional modes, one can *see* the readiness and observe its flexibility and freedom in action. In the hearing/vocal mode, one can only *hear* the action, although visible manifestations of the vocal process may help one see what one hears. But there is no way of hearing the vocal state of being before the sounds are actually produced. Unless overt physical or facial signs signal it, analysis of the hearing/vocal state of being must be largely retrospective.

The mode most likely to interfere with the other modes because of a lack of readiness is the kinesthetic. The general rule for positive mode interplay is for the kinesthetic to remain in a state of readiness when the other two modes are the primary communicators. If the kinesthetic mode is not in a state of readiness, it interferes with the hearing/vocal mode through glottal alteration of the vocal process; this seems to be an attempt to show emotion through vocal interference, which also interrupts and interferes with the breathing process. It also makes the facial/emotional mode less communicative and mobile in some cases, and it causes it to be overactive, to indicate and to mug, in others. In neither instance does it allow the other mode to communicate freely.

If not in a state of readiness, the kinesthetic mode interferes with its own functioning, especially in the use of gesture. It is not only the slowest of the three systems, it is the largest, and there is much opportunity for intramode interference between head, neck, and shoulders; between shoulders and rib cage; between legs and pelvis girdle; between pelvic girdle and rib cage; between hands and arms; and between all of these and the vocal process.

If not in a state of readiness, the facial/emotional mode interferes with the hearing/vocal mode. A tense, overactive, or blank face interferes in subtle but significant ways with the vocal process through the interrelated physical tensions between the two systems. A tense, anxious face often signals interruption of or interference with the breath. The mode also signals the kinesthetic mode that all is not well, causing sympathetic tension in the body generally and in the vital head-neck-shoulder girdle area particularly.

If not in a state of readiness, the hearing/vocal mode and its breath support system arouse sympathetic tension in the rest of the kinesthetic mode by interfering with the breathing and the production of sound. The hearing/vocal mode also arouses sympathetic tensions in the facial/emotional mode that interfere with its mobility and communicative power.

There is clearly a feedback process between the three systems. Using Arthur Koestler's term, each mode is a holon, a system complete in itself that also interrelates with other systems. Each individual holon-system has its own internal feedback process: it has self-assertive tendencies as well as integrative tendencies. The self-assertive tendencies are those that fulfill the internal workings of the system; the integrative tendencies relate to other systems. Each mode thus relates to its own needs and energies, and it interrelates with the energies of the other two modes in forming a larger system. When this interrelationship is functioning healthily, when the energy exchange is free, open, and supportive, we have a state of high synergy. When any mode is not in a synergistic state, the whole system is adversely affected. As we have said, only partly in jest, no mode is an island: touch any aspect of one of the modes and you affect them all.

We have concentrated thus far on self-assertive exercises that develop the needs of each mode in isolation. In this chapter, we concentrate on developing the integrative tendencies in each mode, ways of interrelating that develop the capacity of the total system. Moving beyond the concept of readiness, we can identify some of the ways in which each mode can help the others.

The kinesthetic mode helps the hearing/vocal mode by relating to the musicality energies in a supportive, punctuating, underlining way when it is appropriate. One runs the risk of conducting one's self or Mickey-Mousing (mirroring the music with physical movement), but there is risk in all uses of energy, and both of these problems are simply faulty technique. The mode helps the audience hear better by what it shows them, and it also helps performers to sing better by giving them a physical awareness of the flow of the music. The kinesthetic mode helps the facial/emotional mode by allowing it to express itself freely without accompanying tension and by supporting the facial/emotional statements with appropriate gestural or movement statements (which must not be held in a state of tension).

The facial/emotional mode helps the hearing/vocal mode by allowing its own energies to flow freely, thus releasing the hearing/vocal energies that are in such close proximity. By making clear, vulnerable statements, the mode also eases the hearing/vocal responsibility of carrying the total burden of communication. The facial/emotional mode helps the kinesthetic mode by defining clearly the emotional meaning of the action or the music; it thus takes the tension burden literally off the kinesthetic's back. The more clearly and freely the facial/emotional mode is able to express its meanings, the less the kinesthetic mode needs to justify by tension.

The hearing/vocal mode helps the facial/emotional mode through its access to verbal-intellectual meanings, as well as in its free-flowing, nonverbal use of musicality, both spoken and sung. Like the other modes, it lends assistance by clarifying the communication so that no gaps need to be filled. The more easily energy flows through the vocal process, the more easily the facial/emotional mode can release its own energies. The hearing/vocal mode helps the kinesthetic mode by specifying the nature of the action, by clarifying the meaning of the situation, and by releasing the kinesthetic mode from any need to contribute additional meaning through tension.

Each mode helps the others most by helping itself. If each mode expresses its own needs with the greatest freedom possible, with no additional or superfluous tension, it is better able to interrelate effectively with the other modes. The better the self-assertive needs of each mode are fulfilled, the better they are able to serve the integrative needs of the total system. Because the burden of maximum communication falls on all three modes, they help each other the most by taking on themselves the most appropriate aspects of that total burden—allowing the other modes to do what they do best, and always keeping their own flow of energies as free and open as possible.

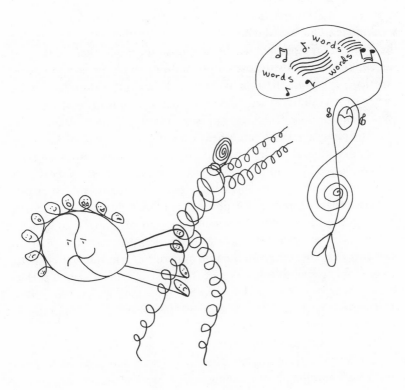

Exercising Mode Combinations

With the concepts of readiness and cooperation-in-action in mind, let us summarize the exercises we have already described and discuss the working relationship between the modes.

Exercises for the Kinesthetic and Hearing/Vocal Modes

One can physically describe the music (sometimes called Mickey-Mousing) while singing it, or conduct it extravagantly or physically manifest it in other ways. These ways of experiencing the music kinesthetically have to be altered for performance, but they offer insights and release relative to the interrelationship between the kinesthetic and hearing/vocal modes. One can also do the physicalization before singing, letting the body "do the singing" to the accompaniment and then adding the singing plus the newly discovered physicalization; or one may simply re-experience the physicalization in the mind as one sings. These techniques release what I call the closet kinesthetic dominant in many of us. Ristad's book *A Soprano on Her head* speaks to this area in useful ways.

Any physical task accomplished while singing is a way of exercising this combination of modes. It is a primary exercise area, but one that is seldom utilized by performers when warming up. As often as I see singers vocalizing in warm-up studios, I rarely see a vocal warm-up that creates a positive relationship with the physical and facial systems. Singers make singing-metaphor gestures (gesturally trying to draw the sound out of their mouths, or conducting themselves or using themselves physically in ways that relate negatively to the task of performing), thus actively practicing mode relationship habits that they have to deny in actual performance. If they used those physicalizations as consciously chosen exercises, as suggested above, they could be useful; but I have never found this to be the case.

We have suggested that the arbitrary gesture exercise be practiced daily, independently of singing. There is no reason why it cannot be practiced while warming up and singing as well; the same is true of the face-space-body exercises (see chap. 6). But performers must take the responsibility for exercising the total system each time they exercise one part of that system. They really have no choice, for that is what they are doing in any event: the modes cannot be totally isolated from one another. The only question is whether performers can develop the systems relationship and place it under their own control or whether they will continue to be creatures of history and habit. They can choose to be free, to be enlightened performers by progressive mastery of their uses of energy; or they can remain victims of the past, with growth and development dependent upon accidents of birth, upbringing, and situation. The only way to free one's self of a dependence upon situation—upon having a good director or conductor in the next show, finding a good class, encountering a new teacher—is to learn to work with one's energies on one's own. One should seek out good teachers, good directors, and good situations, but we are fundamentally responsible for our own growth and development. We only grow by working on our own, and our real challenge is the integration of skills, the integration of the modes. It is the integrating skill that singers must develop on their own.

Readiness can be exercised while singing. A person's ability to move in any direction at any moment is one way of testing this readiness. Simply ask another person to signal you to move arbitrarily while performing, and find the physical state that allows you to do so freely and easily. Another technique is to imagine that you are an athlete playing a game while singing, but without going through the actual physical moves. Whatever your game—tennis, basketball, or fencing—you may be in a better readiness state when prepared to play that game than you are as a performer ready to sing and act.

Exercises for the Kinesthetic and Facial/Emotional Modes

In theater and music theater, there are few moments when the kinesthetic and facial/emotional modes are not functioning simultaneously with the hearing/vocal mode. But those few moments are often key ones that create unique challenges for the singer-actor. These challenges occur with greater frequency in music theater than in theater. If you can imagine an actor in the midst of a passionate monologue or dialogue, pausing every so often for five or ten seconds without losing energy or developing tension, you have described a common situation for the singer-actor. Every introduction, interlude, postlude, or sequence in which the singer is not singing is a specific exercise for the kinesthetic and facial/emotional modes in total isolation from the hearing/vocal mode. The reverse isolation is not found: when the hearing/vocal mode is in action, the other two modes continue to exist and send messages whether we like it or not. Thus, for purely practical reasons, the kinesthetic and facial/emotional modes partnership is an important relationship to develop.

The facial/emotional mode should be able to communicate powerfully without any overt kinesthetic contribution. The kinesthetic impulse toward justification by tension needs to be inhibited even while the body maintains its readiness. This particular isolation of function—a kind of benign incongruency—may be one of the most important capabilities to be developed by the singer-actor. The other vital skill is the ability of the voice to function with maximum energies while the body is in a similar state of supportive readiness—also a benign or cooperative incongruency, to be acquired (like the other) through exercise and practice.

The reverse relationship is different. The facial/emotional mode should always aid the kinesthetic mode in clarifying the meaning of its messages. Gestures are potential energy statements to be actualized by hearing/vocal, facial/emotional, or situational meanings. For the facial/emotional and kinesthetic combination, this means that all physical statements need meaning messages from the facial/emotional mode in order to realize their full power.

One exercise is to take a list of attitudes and communicate them with the facial/emotional resources while maintaining the kinesthetic mode in a state of readiness (see chap. 5). Music is helpful here, because that is the actual situation during performance. As the intensity of the facial/emotional communication increases, the kinesthetic justification by tension wants to come into play. Freeing the body of this need, even as the face develops its maximum communicating power, is the core of this exercise.

One may exercise the kinesthetic modes's gestural capacity but allow the facial/emotional mode to actualize the potential meanings. One can perform mirror incorporation exercises, use arbitrary gesture cards, face-space-body sequences, or any other gestural assignment. The point of the exercise is to allow the face to define the meaning rather than calling full-body tension into play. In doing so, the performer may come to realize that anything the kinesthetic mode does, no matter how unusual, can be aided and justified by the facial/emotional mode so long as the two modes are not entangled. While the facial/emotional mode can and should be exercised independently of the kinesthetic mode, the latter always profits from the actualizing energies of the former.

The kinesthetic mode can act in combination with itself. There is always the possibility that the full body will attempt to justify or give meaning to gesture by overall tension. In practicing the second exercise above, it is important to inhibit the initiation of full-body tension, keep the kinesthetic mode in a state of readiness, and allow the facial/emotional mode and the gestures to do their dance together, free of overall interference.

Exercises for the Facial/Emotional and the Hearing/Vocal Modes

Because of the proximity of the facial/emotional and hearing/vocal modes and the relative subtlety of their energies, the relationship between them is especially significant. Kinesthetic statements and interference are relatively easy to perceive and to work with. But the energies that interrelate between the other two modes are delicate and difficult to detect, and they are also powerful in their effect on each other.

An inhibited, neutral, or blank facial/emotional mode can block the voice in subtle ways without the audience or singer being aware of it. A young singer whom I had advised to do facial/emotional exercises every day began incorporating them as part of her vocal warm-ups. She realized that she had been programming her face to be "a vegetable" (as she put it) while she warmed up vocally, and it was unreasonable for it to do anything else when she performed. That gave her a good, logical reason to do the exercises, but there was a dividend: her vocal warm-up time was cut in half. Releasing the facial/emotional holds that had kept it deadpan also released the voice and allowed it to warm up more quickly. This demonstrates again the holistic nature of the modes system: release a tension in one area, and you release it in others. Free the facial/emotional mode from its deadpan hold — or from the opposite of that, the entanglement of facial musculature with the act of singing — and you release the voice along with it.

Many exercises can develop the flexible interrelationship of the two modes. The use of arbitrary attitudes while singing, which often begins as an exercise in intentional incongruency, ends with the realization that all emotions are blends to begin with and that no matter how foreign the attitude may seem, it blends easily with those of the aria. The essential point of the exercise is the capability of the facial/emotional mode to send messages that are seemingly different from those of the hearing/vocal mode.

The B. S. round, (with apologies to Ms. Sills) is an exercise that tries to do what Beverly Sills was able to do so brilliantly: send smiling facial/emotional messages of incredible warmth, sustaining them for as long as possible. This is often an exercise in cooperative incongruency, depending upon the song or aria. Even if it portrays a grief-stricken state, the facial/emotional mode should be able to send a positive message without interference.

I have already described the exercise that uses a facial mirror while singing (chap. 5). It is designed to develop the mobility of the face while singing, preparing the facial/emotional resources to serve the communication of emotion with no interference by the effort of the hearing/vocal mode.

The use of Kabuki or commedia masks while singing is the equivalent of the kinesthetic exercise, in which a powerful gesture is initiated and then sustained without the tension that initiated it. The performer makes a mask, as extreme as possible, then sustains it with as little tension as possible while trying to let it feel "real" again, without losing the mask itself. At the same time, the performer keeps singing as one would without the mask.

Allowing the facial/emotional mode to communicate the energies of the music while singing is a version of the kinesthetic exercise in which the performer physically demonstrates the energies and structure of the music. It is a kind of Mickey-Mousing or facial duplication of the form of the music and also a form of mode congruency (the face reflecting what the voice is doing) that should ordinarily be avoided by singers. But it

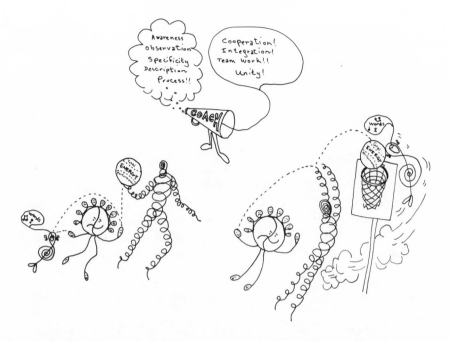

is a useful way of activating facial/emotional involvement with the music. Observers should watch closely to see that the kinesthetic mode remains in a readiness state and does not attempt to join the descriptive process.

Tri-mode combinations

In working with triple combinations, the interconnectedness of the three modes is demonstrated repeatedly. In one of my university classes, three successive performers had a state of being that was not congruent with the implicit demands of performance. To put it more simply, they were not in a state of readiness physically. In addition, their facial/emotional communication was not strong (although they were consciously trying to use it), and there were other tensions in the body. But then they found a state of readiness with their bodies. In all three cases, this involved an adjustment in the basic stance itself. Two of the performers had been leaning off on one leg; the third was back on his heels and sitting into the hips. When a readiness state of being was achieved kinesthetically, it dramatically improved the energy flow in the other two modes. Tensions within the kinesthetic mode, which were not a concern of the exercise, also disappeared.

This kind of experience raises a number of questions. How many physical tensions are created by the body in an attempt to compensate for what *it* knows—although the intellect does not—to be an incongruent and inappropriate state of being for the scene or song in question? How many facial/emotional or hearing/vocal tensions or deficiencies stem from *their* mode-mind awareness that the body is in a state of performance incongruency, so that a free flow of energy in the other modes is blocked?

A particularly interesting case of trimode entanglement with the intellect occurred with a soprano in my San Francisco classes. She asked if she could sing Mimi's aria "Si, Mi Chiamano Mimi" from Puccini's *La Boheme* in gibberish instead of Italian. That is, she wanted to improvise a language to replace the original. I readily agreed, adding my usual proviso that the only thing wrong with the question was that she felt she had to ask it in the first place. I always encourage the singers with whom I work to do whatever they want to do. Young singers need badly to flex their independence; this singer was particularly judgment and control oriented, and she needed to assert her rights to do what she needed to do.

She began to sing, and it was astonishing to her coach and me what a remarkable improvement there was in her sound. It was also gratifying to see the marked improvement in her facial/emotional and kinesthetic communication, both of which were blocked to some extent by tension holds. The singer felt an exhilarating flow of energy and was delighted with her new sense of freedom. All three of us were euphoric.

Then I suggested that she try singing the aria in the original Italian while maintaining her newly acquired performing freedom. To the surprise of all three of us, the tension returned, the new vocal beauty faded, and the performance lost its previous impact. The hearing/vocal mode concern with Italian pronunciation and diction—strong judgmental areas for many singers—not only created a beauty-robbing tension in the voice, but brought tension patterns to the face and body as well. It was a remarkable demonstration of the intellectual judgment center creating hearing/vocal mode tensions that interfered with the other two modes as well: a laboratory experiment that demonstrated the holistic interaction of the modes system.

We cannot leave the situation without describing the exercise that allowed the singer to solve the problem of singing the original Italian without losing her vocal, physical, and facial performing freedom. It was a simple matter of moving back and forth between the freedom-bestowing gibberish and the tension-producing Italian until the singer became aware of *how* she was creating the tensions and was able to release the need to do that. Her next public performance was a stunning demonstration of what the exercise did for her.

Yet another interesting case of mode awakening affecting the intellectual thought process was the case cited previously of the young singer who was concentrating on developing her facial/emotional mode system, which had always remained a relative blank while she sang. The exercise we assigned was simply to send specific messages of any kind through the facial/emotional mode while singing. The content of the messages was less important than the fact that a message was communicated. She performed the exercise with good effect; then she stopped and said, "I started to think about *what* I was singing about for the first time!!" The "thinking" she did with her face triggered a parallel thought process in her intellect; when her face was blank, it apparently inhibited her thought processes as well, leaving her mind unfocused on the situation of the character. When the face began thinking, other mode-mind processes were initiated as well, including those of her voice and body; observers noted a distinct improvement in vocal quality, physical freedom, and overall communication when the facial/emotional mode was activated.

A Closer Look at Incongruency

Mode incongruencies are a typical state of being for many performers. Unfortunately, the incongruency is not a matter of choice but of tension habits that are below the level of awareness. We must first free the performer of the unintentional incongruency, develop the modal interplay ability, and finally arrive at a stage where the performer can make characterization choices that involve incongruency from a point of awareness and freedom.

Long before the performer begins to learn a score, the composer has made decisions that establish either a congruent or incongruent relationship between the words and the music. In chapter 3, we noted that the hearing/vocal mode is capable of being incongruent within itself; the words can suggest one sort of emotional meaning, while the music suggests another. Sarcasm of any kind usually employs some kind of incongruency between music and meaning. It occurs with some frequency in the theater, but it is rarely found in opera or music theater. When it does, it is created by the composer, not the performer.

When a composer works with incongruency, it is usually subtle and rarely identified as such. At one point in Mozart's *Cosi fan tutte* (which is filled with hearing/vocal mode incongruencies), the sisters, disconsolate at the absence of their beloved sweethearts, are using words expressive of grief and melancholy. At the same time, the music (at least according to Deryck Cooke's carefully developed vocabulary of musical meaning, not to mention the plot and character developments that reveal the incongruency in retrospect) is expressing a sense of excited anticipation — perhaps at the presence of their new, exotic suitors. Society demands that the ladies express the words they do, but their hearts insist upon the music. Critics, while not identifying the incongruencies specifically, have always had problems with *Cosi* and with its "ironies" and "contradictions." It may be one of the earliest intentionally incongruent music-theater statements, and, therefore, one of the most sophisticated scores, psychologically, ever written.

Later composers worked more freely with the ironies and contradictions of incongruency, drawing upon the contrasting power of words and music to make complex musical-dramatic statements. The vast majority of music-theater experiences, however, are congruent. The power of the music theater form, particularly of the operatic sector, tends to reside in the intensity of emotion rather than in its complexity. In fact, the more emotionally complex the operatic experience becomes, the less popular it tends to be. Emotional complexity is dramatically acceptable if it does not lose its intensity. Incongruency, by definition, implies a contradiction

that tends to mute the singleness of purpose and intensity of the emotional statement.

The understanding of this factor is vital for the performer, who must
perceive clearly the intensions of both the language and the music. If they
are incongruent, the performer may underline words or music with either
or both the facial/emotional and kinesthetic modes. In the example used
above, the facial/emotional mode of the *Cosi* sisters would probably obey
the demands of social convention and portray sorrow. If they were to
smile and be gay, it would betray the unconscious nature of the irony,
for the sisters are not consciously aware of their underlying hypocrisy;
they believe they are unhappy and would be deeply offended if told
otherwise.

The kinesthetic mode, however, is more like the music; its meaning
is defined by the specific emotional meanings of the face. Therefore this
mode can express the "excited anticipation" of the heart so long as the
facial/emotional mode continues to send melancholy messages that reinforce the verbal needs of society. Little bursts of physical excitement
might occur, combining with the sad faces and sad words to express the
frustration of not being able to properly express one's grief or melancholy. Or the erotic anticipation of the sisters could be expressed by
languorous, caressing movements that, in the societal context, become
mournfully sad instead of sensual. The number of possible choices is
immense.

Ultimate incongruency is psychotic. In such cases the face, the body,
and the voice are expressing messages totally at odds with each other: the
killer with the relaxed, shambling approach, knife in hand, smiling, his-
sing intensely. This kind of incongruency includes the intent behind the
messages as well as the incongruency among the messages themselves.
But the incongruency reflects high-intensity emotion that has not found
a healthy or normal channel for expression. That description applies also
to many operatic characters, who, by and large, are not healthy, well-
balanced individuals.[1] That is precisely why we find them so fascinating.
But for the performer, these incongruencies and unhealthy ways of being
must be consciously and coperatively controlled. There is a real danger
in the performer losing control to the unhealthy state being portrayed.
Because that performer is dealing with the expression of human energies

at their most powerful level, there is great potential danger to the performing system unless they are under in-process control. I have observed performers who were unable to portray character tensions and negative mode relationships from a point of freedom and cooperative choice, and they destroyed their voices by the creation of kinesthetic character tension. A proper understanding of mode interplay can ease such problems. But if the tension patterns of the character are simply thrown into the modes system before the performer has learned to isolate them, it is almost impossible to keep those tensions from infecting the total system.

Some of the exercises we have already described involve incongruency. The arbitrary attitude exercise, for example, often finds the facial/emotional mode delivering messages opposed to or different from those of the hearing/vocal mode. Smiling through tears and whistling in the dark are examples of incongruencies that have become commonplace communication concepts. The intriguing aspect of most incongruencies, however, is that they are more difficult for performers to coordinate and project than they are for observers to understand and accept. To the observer, the performer seems to be making perfect sense out of whatever unusual exercise is being attempted—and most "unusual" exercises involve incongruencies of some kind. But suddenly the performer stops and says, "This doesn't make any sense at all." And the observers reply in unison, "Yes, it *does*!" The mode minds were making sense of it for the observers, and only the intellectual-verbal mind of the performer was trapped by old habits, new shoes, and the predictive, judgmental rationalizations of word logic. I find working with incongruencies with performers to be the most creatively demanding, imagination-freeing, mode-flexing challenge of all. We are accustomed to perceiving performance as a whole and are largely unaware of the individual communication potential of the parts—the modes. Incongruency exercises compel us to come to grips with the actual complexity of modes interplay and open up creative possibilities that are not readily apparent when we view performance as a generalized gestalt.

In exercising mode incongruencies, one can simply ask the performer to deliver contrasting messages in two or more modes and describe what happens. The interest is more in what the performer does with the challenge (or what the challenge does with the performer) rather than the challenge itself. The performer may be asked to send facial/emotional and kinesthetic messages that are incongruent with the musical-verbal statement of the hearing/vocal mode. In opera, those are the only two modes that *can* exercise incongruency because the music and the words are set. The hearing/vocal mode efforts of the singer in that case are recreative, whereas the facial/emotional and kinesthetic modes contain the creative potential.

With spoken language, the situation is slightly more complex. The words are set, but the music used to speak those words can oppose them, agree with them, or be neutral. Add to that complexity of choice the facial/emotional and kinesthetic choices of opposition, agreement, or neutrality, and one has an enormous range of exercise potential for the most advanced actor.

An even more complex form of incongruency lies within the modes themselves. An example is the separation between the words and the music with which the words are spoken. This intramode incongruency happens in the kinesthetic system whenever different messages are sent by different parts of the overall system. For example, tense shoulders but relaxed hands; an erect upper body but a tilted-off, relaxed head; and knotted fists but a loosely flowing body. The same possibilities occur within the facial/emotional mode on a more restricted scale: the angry eyes, the smile to cover; the gentle eyes, the sarcastic mouth; and the blend of crying and laughing. But these are subtle and special cases, for the most advanced kind of work. In my experience, the difficulties of releasing unintentional incongruency, developing individual mode strength, and promoting congruent mode interplay have provided challenges enough for most training periods. I look forward to extended, indepth work with performers who are prepared to be challenged by these more advanced concepts. But even when that time comes, the fundamental process remains the same: to allow the singer-actor to do whatever he or she wishes to do with greater freedom, greater power, and greater flexibility.

Case Studies of Mode Combinations

In exploring the combined messages that can be delivered by the modes, we will examine two arias: Tamino's "Dies Bildnis" ("This Portrait") from Mozart's *Die Zauberflöte* (*The Magic Flute*) and the Countess's third-act recitative and aria from Mozart's *The Marriage of Figaro*. We will first explore the thought-process messages that the facial/emotional mode can deliver; then the emotional, attitudinal messages that could inform that thought process; and, finally, the kinesthetic messages that could accompany those of the facial/emotional mode. In doing so, we will relate all facial/emotional and kinesthetic mode choices to the hearing/vocal mode musicalities contained in the arias.

It is not my intention to present here Balk's Interpretations of Famous Arias. This has been done in detail by others, and although these interpretations are valid and even useful on occasion, I find the philosophy behind the idea disturbing. Like so much of what goes on in the world of operatic production, preset interpretations can be dogmatic and even stultifying, particularly if they are approached as the only ones possible. Some of the worst cases of held tension and acting interference I have encountered have been performers who were taught *the* way to interpret a given role (down to the last twitch of the little finger) by a former singer who had performed the role. That former great performer (and in many cases these performers-turned-teacher were excellent performers) simply grafted the details of his or her own performance (or what the performer perceived as such) onto the student, who submitted willingly from natural awe of the fame, skill, and technique of the old master. In itself, this is a wonderful exercise; but how much better it would be if, having mastered that version of the character, the student was then given several other interpretations to work with—new shoes to break in—so that at least three interpretive possibilities could be carried into the professional world (along with the flexibility engendered by such a process), rather than a single point of view and the resultant inflexibility of attitude about other interpretations.

In short, our explorations are intended to open up as many possibilities as we can arrive at within the limitations of this format. From among them, the performer and the teacher or conductor can choose those that are most appropriate to the situation and the personalities involved. They may also create other choices. With this kind of thinking as an example, the performer can approach any piece in the personal repertory and create a range of choices. The choices, however, are dependent upon being specific with the mode concept. It is often difficult to come up with a wide variety of choices based on a generalized character description; but once you begin talking about specific choices within the modes context, new ideas emerge with relative ease. The intention, then, is to create a process paradigm for the exploration of any aria, any soliloquy, any dramatic-musical performance in any style.

Tamino: Choices for the Facial/Emotional Mode

In *The Magic Flute* scene, Tamino has just been given a small portrait of Pamina—a woman he has never seen—and his reaction to it is so powerful that it evokes the aria in question. This creates a classic focus problem, for it implies that Tamino cannot take his eyes off the portrait, which in normal reality might be precisely the case. That, however, is a very limited way to approach the performance realization of Tamino's experience, for it does not allow him to share the experience with the audience nor allow his imagination to create a progression of thoughts by use of focus structure. Change of focus is one of the most important elements in communicating thought process, even as the ability to sustain focus is one of the most important means of communicating intensity of thought process. The singer-actor must learn to understand Tamino's thought process and to communicate it with his facial/emotional mind by performing exercises with each choice. He will be greatly helped by observers who describe accurately what he has actually communicated with his projective modes.

As Tamino looks at the portrait for the first time, the orchestra plays two fanfares (bars 1 and 2), the second more intense than the first.[2] Immediate kinesthetic decisions have to be made: When should he look at the portrait before the orchestral chords? What is the nature of his physical reaction to the impact of that first look? Is it the love-at-first-sight thunderbolt? But let us reserve those questions for the kinesthetic-hearing/vocal combination. Confining our examination now to the facial/emotional mode, we see that Tamino could continue to focus on the portrait in his hands for the first two phrases that he sings (bars 3–6):

Dies Bildnis ist bezaubernd schön, wie noch Auge je gesehn!
(This picture is bewitchingly beautiful, like no eye has ever seen!)

At the end of that phrase, Tamino could look up from the portrait and begin a focus search (indicating a mental search) for the specific nature of this experience as he sings (bars 7–8):

> Ich fühl es, ich fühl es. . . .
> (I feel it, I feel it. . . .)

Then, as he approaches the highest note thus far, and the intensity of the words (bar 9):

> Wie dies Götterbild
> (as this God-like image),

an eye shutter might be appropriate as Tamino "goes inside" to savor and control the depths of emotion he feels. He could also continue to focus on the vision of the image that he "finds" at the end of his focus search. If the performer chooses the eye shutter, the length of time the eyes remain closed may vary; but they should probably not open until at least the middle of bar 12, as he sings:

> mein Herz mit neuer Regung fült. . . .
> (my heart with new emotion fills. . . .)

They could also remain closed until the repeat of that phrase (bars 13–14), finally opening as the phrase concludes in bar 15.

At that point, Tamino might return to the portrait for another intense look during the orchestral interlude (bars 15–17). Before the end of that interlude, another focus search might begin as Tamino tries to understand the nature of the experience he is having. The search might continue during the next two phrases (bars 18–21):

> Dies Etwas kann ich zwar nicht nennen;
> doch fühl ich's hier wie Feuer brennen.
> (This something can I certainly not name;
> yet feel I it here like fire burning.)

As that phrase concludes, nothing seems more likely than a light bulb (during the second half of bar 20) — a sudden change of focus that says, "I've got it!" or at least, "I've got a clue!" During the following words (bars 22–25):

> Soll die Empfindung Liebe sein? (repeated)
> (Can this emotion love be?),

Tamino could make a brief focus search of growing intensity that lasts through the repetition of the phrase. The search is rewarded as Tamino finds the image of Pamina (his focus image, not the portrait) and the focus image of Love coinciding. And he sings passionately (bars 26–34),

> Ja, ja! Die Liebe ist's allein, die Liebe, die Liebe,
> die Liebe ist's allein.
> (Yes, yes! Love it is alone, love, love,
> love it is alone.)

During the interlude that follows (bars 34–35), Tamino returns to the portrait itself. Then, on the line (bars 36–37):

> O wenn ich sie nur finden könnte!
> (Oh if I her only find could!),

Tamino focuses on the concept of his physical search for Pamina, which is followed by another focus image on the next phrase that envisions the moment of their first sight of each other (bars 38–39):

> O wenn sie doch schon vor mir stände. . . .
> (Oh if she only already before me stood. . . .)

Another focus shift is possible before the next phrase, and another before the repeated word in that phrase (bars 40–41):

> Ich würde, würde . . . .
> (I would, would . . . .)

It is like a brief search for the image of what he might actually do at the moment he first sees her. On bar 42, he could return to the image of Pamina or possibly to the portrait itself, as he sings:

> warm und rein
> (warm and pure)

This focus could sustain as he sings the question again (bar 43):

> was würde ich?
> (what would I do?)

On the following bar of rest, there might be a gentle light bulb, an easy change of process in the focus. The new focus is sustained during bars 45–49 as Tamino sings:

> ich würde sie voll Entzükken an diesen heissen Busen drucken.
> (I would her filled with enchantment to this loving breast press.)

Given the intensity of the experience, eye shutters are always possible; but their use should be judicious, certainly not to exceed two or three during the course of this or any aria.

As that phrase concluded, a shift of focus to a new image of the two of them together might be appropriate as Tamino sings (bars 50–61):

> und ewig wäre sie dann mein . . . . (repeated five times)
> ("and forever will she then be mine . . . .)

Another shift of focus is possible after the first repetition (bar 51), or the focus may be maintained until the second repetition concludes (bar 54). In either case, once the focus shifts, it should probably be maintained through the last three repetitions because they are inextricably linked by the music into one long, beautiful phrase. As Tamino concludes, there are three orchestral bars of conclusion during which Tamino might return to the portrait, gazing at it as the orchestra concludes and until he is interrupted by the approach of the three ladies.

Now that we have a concept of how the thought-process structure might be communicated, let us examine a series of attitude choices to fill that structure. Let us select as wide a range of attitudes as possible without actually encountering incongruency.

To begin with, we can simply list attitudes that might logically be a part of Tamino's emotional situation as the aria begins. He has just experienced, in rather rapid succession, near-death from a monstrous serpent, acquaintance with a very odd, birdlike creature who seems to be a human being, and a visitation by three unusual ladies who place a padlock on the bird-man's mouth and give Tamino a locket with a portrait inside. Thus, even before viewing the portrait, Tamino is likely to be in a state that includes a combination of some of the following attitudes: uncertain, incredulous, doubting, worried, uneasy, cautious, astonished, surprised, frightened, alarmed, fearful, awed, astounded, shocked, uncomprehending, puzzled, and perturbed. Any of these may be blended, for there is no such thing as a "pure" attitude — only blends of several intermingled emotions.

Besides these situational possibilities, we may add the personal attitudinal characteristics of Tamino that become part of the overall blend: brave, resolute, determined, lively, earnest, courteous, trusting, alert, and the like. Once Tamino has seen the portrait, we may add the following emotional ingredients to the recipe: amazed, passionate, eager, ardent, hopeful, ecstatic, aware, exalted, excited, yearning, jubilant, elated, and joyful.

In following the thought processes outlined above, the first two phrases (bars 1–6), which are focused on the portrait, might center about the astonished-amazed-awed combination; the search that follows (bars 7–8) might include eager-puzzled, growing to ardent-ecstatic on the eye shutter (bars 9–14). As Tamino searches with increasing excitement for the definition of what the feeling is (bars 15–20), the process culminates in the light-bulb shock of awareness and awe (bars 21–22), which in turn grows to the jubilant-elated-exalted outburst of affirmation, "Yes! It can only be love!" (bars 23–33). In the interlude that follows and as Tamino imagines what he might do (bars 34–43), the hopeful-eager-yearning-ardent cluster dominates, followed by a moment of almost playful puzzlement during bars 43–44 ("What *would* I do?"). As he realizes the answer, it is with a renewed sense of passionate jubilation and elation. The whole constellation of possibilities that we have mentioned continues to play and intermingle throughout the rest of the aria, the particular

choice of emotions depending upon the personal makeup of the performer and the preferences of the conductor and director.

The facial/emotional and hearing/vocal modes in combination thus
offer a multitude of choices, a depth of richness in both the focus structuring of the thought process and the emotional energies that fill it. All
those technical resources can be made available to the performer through
awareness and exercise—practice, play, and persistence. Once available,
they can be used in synchronization with the music, the text, and the
situation. The sequence is always the same: analysis of possibilities;
specific choices; practice of the choices; and then, in actual performance,
allowing the flow to take place with a minimum of control and a maximum of nonjudgmental awareness. Once the performance is concluded,
that awareness can be drawn upon in helping one make changes in the
choices, returning to the sequence of analysis-choice-practice.

In actual performance, of course, one does what one does. Performance is not the time to practice things with which one is not comfortable. You don't give yourself a voice lesson during performance—you
can't change your vocal technique on the spot, and you shouldn't expect
to change any of your other performance technique habits without having
practiced them first in a training exercise situation. Nonetheless, there are
times when the confidence in process and in one's ability to deal with
choices has been sufficiently developed through exercise so that relatively
unpracticed ideas can be brought into the performance. This is the state
of true performing power, when spontaneity and control exist together
in perfect harmony. When it happens—as it did three times with young
performers in an actual production during the writing of this chapter—it
is a tremendously gratifying experience. But like all good things, it must
be allowed and not made to happen.

The Countess: Choices for the Facial/Emotional Mode

Before we add the kinesthetic component to Tamino's aria, let us examine a female characterization for the hearing/vocal and facial/emotional
combination. The recitative and aria of the Countess from the third act
of Mozart's *The Marriage of Figaro* serves that purpose, plus adding an

environmental focus possibility to the possibilities we used in analyzing Tamino's aria.

Countess Almaviva and her maid Susanna are plotting to trick the Count Almaviva into revealing his own scheming infidelity. Susanna has gone to the Count to arrange a secret meeting in the garden between the two of them. When the time of that meeting arrives, the Countess will meet the Count in Susanna's place. She hopes that, thus confronted, he will be willing to change his ways. The scheme is a dangerous one, and as the Countess enters she is anxiously awaiting the return of Susanna from her initial meeting with the Count.

The focus process might begin with an environment search of the room that the Countess is entering, a search for Susanna and for anyone else who might be there. The term *search* does not mean a physical search, of course, but a search with the eyes. The accompanying kinesthetic possibilities will be covered below. As she searches, the Countess sings (bars 1–4):

E Susanna non vien! Sono ansiosa di saper come il Conte accolse la proposta.
(And Susanna has not come! I am anxious to find out how the Count received the proposal.)

At the end of bar 4, there could be a sudden shift of focus as if the Countess suddenly hears a sound and is frightened by it. Then, as she sings (bars 5–6):

Alquanto ardito il progetto mi par,
(How daring the project seems to me,)

her focus fixes on the thought-image of their scheme in action. At the end of bar 6, she might be startled out of that fearful contemplation, either by another imagined sound or by the sudden thought of her husband's reaction if he knew.

During bars 7–8, she focuses on that image as she describes the Count:

e ad uno sposo si vivace e geloso . . . .
(to a husband so full of spirit and jealous . . . .)

As that thought concludes at the end of bar 8, the Countess might either flinch away from the image with a sudden change of focus or be startled by another imagined sound.

At the end of bar 9, as she says:

> Ma che mal c'e?
> (But what's the harm?)

she focus-searches for a more congenial image of their plot and finds it during bar 10, sustaining that focus through bar 14 as she says:

> cangiando i miei vestiti conquelli di Susanna,
> ei suoi co' miei al favor della notte.
> (Changing my clothes with those of Susanna,
> and hers with mine under cover of night.)

But the image changes from an innocent plot to that of a degrading masquerade. As that happens, she might respond with an eye shutter to blot out the pain of the image as she sings (bars 15–18):

> oh cielo! a qual umil stato fatale io son
> ridotta da un consort crudel!
> (Ah heaven! to what a lowly, unfortuante position
> I am reduced by a cruel consort!)

Somewhere during that phrase (possibly after "io son ridotta"), her eyes open to a new awareness of the real culprit, her husband. Then, on strongly punctuated chords (bar 18), she has a sudden change of focus— almost a light bulb—to the image of her guilty husband whom she proceeds to chastise in no uncertain terms (bars 18–24):

> che dopo avermi con un misto inaudito d'infedelta,
> di gelosia, di sdegno! Prima amata, indi offesa,
> e alfin tradita.
> (who, with an incredible mixture of faithlessness,
> of jealousy, of disdain! Having first loved, then offended,
> and finally betrayed me.)

As the punctuated chord of bar 24 echoes her indignation, the Countess might shift her focus to the image of herself, the martyr and abused wife. Another choice might be an eye shutter as she thinks of that image, which expresses the intensity of her indignation at the thought of her undeserved humiliation (bars 25–26):

> fammi or cercar da una mia serva aita!
> (forces me to seek help from my servant!)

At this point we move into the aria itself, which begins with two or more focus images related to the Countess's thoughts of the nostalgic past with the Count (bars 1–18):

> Dove sono i bei momenti di dolcezza, e di piacer,
> dove andaro i giuramenti di quel labbro menzogner;
> (Where are the beautiful moments of sweetness and pleasure?
> Where have the promises of those deceitful lips gone?)

Then, for bars 19–27, the painful present becomes the subject of both the words and the focus images:

> Perche mai se in pianti, e in pene (bar rest)
> per me tutto si cangio . . . .
> (Why, if into tears and grief
> everything for me has changed . . . .)

The focus changes from the sweetness of the past to the present; another focus shift could take place within the context of that present during the rest on bar 23, with other shifts possible on bars 25 and 27.

Then the Countess begins a focus search that carries her back to the nostalgic past (bars 28–36):

> la memoria di quel bene dal mio sen non trapasso, (repeated)
> (has the memory of that sweet past not left my memory?)

Thus the pain of the present drives the Countess back to the past, and both the pain and the nostalgia allow the possibility of judiciously chosen eye shutters.

The nostalgic-past section is repeated during bars 37–51; the words are the same as for bars 1–18, as is the music except for the final bar. During this passage of memory, two to four focus images are possible, al-

though a single sustaining focus over the whole long, wonderful phrase
is also possible. Since there is a light bulb denoting sudden change of
process between bars 51 and 52, the contrast would be greater if preceded
by fewer changes.

The new idea, signaled by the sudden allegro tempo and by the
light-bulb focus change, is the Countess's hope for a better future
through the exertion of her personal efforts. Up to this time she has been,
to some extent, a pawn moved by other people's energies; but she now
realizes that she also has power and can take control of her own
circumstances, possibly altering them for the better. The first time she
dwelt upon the nostalgic past, it led her to the painful present; when her
second retreat into the past begins to lead her into the present, she leaps
over that present into a hopeful future where potential happiness can be
actualized (bars 52–63):

> Ah, se almen la mia constanza nel languire
> amando ognor mi portasse una speranza
> di cangiar l'ingrato cor!
> (Ah, if only my constancy, while I am languishing
> but still loving, might bring me a hope
> of changing his ungrateful heart.)

These words are repeated several times until the conclusion of the aria.

The initial focus image of future hope may be maintained for bars
52 and 53, when it is almost pulled back to the image of the painful present as the music shifts to a minor tonality in bar 54. But in bar 55, the
music returns to the future hope tonality as it lifts from the minor third
of E flat to E natural.

On bar 60, focus shifts to other images of hope are possible; but as
there is a focus search of excitement from bars 63–65, a single focus might
be maintained until that point. That search finds a focus for bars 66–68,
followed by another search from bar 68 to bar 70. The focus found on bar
71 sustains through bar 73, where it is almost pulled back to the minor
E flat image for two bars. But on bar 76, the music rises even more strongly
to the E natural. The rest of the aria remains with the image of future
hope, and, given the new rhythmic impetus of the whole allegro section, a number of focus shifts are possible. As always, the focus thought

process should reflect the musical shape of the aria without being rigid.

From bars 76 through 103 (the final sung bar), as many as ten separate focus images are possible (specifically on bars 76, 78, 80, 82, 84, 88, 92, 95, 99, and 100) with all shifts to be made fluidly as the voice moves into each new phrase. Alternately, as few as four or five are also possible (specifically on bars 80, 84, 92, and 99). Each focus image is a *thought*: the mind is very specific in its thought processes, and the purpose of the focus process is to communicate the actual thought-process structure (or the structure you wish the audience to understand from the character) as clearly and specifically as possible.

An immense number of emotional choices are available to the Countess from moment to moment. As she enters the room in search of Susanna, she contains the following attitudinal mixture: worried, uneasy, fretful, nervous, wary, apprehensive, concerned, frightened, disturbed, and doubting, among others. As the recitative progresses, she becomes by turns apologetic, regretful, bitter, pathetic, mournful, angry, scolding, reproving, contemptuous, challenging, bold, and defiant.

When the aria proper begins, the Countess thinks first of the past and is nostalgic, pleading, resigned, dreamy, prayerful, yearning, longing, melancholic. As she is pulled back to the present time of pain and resentment, she has the choice of bitterness, disappointment, vexation, anger, self-pity, and grief. She then returns to the cluster of emotional possibilities associated with the past, but as the second move toward the present is overleaped into the future, a new constellation of emotional states emerges: eager, excited, energetic, vigorous, passionate, ecstatic, rapturous, inspired, hasty, exalted, hopeful, lively, joyful, playful, jubilant, enraptured, bold, challenging, and confident.

Again, there is an astonishingly rich blend of possibilities available to the Countess during these few moments on stage. They need not all be used, of course, but it would be a superb exercise for all potential Countesses to work with different combinations until a dozen possibilities are developed. A dozen would not begin to exhaust the interplay of possibilities for focus and attitude interplay, but it would open the mind to the true potential of performer power when it exercises all the choices available. And what fun it could be to do so, once the performer's product-judgment reflexes are stilled!

The Kinesthetics of Opera

With the hope of opening up even more challenging vistas of performing power, let us add the interplay of the kinesthetic to the facial/emotional mode possibilities we have developed. The intersection between the hearing/vocal and kinesthetic modes is, as we have said, the key to the dilemma of creating human realities from the abstractions of opera. The operatic hearing/vocal mode pushes the level of abstraction as far as it can go without losing touch with human reality, and that is its principal glory and power. But the kinesthetic mode represents the real world of the human being in the most tangible way possible—in the physical being of the human performer. Opera and music theater in general are based on this intersection of human reality and musical abstraction as it portrays a series of human events. The word defines the specific nature of characterization and action, while the music elevates, qualifies, and transports those events and characters to more stylized realms using time alteration as its basic tool. The singer-actor is the unifying force in blending and integrating the reality and the abstraction, in giving specific human life to the transcending powers of music and making the total experience a unit. But in bringing human reality to the music-theater situation, the singer-actor is deprived of two primary weapons: the naturalism of the human voice as it speaks in everyday life and the detailed comprehensibility of human language as it is spoken rather than sung.

The splendor of the operatic voice—the essence of the form—is also its greatest weakness: it is neither naturalistic nor is it easy to understand, particularly with orchestral accompaniment. The elevated, unnatural, but magnificent style of opera places a large burden on singer-actors as they attempt to portray reality. They have the large, visible, real, but abstract energies of the body on one hand, and the large, invisible, stylized energies of the voice on the other. The gap between these energies creates much of the performance pressure on the singer. What are the relief valves?

We have mentioned several of them in discussing hearing/vocal and kinesthetic mode interaction: they include readiness and lack of superfluous tension in the kinesthetic mode and the mental capacity to accept singing-acting energies from the hearing/vocal mode as an acceptable translation of reality. But if one is not a hearing/vocal dominant, the latter can be difficult; and, as we have seen, kinesthetic mode energies need specifying if their meanings are to be clear—a fist has only potential meaning until defined.

The missing link, for both the singer-actor and the audience, is the facial/emotional mode. Its projective communication to an audience may be limited in a large theater, but more important is its interconnection with the other two modes and the effect it has upon them. It makes reality clear to the singer-actor—recall the singer who knew what she was thinking about for the first time when the facial/emotional mode was communicating—and it relieves the other two modes of total responsibility. It serves as the time extender (through focus structure) and the energy specifier (through emotional choice and projection). It gives the abstract, potential energies of the other two modes specificity, it lends the invisible visibility, it grants the highly stylized a measure of reality, and it can do all this because it is the quickest, most nimble, and most flexible of the three mode servants of the mind.

Perhaps the absence of facial/emotional mode specificity leads to the grandiloquent semaphoring and statuesque posing that is sometimes a part of opera. Along with the misunderstood idea of sustaining the music, the body feels it must take up the reality burden and carry it all by itself. Assuming a mistaken responsibility for more than it can do, it ends up overdoing in attempting the impossible.

I dwell upon the interrelationship of all three modes before describing the possible contribution of the kinesthetic mode to the two arias for the reason elaborated previously: the facial/emotional mode can and should be exercised independently of the kinesthetic mode, but the kinesthetic mode needs the specifying assistance of facial/emotional energies to be properly exercised. We do not exercise the hearing/vocal and kinesthetic combination separately; the facial/emotional is an automatic and necessary partner in their relationship. Thus, as we discuss the kinesthetic mode contribution we assume its integrated interaction with the choices made by the other modes.

Tamino: Choices for the Kinesthetic Mode

Let us return to Tamino's aria to examine possible kinesthetic mode contributions. The question for the singer-actor is, "What can I do with my physical being to assist the communication of the meaning of the words and the music?" The implicit follow-up question is, "How can the facial/emotional mode make those statements specific?"

The first kinesthetic decision has to do with the portrait itself: how it should be handled when looking at it, and how to deal with it when focused elsewhere. This involves the nature of the portrait holder: its size, whether it must be opened to view the picture, and where it can be placed in the costume of Tamino. These are all kinesthetic decisions that need to be thought out before performance or even rehearsal because they dictate many succeeding choices.

The first major kinesthetic statement relates to the impact of the first look at the portrait. Possibilities range from actually staggering back under the blow of the sight; to moving forward as if to get closer to it; to simply standing still, transfixed by the sight. The first two ideas are strong, potentially melodramatic choices that could be easily dismissed intellectually. But no kinesthetic decision can be made in the mind alone; it must be worked with so that it is a mode mind, in-action decision. And even if a specific action seems unworkable, trying to make it work is a useful exercise that stimulates other new ideas as well. Never reject a kinesthetic idea on an intellectual basis alone—always test it with the body. Another variation of Tamino's first reaction, for example, would be to have him moving before he first looks at the portrait so that the look stops him dead in his tracks.

Following that moment, as he sings the first phrase (bar 3), his free hand might touch his head or chest as if to say, "What is happening inside me?" The focus search that follows (bars 7–8) could involve a move (a step or two) to suggest the impetus of searching; the free hand might also reach as though wanting to touch the image in his mind. The eye shutter (bars 9–14) might also be emphasized by holding the portrait tight against his chest. As his eyes open (bar 15), he might take another glance at the portrait and then, as the searching focus begins again, take another step or two as his hand reaches for the image. As he says (bars 19–21):

> doch fühl ich's hier wie Feuer brennen
> (yet I feel it here like fire burning),

a logical gesture would be to touch his heart—the likely place for love to burn.

As the sudden recognition of the light bulb occurs (end of bar 21), a hand could touch the head as if to relate to the origin of the new idea. The affirmation (bars 27–28):

> Ja, ja! Die Liebe ist's allein,
> (Yes, yes! It is love alone,)

might well be accompanied by both arms held out in exultation. As he continues this phrase about love, Tamino might relate back to the portrait or hold it up, and then, on the interlude that follows (bars 34–35), he might kiss the portrait.

As he sings:

> O wenn ich sie nur finden könnte!
> O wenn sie doch schon vor mir stände!
> (Oh, if only I could find her!
> Oh, if she only stood before me!)

he might take a step or two in the direction of the two separate focus points, reaching out as though to take action. Then he stops, as he tries to think of what he would do. He might sustain the action gesture, appearing frozen in thought. As he sings "warm und rein" ("warm and pure") in bar 42, he might release that gesture as he returns to the portrait, maintaining that state of being through the question, "Was würde ich?" ("What would I do?") in bar 43.

On the bar of rest following, his head could come up in a gentle light bulb, as he moves from contemplation of the portrait to the focus image of what he *would* do. As he sings (bars 45–49):

> ich würde sie voll Entzükken an diesen heissen Busen Drücken
> (I would press her, filled with enchantment, to my loving breast),

he might hold out his arms and maintain that gesture throughout the phrase, or he might go through the action of seeming to embrace her but ending up embracing himself. In either case, during the concluding phrases the arms—either reaching out for her or actually seeming to embrace her—release to the sides, and Tamino, without any kinesthetic statement except the body, alert and vital, allows the ecstasy to flow through him. On the three-bar postlude, he might lift the portrait again, kneel to it, clasp it to his heart, then look at it again until interrupted by the three ladies.

This is all analytically dry until tested in action by the performer. At that point, his total projective system begins to function and to interact with the perceptual systems of the observers. The act of music theater takes place. Our analysis is useful only in helping the performer make different choices with specific messages behind them. It is up to the observers to perceive and respond to those messages: "I didn't understand that gesture because. . . . " "Your face seemed to be saying . . . , which was different than the words or musical meaning." "Can you release the shoulder tension that seems to come in on high notes?" "Can you allow your face to show more joy while you're singing?" Comments that are appropriate to the individual performance are vital to performer growth, and therein is the action, the fun, and the growth. Our analysis can only give things an intellectual push, but the mode minds have to keep the process going.

The Countess: Choices for the Kinesthetic Mode

Let us now examine the Countess's recitative and aria for kinesthetic possibilities. As it begins, the kinesthetic situation involves the Countess entering the room, carefully and cautiously, on the alert for either the Count or Susanna. The first bar of the recitative has an orchestral motif suggestive of tiptoeing. The fourth, sixth, and eighth bars have orchestral passages that might motivate a startled turn as though the Countess heard someone approaching; the eighth and ninth bars are particularly appropriate for that action. Then she tries to rationalize the scheme (bars 9–14), focusing on the image of the plan being carried out. During that sequence she might remain physically still, although her hand might touch her dress as she speaks of the exchange of clothes.

Then, as the humiliation of the situation strikes her, she might turn away from the image physically, enforcing the eye shutter that we suggested as a possibility (bars 15–18). As she shifts her focus strongly to describe and accuse her husband (bars 17–25), she might give his image even greater concreteness by physically gesturing to it—holding both hands out as if to say, "How could you?"; or with one hand held out to it as if to say, "There he stands!"

As she speaks of being loved at the beginning of their romance (bars
20–21), her hand might touch her face as though remembering his touch,
a gesture that could remain there and relate to the pain she feels in the
present, until, at bar 23, it could sweep out with the other hand as if to
say, "Look at me now!" Or the gestural capacity could remain in readiness
during bars 17–25, but in 18th-century readiness, for the costuming of
the period does not always permit the hands to hang freely at the sides.

One problem in discussing the kinesthetic choices in this aria is its
realistic setting and the likelihood of many different specifics in props,
furniture, and ground plans. Whereas Tamino's aria is centered around
a prop, the portrait of Pamina, his situation beyond that allows fewer
opportunities for relating to furniture or ground plans. Our analysis of
the kinesthetic possibilities for the Countess includes the idea that stools,
chairs, or tables might be available for use but are not indispensable.

As the aria begins, with its soft, sustained immersion in nostalgia,
physical stillness seems to be the most appropriate response, with the
focus shifting to that image area at the end of the recitative. This stillness
could be maintained from bars 1 to 18, or a hand could gently steal up
to the face as though remembering the youthful Count's loving touch.
If so, this gesture would drop (bar 19) as the Countess returns to the
image of the painful present. On bars 20–21, she could hold out her
hands as though appealing for an answer to the Count's betrayal. One
of those hands might then move to her breast (bar 24) as if to relate to
the pain she feels in her heart, remaining there through bars 35–36. A
word about the Del Sartean flavor of all these directions is in order at this
point.[3]

I often encounter young performers who classify gestures as phony or
melodramatic because they are large or because they relate to the body
or the head in some way. This rejection of all gesturing is in obvious
defiance of life itself, which is filled with gestures of every size, description, and destination. The judgment against scale and character of gesture comes directly from held-tension, overcontrolled gesturing as it has
existed on the operatic stage. But it is obvious to anyone who has worked
with gesture that there is none that cannot be effectively and naturally
executed. I have seen performers attempt every conceivable style and scale
of gesture, and I am convinced that the acceptability, naturalness, and
effectiveness of any gesture is a function of its execution and not what it
does nor how large it is. (Refer to the discussion in chap. 6 about the

impulse-initiation phase of gesture, which is where any unnaturalness originates.)

We return to the Countess at bar 35, possibly with her eyes shut and her hand to her breast, caught in the pain of the present. At bar 36, as her thought focus returns to the nostalgic days of young love, her kinesthetic stillness could also return, the hand either remaining at her breast, dropping to her side, or reaching gently to touch her face as she did during bars 1–18. Because the music of bars 37–51 is identical to that of bars 1–18 (with the exception of the last bar of each), the gesture (if one is chosen) might be varied, either using the other hand to touch the face or creating even greater stillness as a contrast to the higher energies of the final section.

The new idea, the light bulb that occurs between bars 51 and 52, could be made stronger if the sudden shift in eye focus is accompanied by a kinesthetic shift of the head as well. As the image of a happier future grows (bars 52–63), one hand might reach out as though to caress it. In bars 63–65 there is no singing, and the Countess might move as though to leave and put her plan into effect, but stopping before bar 66 to re-examine the idea briefly (bars 66–69). Stillness-readiness is always possible in those places where the possibility of movement is suggested. Where the facial/emotional mode focus may move a great deal, the kinesthetic mode may remain in a position of pure readiness for lengthy periods. Thought process is always active, always involved with meaning messages; but for the physical being, readiness may be sufficient.

Another nonsinging section in bars 68–70 may elicit either a move or stillness. If a move is chosen, it should probably have a different rationale from the previous one: another direction and another intention. If it were a move to seek out Susanna in the direction of the images of present pain, the timing might also relate to the momentary musical shift to the doubt or worry of the minor E flat (bars 74–75). The rejection of that painful image could be communicated by an actual physical turning away from it.

The rest of the sung portion of the aria (bars 76–102) is a continuing affirmation of the Countess's new hope. The sense of growing confidence and excitement might also be conveyed kinesthetically by mental images of growing taller and stronger, of extending one's physical being, allowing the body to expand into a larger space, floating buoyantly beyond one's self. All of these images, of course, are to be used without physical tension.

When the Countess has finished singing, there is an exuberant and decisive eight-bar postlude. The Countess could begin her exit with great energy (bars 102–105) but turn back just before doing so to make a final physical and facial reaffirmation of her new sense of hope (bars 106–107). Her exit would follow on bars 108–109.

To illustrate the problems of sketching the kinesthetics without knowing the specifics of a production, consider what the addition of one prop could do. I created a prop sequence for *The Marriage of Figaro* that I call the Progress of a Rose. It culminates in the Countess's aria. The progress begins when Susanna brings in a bouquet of white roses to the Countess following her first aria, "Porgi Amor." When Figaro enters to tell Susanna and the Countess about his scheme to trick the Count, he demonstrates the plan, story-theater fashion, with Susanna's assistance. At one point he plucks a rose from the bouquet and presents it to Susanna as though he were the Count. Susanna then wears the rose in her bosom for the rest of that act, possibly using it when she emerges from the closet in place of Cherubino to confront the bullying Count—either playing with it, holding it in her teeth, putting it in her hair, or mock-fencing with the Count.

In the third act, when the Count is trying to embrace Susanna at the end of their duet, she escapes by pulling the rose from her bosom, kissing it, and giving it to the Count. She then slips away as he accepts it. But when the Count overhears Susanna and Figaro laughing about the scheme only a moment later, he realizes that her ardor was a lie. Enraged, he sings his aria, "Hai Gia Vinta La Causa" ("You have won the decision?"). In the course of it, he crushes the rose he accepted so eagerly, hurls it to the ground, grinds it beneath his heel, and stalks out. There it lies, the bruised remnants of what had been a beautiful flower.

The Countess enters. Of the many possible uses that could be made of that symbol of her dying relationship with the Count, two stand out. At the conclusion of the present pain sequence (bars 33–35), the Countess could see the crushed fragments for the first time. She could kneel down, touch them gently, lift them up, and sing the recapitulation of the nostalgia for lost love (bars 37–51). Another place to relate to the ravaged flower would be just before her exit, turning back to look at it briefly but rising above the vision of despair it offers to her own vision of potential happiness.

The props, the furniture, and the ground plans—all conceived in large part by the director—relate to the kinesthetic potential of the scene. Performers do not ordinarily become involved with the creation of ground plans, but the way they use the space provided is a significant aspect of their kinesthetic communication. The same is true of the way they use props and furniture. In both areas, performers should be encouraged to become involved in the search for useful ideas.

All three modes are always acting in combination, whether positively or negatively. To ask a performer to use all three modes in performance at the same time is simply asking him or her to be visible and sing. The performer is always using the facial/emotional and kinesthetic modes simply by being there, even though the messages delivered by those modes may not be useful. But to ask for a *triple dominant performance* is to ask for maximum expressivity in each mode when it is appropriate. The communicating burden can shift from mode to mode depending upon need, and it can also give double and triple mode "salutes": the face smiling with joy, the voice singing a ringing high C, the arms and body stretching to the heavens in exultation. But the ability to make the quick and flexible shift from mode to mode, and the ability of any mode to make a strong communicating statement as the other two remain in readiness or as cooperating partners, are the strongest signs of performance power.

A basketball team of three people, all equally skilled at handling and dribbling the ball, shooting and rebounding, always beats a team with one star and two other players who can pass but not shoot. In the same way, a person possessing a modes "team," all of whom are capable of communicating powerfully at any moment, is always preferred over a person with a modes team having only one strong communicator. If that single mode happens to be one of the best in the world, the performer may triumph. But how much more power would the performance possess if other modes were also developed and integrated with the major mode?

The combined modes, then, are really the recombined modes. We

have suggested a three-part process: release the modes from entanglement or interference with each other, develop the strength of the weaker
modes in isolation to achieve a better balance between modes, and
recombine and reintegrate the three modes by exercising their ability to
work flexibly and freely with each other.

Chapter 8
The Annotated
Disappearing Diva

In 1980, before I encountered the theory of perceptual modes, I became aware of another phenomenon. It was the diminishing vocal health of many young singers who had appeared to have a bright career ahead of them. In their middle or late twenties the decline began, and by their thirties many of them had disappeared. The analysis I made at that time seems even more valid now than it did then. Without modifying those conclusions, however, the modes concept allows another perspective. Because the concept is not an acting system but a facilitator to all approaches, it may allow us to see the issues more clearly in reexamining the Case of the Disappearing Divas.[1]

The kinesthetic mode is often called into play to fulfill what I call the acting-showing demand, even when the performer is not a kinesthetic dominant. The acting-showing demand is the necessity a singer feels to do something to show that he or she is acting as well as singing. The question of kinesthetic interference with vocal production has become a potentially crucial issue in the past two decades, suggesting that kinesthetic interference with the voice is a far more widespread phenomenon than it would be if that interference depended only upon kinesthetic dominance.

The Case of the Disappearing Divas

There is a mystery afoot in American opera, and no one seems to know what to do about it. The future great voices of opera, the prima donnas and prima uomos of tomorrow's opera stages, are missing. Young singers

who might develop such greatness seem to be threatened by some un-
identified villain or villains, but no one knows the why, the who, or the
how of the crime. Opera producers are increasingly aware of this diminu-
tion in vocal quality of the young American singer. In the annual Opera
America auditions, which assemble some of the best young singers in the
country to audition for the collective professional opera managers, it has
become commonplace to hear evident vocal deterioration in some of the
singers over a period of two or three years. Observers are distressed to note
that many young singers of ten years ago have failed to survive a decade
of singing: there are fewer and fewer mature singers in their thirties and
forties. And lest one be accused of too short a perspective, opera managers like San Francisco's Kurt Herbert Adler are adamant in their convic-
tion that vocal standards have declined in the past twenty years.

Few who have listened carefully and consistently would disagree. But
if there is general agreement on the nature of the crime—that the potential great singers are missing—there is little to go on in solving the mystery. Everyone has theories, of course, especially those directly involved
in opera production. At the annual meeting of Opera America in
December 1979, James Roos of the *Miami Herald* pursued this issue with
six of the country's leading opera producers.[2] According to his report,
they "hedged and hemmed and hawed when confronted with the dearth
of great voices." The late Robert Collinge of the Baltimore Opera was
quoted, "There probably aren't as many great voices today. There are too
many singers singing too soon and too much. You can't expect voices to
hold up the way they used to." This raised the central issue of who is
hiring the singers to sing "too soon and too much", but, as Mr. Roos put
it, "nobody was willing to pick up that gauntlet." We will explore that
issue in greater detail, but several other comments should be noted.
David DiChiera of Michigan Opera Theater said, "It's the range of what
singers can do well that is greater now. This is the age of the ensemble
singer." Presumably this "ensemble singer" can't sing as well but can act
and move better than used to be the case. The important questions for
us are whether the practice of these additional skills actually interferes
with the singing or whether the demand for complete performance excludes those who can only sing well. Michael Bronson of the Metropolitan
Opera insisted, "Opera singers today are more flexible and much better
prepared. They have to be very good actors besides having a voice—today

it's total theater that counts." Again, the question is whether being more flexible and better prepared for total theater excludes voices of the best quality.

Mr. Roos was not convinced by the implied argument that possession of these other skills compensates for a lack of vocal excellence. He believed, and it is difficult to disagree, that the primary basis for opera must be the voice: when that factor is compromised, nothing else can make up for it. This assertion was not denied by the managers, but there seemed to be a general acknowledgment of the decline in vocal quality over the past two decades. However, no explanation was advanced to account for it besides the "too much—too soon—too often" syndrome. And that does not tell us why a great voice does not exist, only what might have been done to damage it.

COMMENT: *In terms of the mode concept, the demand for kinesthetic and facial emotional skills in addition to hearing/vocal mode skills may have raised the qualifications of singing-acting too high. Or something may have interfered with the hearing/vocal mode skills and not allowed them to develop as they should.*

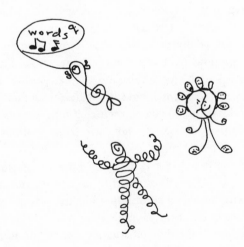

In the *New York Times* of 20 April 1980, Peter Davis also investigated the problem. His survey of "impressarios, managers, voice teachers, coaches and administrators of organizations that assist budding musical talent" indicated that "potentially great voices are reasonably common . . . but that conditions in the music world today are not conducive to their recognition and development." The too much—too soon—too often syndrome was noted once again, with a stress on the need for a long-term developmental period during which the sophisticated muscular strength and coordination system necessary for great singing can be built up. It takes years to develop a great athlete: how much longer to develop the capabilities involved in the infinitely more complex task of singing-acting?

In both articles, the managers—those who hire the singers for too much, too soon, too often—seemed to be held responsible for many of the problems. In addition, the *New York Times* article discussed another aspect of possible managerial culpability. Opera managers in general were accused by Conrad Osborne of hiring "a certain type of mechanically facile young performer (a quick study and top reader, obediently flexible in rehearsal) whose singing is neat and unthreatening and who can be described with the oft-heard phrase 'attractive, moves well, excellent diction.' " One might ask why such singers should not be hired, and the answer follows: because "we cannot care about, or believe in, a note they sing or a word they say, for much the same reasons that in life we often do not believe or trust persons whose preoccupation is with being attractive, moving well and possessing excellent diction." The unusual logic in this accusation will be pursued below, but for the moment it seems that there are two injurious syndromes: opera managers are hiring singers to do too much, too soon, too often; and they are hiring singers for the wrong reasons—for their good looks, their flexible acting capacity, their easily assimilable (natural?) voices, their charming personalities—and as a result rejecting singers who do not have these qualities but who, by implication, have better voices.

Accepting the fact that it is not good for a young singer to do too much, too soon, too often, what about the second argument? Is there any good reason why beauty, a flexible personality, acting talent, and ensemble performance capacities cannot coexist with vocal talent? The argument seems to imply an either/or situation: either you have great voices *or* great singing-acting, vocal excellence *or* total theater, divas *or* ensemble performers. At present, young singers seem to be endowed with the latter of each of those virtues. One kind of value has superseded the other, and this suggests a relationship. Is there a connection between the ascendance of one phenomenon and the decline of the other, between the rise of the charming and beautiful, complete singer-actor and the disappearance of the disgusting but divinely endowed diva? And who is responsible? Although there may be no guilty parties, only a series of communally misguided intentions, faulty perceptions, and compensatory rationalizations, let us examine each member of the operatic family as though we were all potential villains, beginning with the collective voice teachers of America.

Voice teachers are responsible for the vocal health of their students. If we assume that there are the same proportion of potentially great voices in the general population at all times (and no one has advanced a genetically valid reason to assume otherwise) and that the same proportion of those potentially great voices are actually taking voice lessons at any time (a more questionable assumption for sociohistorical reasons to be discussed below), there should be more great singers than ever before. Since this is evidently not so, there are three possible assumptions: (1) there are fewer singers with potentially great voices taking voice lessons; (2) they are being taught badly by their voice teachers; (3) they are being destroyed at a later stage in their careers.

To take the first of these possibilities, it is evident that pop, rock, and musical comedy opportunities in the past two decades have never been more tempting and available to the young singer. Some young singers have doubtless been lured to these more commercial opportunities before their voices were developed sufficiently to demonstrate operatic potential. Only in the past few years has the glamour of opera via the Sillses, the Pavarottis, and television made it a cultural phenomenon competitive with more popular forms of singing. But the lead time for developing an operatic voice of superstar stature is so long that the effect of this new popularization will not be felt for at least another decade. Looking at the preceding decades, the anti-elite, egalitarianism of the sixties and seventies may have spoiled the appeal of opera (certainly the most expensive, elitist art form extant) for many potential young singers of that time. But although both of these factors may have siphoned off significant numbers of singers from the operatic pool, there is nothing we can do about either of them. We have little choice but to accept the sociohistorical context of opera at any given time and work within it.

Having noted the existence of such factors, let us move to the second possibility: that the voice teachers of America suddenly began teaching badly en masse about 1955. Such a proposition is palpably absurd. And even if it seemed plausible, there is no way to prove or disprove it, and nothing could be done about it in any case. Collective voice teachers are no more guilty of improper teaching than they have ever been, and our energies can be best spent investigating other suspects.

Another collective body closely involved with the training of the young singer is that of the producers of opera in academia. By their own admission they feel compelled to produce operatic classics to sustain interest in their programs by administrators, performers, audiences, and themselves. For the average opera producer at Performance U, it is more fun and more prestigious to do *La Traviata* than a double bill of *Hin Und Zurück* and *The Maid as Mistress*. But if the producer decides to produce *La Traviata*, it must also be cast—presumably from the student body (as well as faculty colleagues.) This kind of academic competition with the professional world saw a rapid increase in the sixties and seventies, and it may contribute more to the too much—too soon problem than anything found on the professional level. Young singers who know that great classic roles are available practice those roles endlessly in the hope that they will be cast. And while the study of appropriate classic roles may be the best possible training for the young singer-actor, the proper vocal, musical, and dramatic guidance is essential. Otherwise, young singers not only overwork their voices during a vital developmental period but also have illegitimate expectations about how they should be cast after graduation from Performance U. They begin their rounds of professional auditions singing inappropriate literature, causing professional managers to roll their eyes to heaven bewailing the incompetence of the teachers and producers at Performance U who permit and encourage such folly. Whatever damage is done, most of it occurs on the academic level because it is unlikely that those professional managers will cast young singers in the very roles they are criticizing them for using to audition.

But even on the academic level, too much—too soon is probably an accessory to the crime and not the culprit, for not all young singers are given the questionable opportunity of performing roles before they should. We can compare it with the problem of oversinging in large halls: it happens for a few singers, but it is by no means a deteriorating stress factor for all of them. To isolate the primary villain we must return to our third possibility, that singers are being damaged at a later stage in their career. We must locate a factor that affects all singers regardless of roles or hall size, a factor that is historically unique and not the fault of individual voice teachers or opera producers.

Although none of the suspects we have isolated thus far matches this description perfectly, there is such a factor. It is not a person, nor a group of persons but rather a point of view about opera. This view has come to be accepted by virtually everyone working in the art, and it was implied if not spelled out by the managers quoted at the beginning of our search. It is the belief that opera should be total theater and that the performers of opera should be complete singer-actors. Very few understand the implications of such a belief, but even fewer would argue against it. It has become a virtual cliché that needs to be reexamined to find out what it means and how it affects those professing it.

Paying the Price for Opera as Theater

The cry for a more believable, more theatrical kind of opera and for a more attractive, complete opera performer began as a murmur in the fifties, grew in volume during the sixties, and became a full-throated aria, a part of the standard repertory in discussing opera production, in the seventies. For the first time in history, young opera singers have been informed during their training that there is a new and special importance attached to their ability to act. Seldom have the educational and professional worlds, usually at odds with one another, sung together in such harmony extolling a new view of singing-acting. There have always been a few great singer-actors in opera, but this new point of view has been applied to all singers, not just the gifted few.

Why is this so? More than anything else, I suspect, it began in the forties and fifties as a result of the increasing competition with the realism

of theater, movies, and television. The world of opera felt the need to
capture a semblance of the visual excitement and acting reality that were
becoming part of the mass public's theatrical awareness. Opera as total
theater, opera as true music-drama, an ancient idea more honored in the
breach than the observance, was being promoted once again. Hardly a
year has passed without a book or article about the need for total music-
theater or the complete singer-actor. But although these ideas are as old
as opera itself, opera has never found itself in competition with forms as
powerful as those created by technology. And so in the fifties, for the first
time in history, a new, mass awareness of theatrical possibilities was
created, theatrical forms began to be compared, and realism—the aesthetic opposite of what opera had come to represent—began to be the
dictating influence on virtually everyone, including singers. Suddenly
they were asked to be real (and natural and believable) in a form that
begins as the virtual antithesis of dramatic realism.

*COMMENT: Movies and television are seeing-mode media per-
ceptually and facial/emotional media projectively. This
demand for realism from the singer-actor was made
additionally difficult by the difference in intimacy
between film and television and the operatic stage.
Even theater, which is considerably more intimate than
opera, is a hearing-mode medium as well. The average
low-key, realistic play has a difficult time on Broadway
because it demands seeing-mode intimacy—the
facial/emotional communication is vital—to be fully
appreciated. Furthermore, realistic plays are often not
comfortable with strong hearing-mode values, and performers are seldom able to take full advantage of the
fact that they are played in a hearing/vocal mode
dominant form—live, spoken theater.*

Along with the demand for realistic acting came the desire for pretty
faces and figures, also a product of movie and television orientation. The
three-hundred-pound soprano was out, the svelte soubrette with a

model's face was in. A whole generation of potential sopranos was and is being affected by this judgment. At one time, large and not conventionally attractive girls had very few ways to gain esteem, but vocal beauty was one of them. Kate Smith is a good example of the type, but since that time one can think of very few amply proportioned yet popular female singers. And one should remember that Ms. Smith was a radio star who never became popular on television. Singers of generous physical endowment tend to be either recording artists or they sing with a group where they are absorbed visually in the ensemble. Sometime in the fifties, then, fat girls were given to understand that their voices, no matter what their beauty or character, were no longer sufficient to compensate for the unviewable condition of their bodies.

That was and is a lie given the number of large and less than conventionally lovely women who have always trod the operatic boards of the world because of their opulent vocal gifts. But the truth or falsity of a statement has little to do with its effect. It would take a rare individual to continue working in a performance art when she is told that she will not perform, that she is too large to be used, and that the cute 110 pounder who didn't sing quite as well would be cast instead in all major productions at Performance U. At that age, when the difference in vocal quality between one girl and another is less obvious than it would be after years of careful development, such a decision seems more logical than in retrospect. It takes a skilled ear, a great deal of experience in having followed young, unformed voices through the stages of development, and a lot of luck to make accurate judgments on their potential future greatness at age twenty-two. It is easy, however, to tell whether a twenty-two year old fits the description "attractive, moves well, excellent diction." So attractive wins.

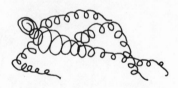

COMMENT: Here the third mode of communication — the kinesthetic — is added to the overall demand. Although the emphasis in the investigation is on the attractive body (the instrument potential), the urge and the skill are also considerations. The person without any kinesthetic instrument potential or urge to use it probably feels very uncomfortable in skill-developing situations and avoids them.

By adding this demand for being pretty and petite to the necessity for possessing acting skills, we may have created a set of conditions that has decimated our young singer population and rendered inoperative any number of glorious voices imprisoned in what we have designated as unsuitable and unskilled bodies. And it isn't just the girls who are being affected. Pretty women demand appropriate partners, and the same selection factors may operate on the young male singers, although perhaps not with the same rigor. In any case, it is precisely at that age that the most encouragement and support is needed for the long developmental struggle for vocal maturity. All young singers need this support, not just the good-looking ones. Not being cast in a leading role can be a blessing for a singer if the free time is used to learn how to sing properly, but the stigma of not being cast at Performance U is tantamount to being judged unworthy. Few have the fortitude to ignore that judgment and simply grow.

Whether these two demands have been major factors in the increasing scarcity of great voices would be hard to prove. Here again it become a question of public taste. If the public is trained by technology to demand certain standards of theatricality and beauty, is it not economically necessary to cater to that taste? Perhaps, but the path is broad that is dictated by the demands of the marketplace. The logic that leads us down that path is very simple: there is a much larger public for movies, television, and theater than there is for opera; if it takes better acting, prettier faces, and slimmer figures to capture that audience, let us make acting, beauty, and size important factors in our casting decisions. The rub comes in the third step of the equation, and we ignore it at the peril of the art form. That step suggests that we make compromises in the vocal area for the sake of visual and acting needs. And that leads us into difficult and potentially dangerous areas, particularly as they relate to the development of the young singer. At the very age when it is the most difficult to tell about the eventual quality of the voice, the young singer is being encouraged or discouraged on grounds that have nothing to do with the voice.

COMMENT: One sees *and judges both the kinesthetic and the facial/emotional modes, but the hearing/vocal mode is judged by ear. Almost everyone can agree as to the quality of the physical and facial attributes of a young performer, but there is great divergence of opinion about the vocal quality and potential of the young singer. I have been repeatedly amazed by the subjectiv-*

ity of hearing/vocal mode judgments on a very high level, from the very coaches and conductors you would expect to agree unanimously: one coach actively dislikes a voice that another coach adores. At the same time, this does not imply that the agreement on physical and facial instrument potential allows all viewers to recognize clearly what the performer is doing to maltreat or interfere with that potential. Nor, oddly enough, do the hearing/vocal mode dominants always hear clearly the vocal interference factors created by the other modes. The field as a whole needs a crash course in mode reeducation.

Let us follow the history of our 110-pound beauty a bit further. Like all singers, she grows old, and the grounds on which she was originally encouraged—her youth, beauty, physical attractiveness, and vitality—become increasingly less meaningful. Just at the age when her voice, if carefully developed, should reach its fullest power, the very virtues that allowed her to become a performer in the first place begin, with rare exceptions, to fade. If her voice has developed some substance, all is well; if not, she retires. Unfortunately, a vocal talent that was just sufficient when combined with attractive nonvocal assets seldom survives an aging process that steals them away. It is hard to conceive of an operatic superstar of the media variety who does not combine unusual physical appeal and acting charisma with a considerable vocal talent, plus the ability to age gracefully. For all Ms. Sills's immense vocal and musical talent, it is undeniable that much of her superstar status grew from her amazing stage warmth, her acting energy, and her attractiveness as well as the gracefulness of her aging. But even in her case, the talent was grounded in the voice, as it must be in opera. Anything that makes compromises relative to the voice, for whatever reason, is a danger to the future of great singing.

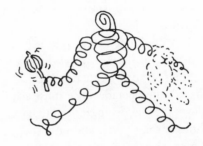

COMMENT: *It is interesting to contemplate the relative staying power of each mode. The kinesthetic mode, which relates to ideas of youth when it is most active, tends to fade the earliest as a performance weapon. The hearing/vocal and the facial/emotional modes, on the other hand, last indefinitely. Of the two, the voice is likely to give out first; but it is surprising how long the sound can remain vital if it is not interfered with by the other modes. The face, of course, can be a potent communicator under any conditions depending upon its exercise and use.*

There is another issue as well. The mass American public has a long-standing aesthetic quarrel with opera, as reflected in the thousands of cartoons and theatrical parodies of the form. And the quarrel is not only with bad acting by oversized, unattractive singers. There is a basic uneasiness with the sound of the genuine operatic voice. It must be larger than the average voice to begin with, and it is often perceived as being pompous, pretentious, and essentially unreal. Part of the problem has to do with the technique of amplification used in all popular forms of singing. No popular singer is ever required to push the sound, to work to project it; electronics does it instead. The relaxed sound, the easily produced sound (with the exception of certain rock screamers) has become highly valued and may have affected judgments of the operatic sound. Thus, along with a demand for natural acting and natural physical beauty, a desire for a "natural" sound may have affected our judgment of young opera singers.

We want the voice to sound natural, just as we want the acting to look natural. But opera is a highly stylized art form, an "unnatural" one, if you will. Depending upon one's view, that is its greatest weakness or its greatest strength. One of the unnatural demands of the form is for voices that can do things no voice can naturally do. Beginning with a size that is larger than life, the operatic voice must acquire a technique of production that allows it to use its maximum range and volume without damage. The technique comes first, and only then can we make other kinds of discrimination. A natural sound is unlikely to result from a concern with unnatural size and highly technical production. Occasionally it does, just as some gymnasts look almost natural in performing their extraordinary but unnatural feats, and then we have another phenomenon of mass popularity. In such cases, attractiveness, personality, and talent combine to seduce us all into a new appreciation of the art, whether it be gymnastics or singing. But apart from such rare examples, it takes prolonged exposure to understand and to appreciate any highly stylized art. If one alters the style of opera to communicate with the musical comedy denominator, one has opera that is simply second-rate musical comedy (just as overaspiring musical comedies sometimes wind up as second-rate operas). In attempting to reach broader, nonopera audiences, we must not permit their uninformed understanding of the art to persuade us to alter it in ways that undermine its substance. This is not a plea for the pompous, the pretentious, the badly acted, and the overweight. But it is a plea to avoid throwing out the unnaturally powerful and unusually gifted vocal baby with the phony, pretentious, and unreal bath. In making the form palatable to the general public we must

not alter the basic components of the form itself, principal among which
is the operatically gifted singer.

COMMENT: *Within the hearing/vocal mode itself, there are*
   strong stylistic demands made of the voice by the oper-
   atic situation — some more natural, some more stylized,
   some lower in energy, some gigantic in scale. But one
   must not give up the hearing/vocal capacity to make
   extreme stylistic statements because of the naturalistic
   demands of the other two modes. The need of the
   kinesthetic and facial/emotional modes to appear to be
   natural tends to place the pressure on the hearing/vocal
   mode to be natural as well. It is seldom the other way
   around, where the kinesthetic and facial/emotional
   modes are highly stylized while the hearing/vocal mode
   is used naturalistically and pulls them toward natural-
   ism (although it is a very useful exercise). We are our
   body, we are our face, but our voice cannot be seen and
   can only be perceived when it is actually used. Once it
   is produced, it remains somehow apart from us: we can
   conceive of ventriloquism, but when was the last time
   you saw someone "throw" their body or face? The voice
   is more manipulable stylistically than the body or the

face, and it can explore stylistic realms that the other
two modes can only hint at. This capacity is what lends
opera its power. To retreat from its dependence on
hearing/vocal power is to lose its essence.

Bigness in one mode of expression (the voice) often seems to promote bigness in egos and emotions as well. As Matthew Epstein, a manager of more than sixty artists, noted in the *New York Times* article, "Big voices, especially in young singers, generally come with big problems—emotional as well as technical ones—and these people need the sort of special care and time to develop that most of our companies are not equipped to give." Or perhaps not willing to give? In the same article, Conrad Osborne suggested that neither managers nor the educational system cares to deal with the larger energies and the volatile, independent temperaments that potential great performers very often have, perhaps *must* have. "Verdi and Wagner increasingly cannot be cast, or the big spaces filled, because the goals of our training are not right to start with, and because the educational system and lower rungs of the profession are not congenial to the bigger mistakes, the more abrasive temperaments, and the rougher independence of the truly individualistic dramatic artist." The names of Chaliapin and Callas are invoked in the article as examples of the kind of temperamental artist whose native talents cannot be contained within the mechanically facile, obediently flexible, quick-study type that is said to characterize the current young complete singer-actor.

COMMENT: *The hearing/vocal mode is the only one that is*
shared by left- and right-brain capacities. The words
themselves tend to be governed by the left brain,
whereas the right brain deals more with the musicality
of those words. The more stylized the use of the voice,
the more the right brain is called upon to participate.
At the same time, studies indicate that as music is
practiced professionally, the left brain is given more

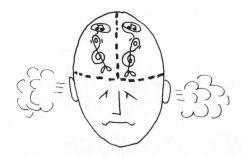

authority in dealing with what would ordinarily be right-brain musical capacities. Opera singers are literally torn between two demands: their art is the most highly stylized hearing/vocal mode art, which pulls them toward the right brain; but they study that art professionally, which pulls them back toward the left brain. This may help us understand why the history of opera is so peopled with seemingly irrational performers, given to extraordinary displays of temperament: it is not only the intense emotion of the form, it is built into the tension of opposing forces within the performer as a person. There seem to be fewer temperamental divas than in the past, and there are also fewer golden-throated divas as well, that is, voices that have the capacity to push the stylizing potential of the hearing/vocal mode to its limits. Is the left brain, the intellectual-vebal fortress, winning the same battle within the performer that it has won in intellectualizing the other arts in the twentieth century?

Another factor worth considering in explaining temperamental outbursts in opera is the expression-repression equation. Opera asks for intense emotional expression almost continually. Much of this high emotion is expressed-repressed for the reasons we have clarified above, creating a pressure that cannot be released in performance but must go somewhere. That somewhere may be the temperamental outburst.

These rough-edged dramatic giants with voices to match are perhaps being rejected by the educational system along with those who are too fat and unattractive, but there is also some question as to whether the operatic temperament is created by working in the operatic form or whether the form demands the volatile temperament as a sine qua non. In any case, experience with many young singers today indicates that not all of them are, in fact, facile, flexibly obedient, nor quick to change, however attractive their body, face, or diction may be. Whatever we have gained in performers with great external beauty, many of them seem to have been conditioned by their experiences in the world of opera production to react with all the tiresome kinds of temperamental inflexibility, laziness, and lack of concern for the art that we have associated with the arrogant prima donnas of the past.

We have another possible accessory to the crime: if the singers are good, we wear them out by the too much — too soon — too often route; if they're fat, homely, or stiff, we reject them on visual grounds; and if they're temperamental, abrasive, and independent, we spurn them on emotional grounds. In all three cases, the voices have not been the primary consideration, and we have no idea how they might have developed. All of these approaches to the young singer undoubtedly contribute in some measure to the disappearance or early attrition of vocal talents that might have developed to greatness.

How the Singer "Shows" Acting

What of the singers who survive these initial tests of endurance and genetics? Can we find a factor that affects them all in their struggle for an operatic career? Before pinpointing the villain, if in fact there is one, we must take short digression into my own Holmesian credentials for investigating the case of the disappearing divas. I began my own career as an opera director and trainer of singer-actors about the same time that the cry for the theatricalization of opera was heard in the land. Adding my own voice to the tumult, I began attempting to realize the idea of opera as total theater. My interests were focused in two areas: new direc-

torial and scenic concepts, and better operatic acting. The latter relates
directly to our investigation.

Most of the opera I had seen before becoming professionally involved
with the form was, with rare exceptions, badly acted. But, like many
other nonprofessional observers, I wasn't particularly bothered. That was
what one expected from opera. When the rare exceptions integrated their
singing with genuine acting, they transcended everything going on
around them and there was cause for celebration. But somehow one did
not impose acting requirements on those singers who seemed incapable
of it. Until I began directing opera and working with the problems of
singing-acting, I accepted opera as a singing form that could tolerate bad
acting but not bad singing. This basic view has not changed, only my
degree of intolerance toward bad acting. At the same time, I became
aware that the uninvolved observer of opera (the average, nonprofessional
audience member) has little understanding of what constitutes good or
bad acting by a singer. Operatic singing-acting is so complex and is surrounded by so many variables that judging it accurately on an absolute
level is terribly difficult. And this is true for operatic professionals as well
as for the lay person.

*COMMENT: Good acting, as defined in the intimacy of the
rehearsal hall, is often based on the facial/emotional*

mode. But those same messages are not perceived by the audience in the typically large opera house. If the audience could actually see the facial/emotional messages, they would be capable of judging the quality of acting; they are certainly well prepared to do so by years of training with television and films. But we have no standard for judging acting (as opposed to dance) as a function of the kinesthetic mode. But judging the quality of kinesthetic interplay with the hearing/vocal mode stylization of opera is extremely difficult, as witness the inability of opera critics generally to specify what is or is not good operatic acting. The skill is so special in its demands and so seldom realized that we have no total standard upon which to base our judgment—only one which is exclusively vocal. We know a good combination when we see it, but we have trouble knowing why.

Over the period of years I have worked with singer-actors, my questions about the art have boiled down to one basic issue: What happens to singers when they try to act in the first place? I am assuming here that the acting being attempted is operatic in nature, or that which attempts to cope with the complete spectrum of vital operatic performance—with the demand for believability as well as for large-scale experience. Unless both demands are met and operatic opposites are integrated in the singing-acting performance, operatic acting can degenerate into form-denying naturalism on one hand or truth-denying pretension on the other.

As I worked I became increasingly aware that the young singer, when called upon to act, almost invariably responded with some forms of physical or vocal tension. These are different from the physical tension habits (facial and shoulder girdle tensions, for example) that many singers are allowed to develop in learning to sing. Singing-associated tensions are important problems that exacerbate the acting-demand tensions. But even singers who have learned to sing with little superfluous tension often repsond to the operatic acting challenge with some sort of induced tension. Why is this so?

Foremost among the possible reasons may be the singer's need to "show" something when asked to "act." With the "showing" capacity of the naturalistic speaking voice taken away, and thus deprived of that important avenue of acting expression, the singer must use emotional or physical resources to show this thing called acting. But very few young singers (or actors) can project, portray, or otherwise communicate the range and scale of emotion inherent in the intense and stylized situations of opera. In fact, the whole issue of the actor's relationship to emotion in performance is highly controversial and difficult to define. At one end of the spectrum are those who insist that the actor must feel the actual emotions of the character; at the other end are those who are equally convinced that an accurate external simulation is sufficient. Somewhere in between are those who are not as concerned with the means used so long as clear communication with the audience is achieved.

If young singers approach the playing of emotions from the actual-feeling end of the spectrum, they have the enormous challenge of summoning up the operatic peak experience. In doing so, they must remember that they cannot *make* such emotions (or any other emotions) happen, that arousing them on cue is a subtle and complex process of *allowing* them to happen in response to specific sensory stimuli. If they approach the problem through the use of external technique, they have a challenge of equal complexity if the portrayal is to avoid empty posturing and seem believable. Whatever blend of options is chosen from this spectrum of emotional communication, integrating the portrayal with the scene in question is made even more difficult because singers usually learn the music first. They are then faced with the difficult task of coordinating the portrayal of the volatile human passions of the scene with the abstractly learned music.

Unless a young singer has unusual instincts in dealing with the portrayal of emotion, he or she is not likely to have access to the actual-feeling end of the spectrum. Deprived as well of naturalistically expressive vocal resources, the singer has one avenue left to achieve the acting-showing demand: the body. Although this resource belongs to the external-expression end of the spectrum, such physical technique is taught nowhere to my knowledge. It is generally rejected as being phony and old-fashioned by young singers conditioned to television realism who, despite their scorn, are totally unable to handle the technique. Regardless of which end of the spectrum is employed, the use of the body remains the issue. Although this conclusion is obvious with regard to external expression, what about the actual-feeling end of the spectrum?

It has been my continuing and consistent experience that the vast majority of young singers (and actors) try to show acting emotion through physical tension of some kind, usually in the shoulder girdle, arms, hands, or thighs. And once such tension is initiated, it must be sustained, for if it has been equated with showing something, a lack of tension is automatically equated with showing nothing.

This fallacious but well-nigh universal approach to the self-imposed demand to "show" acting is made additionally difficult by opera's extension of time. Real time is altered, usually extended, in opera, creating an even greater sense of need to sustain whatever tension has been initiated. Actors experience precisely the same showing-emotion-through-tension syndrome, but they do not have to cope with the time-extension problem that continually challenges the singer and can thus more easily dispose of any tension they initiate. Actors also have the overriding advantage in their artistic efforts of referring to life for their model. They speak their lines, just as people in life speak their lines; actors are imitating an action that is life itself. Singer-actors are also imitating the action of life, but they are doing so with means that are not those of life: with the singing voice, and, in opera, with the most unnatural, unlifelike voice of all. Absolutely nothing in a singer-actor's life experience prepares that person for the improbable challenge of appearing to be a natural human being while singing with unnatural power and style in a form that alters the time flow of seemingly real events in unnatural ways. It is a problem of aesthetic coordination equaled by no other performing art and a problem that poses training challenges we have barely begun to address.

Because the actor has the natural speaking voice as an acting tool, he or she is more prone to show emotion through vocal indicating, a term I use to describe artificial tension in the voice that produces a sense of emotional intensity. This kind of tension is as meretricious and harmful as the visible kind, but it is less often diagnosed accurately by theater people. It is overlooked precisely because it is a tension that cannot be seen but that must be heard, and theater people tend to be better see-ers than hear-ers. An actor can also survive a great deal more tension-abuse of the voice than can a singer. For both of these reasons, American theater training reflects little awareness of the vocal indicating problem. Vocal tension is tolerated and even encouraged by theater directors whose ears have not been trained to detect the vital distinction between vocal indicating through imposed tension and the free voice affected by emotion. Singers who make the same error are usually corrected very quickly, either by the accompanying pain in their throat and the impaired ability to sing or by coaches, conductors, and directors who hear the problem. But even such an obvious error for singers has become more common in recent years as these same teachers put increased stress on vocal characterization and realistic emotional vocal effects and neglect the techniques needed to accomplish such things without vocal damage.

COMMENT: Vocal indicating can also be viewed as the kinesthetic mode trying to join the communication process by interfering with or altering the way the voice is pro-

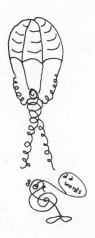

duced. Whether it does so only in kinesthetic dominants or is the response of virtually all performers to the acting-showing demand is open to question. In either case, it is the kinesthetic mode interfering with the hearing/vocal mode.

When Beverly Sills said, "If a character is best portrayed by a cry or a scream, that is what I'll give. I'm not on stage just to make pretty sounds," I cheered. But I also tremble at the possible vocal damage young singers might suffer in attempting to emulate Ms. Sills's ideas without Ms. Sills's (or her teacher's) personal help. It is a sufficient challenge for most young singers to simply produce healthy singing sound. In general, the problems of vocal characterizations can be left to the composer, who specifies a great deal if we attend to the score carefully; to coaches, who can help the singer realize the implicit instructions of the composer and add a wealth of characterizing musical detail; and to the physical and emotional resources available apart from the alteration of vocal production. To sing operatically places the voice under a stress exceeded by no other vocal activity. Like gymnastics, if the form is not perfect, if the alignment of parts is not exact, if the various stresses and strains are not balanced exquisitely along the physical leverage system, a sprained and damaged system can result. The gymnastic form makes ultimate demands on the physical strength, agility, and flexibility of the entire body; the operatic form makes similar demands upon one of the tiniest muscle systems in the body. If it is not perfectly coordinated within itself, and with the breath support system it depends upon, nasty things can happen. If one can imagine a gymnast being rated not only on physical moves but also on ability to project emotional states and recite complicated poetry at the same time, one gets some sense of the immensity of the operatic challenge.

Conrad Osborne described this challenge in the *New York Times* article:

Singing is a highly sophisticated coordination process that involves muscular balance, precision and delicacy. Heavier sounds are achieved by using a heavier mass of vocal cord combined with additional physical alignments in the vocal cavities. If the correct muscles are not sufficiently developed to cope with the extra pressure to produce a big tone, a secondary, less fully developed muscular group will take over as the body compensates for what it is being asked to do. This inevitably creates tension and stress that could eventually lead to a malfunction in the entire athletic mechanism.

This speaks only to the singing process itself, but it follows that any tension or imbalance in the surrounding musculature also interferes with the delicate coordination of the singing process. The tension or imbalance is most likely to occur in rehearsal situations where the singer-actor is trying to integrate all the physical, emotional, and vocal demands of the operatic form. It is a situation to which the voice teacher could contribute vital feedback. But Mr. Osborne and his voice-teaching colleagues are seldom, if ever, present at the very rehearsals where they could help the singer deal with the problems of acting-demand tension. In the vocal studio, the voice teacher can deal with the intricacies of the coordination process insofar as they relate to pure singing. But in the rehearsal room, the singer is asked to "show some emotion" and immediately throws the whole delicately balanced vocal system out of synchronization through induced tension-indicating. Even if the vocal teacher were present, would that teacher perceive what was happening and be able to suggest a solution? Would the director of the rehearsal be tolerant of the teacher's suggestions, helpful or not? It is not merely the singer's vocal process that is in need of highly sophisticated coordination; it is also the relationship between the teachers, coaches, conductors, and directors who work with the singer-actor.

The whole question of vocal technique as it relates to the emotional use of the voice while singing has scarcely been touched. Good coaches do much to elicit a meaningful emotional performance, but their work is seldom correlated with that of the singing teacher who should, of course, be intimately involved with the process. It is an area deserving a great deal of thought and collaboration among the various interpretive teachers of the form.

But while harmful vocal indicating by a singer is generally perceived and corrected, habitual physical tension, which also leads to vocal attrition, is less easily detected and corrected and may for that reason be the more destructive villain of the two. Habitual physical tensions are often accepted as a part of the performer's personality or way of being, and they are either ignored or tolerated. Sometimes the tension problem is not perceived at all. There is good evidence that physical tension in any part of the body sets up corresponding tensions in other parts of the body, specifically in the vocal mechanism. Maintenance of tension in any set of muscles without setting up a corresponding tension in neighboring muscle groups is virtually impossible. Sustained muscular tension in any part of the body thus has a direct effect on some aspect of the singer's vocal production, whether it be on the breathing and support mechanism or on the vocal apparatus itself. This is particularly true of the "emotive tensions" of acting, those false physical indicators of emotional turbulence in the actor that are invariably localized in the shoulders, back, chest, and neck. Tensions set up in these areas virtually surround the breath support system and its tiny vocal beneficiary. Although the tensions may not destroy the delicate functioning of that interlocked relationship, they interfere with it in a serious and insidious way: the vocal attrition is gradual and can go unrecognized until it is too late to undo the harm. If this tension is practiced during the young singer's formative years, the sustained vocal interference that results will prevent the full development of the voice.

In dozens of experiences with young singers, I have learned about the subtle but specific effects of physical tensions on the voice. All of these young singers sang with reasonable skill, and very few were victims of obvious, perceptible physical tension. But when the unnoticed physical tension was removed—sometimes by application of the Alexander Technique while singing, sometimes by exercises that also diverted the singer's attention from "acting"—the voice blossomed, filled out, or acquired a new sheen that was obvious to everyone present. A distinctive change in vocal quality followed the removal of tension. The singers had obviously been doing something to themselves in order to "act," a something that interfered with their vocal produciton but that was not noticed until it had been removed.

It became strikingly clear that some subtle but powerful factor was preventing optimum use of the voice. It was not inadequate vocal technique, for no Alexander session or physical exercise can alter the singer's vocal technique on the spot. But the factor could have been something that interfered with the vocal technique by creating an obstacle to the free use of the voice. And if that obstacle were maintained over a period of years, if the obstructing tension were regularly induced whenever the singer-actor performed, it would do precisely what we have been suggesting: erode the natural beauty of the voice, wearing it down in a gradual process of attrition until there was no blossom left to open. It would subtly but effectively destroy the potential of the voice for development to greatness. And yet at any given moment in the singer's history of performance, the attrition factor would be difficult if not impossible to detect except through exercises having nothing to do with singing or acting techniques per se and that could not be practiced during performance in any case. This attrition factor might involve any number of different interlocking physical tensions, depending upon the individual singer-actor, but all such tensions proceed from a fundamental misunderstanding of the acting half of the the singing-acting process.

Integrating Voice, Body, and Mind

Our search may be at an end. The primary villain in the case of the disappearing diva has perhaps been identified. The clues are as follows: Clue 1: All young singers today are under pressure to give more complete acting performances. Clue 2: Most young singers who try to act out the passions implicit in music-theater literature do so by inducing sustained physical or vocal tension. Clue 3: Any unnecessary, sustained physical tension adversely affects the growth and development of the vocal mechanism and its support system. These clues lead to a very disturbing conclusion: that most young singers are trying to perform in a manner that adversely affects the growth and development of their voices.

COMMENT: *The villain could be seen as the kinesthetic mode, but that mode appears to be merely a tool of the demand to show acting. Rather, the facial/emotional appetite created by films and television has placed a burden on opera, which is dominated by the hearing/ vocal mode; but opera cannot satisfy those demands with facial/emotional mode means. The demand had to be satisfied nonetheless, and the only available means was the kinesthetic mode. But because that mode was unable truly to satisfy the facial/emotional*

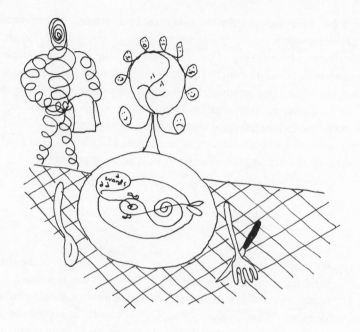

appetite, it was driven to efforts that interfered with the
very mode, the hearing/vocal, that it was trying to help
in the first place.

The coincidence of this sequence of facts with the historical patterns we have discussed (the demand for the acting singer that began some twenty years ago, and the recently noted decline of great, mature voices) seems inescapable. It satisfies the character description of the unknown villain specified earlier: the demands are new and they affect all young singers regardless of roles or hall sizes; regardless of their individual voice teachers, coaches, conductors, or directors (except for those rare few who can help ameliorate the problem); regardless of frequency of performance; and regardless of physical attractiveness, excellency of diction, psychological flexibility, personality, and all the rest.

This is not a plea for a return to the good old days and to the singer who moves neither mind nor body in performing a role. On the contrary, the complete singer-actor remains a goal to be sought. But "complete" does not have to mean the same ratio of physical-vocal-emotional skills in all singer-actors. To move well is an art as well as a skill, to act and project emotion is an art as well as a skill, and to sing is an art as well as a skill. So long as this is true, physical artists will strive to acquire vocal and emotion-projecting skills; emotion-projecting artists will strive to acquire physical and vocal skills; and vocal artists will strive to acquire physical and emotion-projecting skills. An occasional performer is gifted in two out of the three skill areas; rarely, an artist possesses all three.

It goes without saying that all artists aspiring to opera performance should make every attempt to improve their art and skill in deficient areas. What is less clear is the need for developing the interacting, coordinating, integrating capacity of all three areas. Although this improvement in integration may lead to a better performance, as well as improving one's physical or emotion-projecting skills, its primary function is to enable the singer-actor to *sing* more easily in an operatic context. Singing is the basis of the form; although the physical and emotion-projecting skills are also vital aspects of it, the most important reason for isolation and reintegration of the three art skills is to allow the singing function to be optimally supported and aided by the other two. In short, it appears that the coordination and integration of the already existing physical and emotion-projecting skills with the vocal skills is more important than improving any one of them, even though that improvement is also vital to the singer-actor's growth. It is simply a question of priorities.

COMMENT: *By increasing the coordination of the three modes, one is automatically strengthening them individually. Developing coordination requires an understanding of how each mode functions, why it functions as it does, and what it is capable of communicating. All of these capacities develop individual mode power as well as coordination.*

If the integrating and coordinating step is the most important, then the burden is upon those of us who are helping young singers to develop the three skills separately. We are the ones who must lead the performers

through the maze of apparently conflicting demands, seeming contradictions, and puzzling ambiguities. Performers cannot usually do this themselves; they desperately need our combined help. Collectively, we must find out more about the integration of the physical, emotion-projecting, and vocal skills in performance. It is the height of amateurism to ask a young singer to integrate three separate and complex skills into one non-interfering whole without careful observation and assistance. Some performers can do it on their own: I referred earlier to those integrating prodigies as instinctive cooks, able to take ingredients from our academic supermarkets and, without the help of a cookbook, combine them into a superb gourmet performance. But these prodigies are no more than 1 or 2 percent of the singer population, and the health of the form depends as much (if not more) on the kind of recipes we can teach the other 98 percent who are preparing for our operatic stages.

If we continue to ask for the so-called complete singer-actor and total music-theater performance without a better understanding of how that ideal can be achieved, we will continue to see the gradual attrition of young singers as they try to do what we ask without proper guidance. We must become complete observers and total analyzers of the singing-acting process to remedy a failure that exists on all levels, both academic and professional. A recent Opera America audition had an interesting example of the profession's confusion about the interrelationship of the three skill areas. The collective managers had asked to audition an occasional comprimario (a character singer-actor whose voice is not of the size or quality for major roles and from whom special physical and acting skill is expected in compensation) as well as leading roles. Two such comprimarios were selected. Perhaps they were the best available (certainly they exhibited a great deal of energy), but they were even more misguided about the nature of singing-acting than were many of those auditioning for leading roles. Extraordinary tension and vocal-indicating were two of the most obvious problems.

The real point here is that the performers in question were selected to audition at all. Either the problems were not perceived or they were not considered important, both highly erroneous and damaging judgments but indicative of our problem. Perhaps the performers were simply the best of a bad lot, in which case the mistake was to take something bad rather than nothing at all. Whatever the reason, professionals as well as academicians have much to learn about what singing-acting is and how singer-actors can best function and develop before the burden of achieving total music-theater performance is placed on another generation of young singers, condemning still more of them to the file of disappearing divas.

COMMENT: The problem is related to the perceptual dominance of those who work with the young performer. From the perspective of modes, we see that we must devise training for all hearing/vocal mode dominants that will heighten their awareness of the other two modes and of the interrelationship of those two modes with the dominant mode. For the facial/emotional and kinesthetic dominants, we must find training methods that similarly increase perceptual comprehension of the hearing/vocal mode and develop its interrelating capacity with the other two modes. The most useful thing about the modes concept is that it makes these possibilities specific. We can devise such training. As opposed to the more general and unspecified cry for integration, we are able to work with specifically defined, projective capacities. It is a step we should take as soon as possible—ceasing our reliance on the unschooled mode

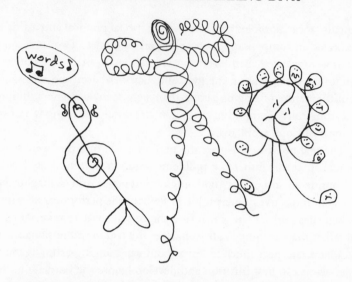

makeup of all individuals and dealing instead with real-
ity. No individual possesses a mode makeup that, with-
out training, makes the reality of the operatic form
accessible to totally integrated performance. Varying
mode makeups, limited to some extent by their na-
tures, create the kind of reality that the form is allowed
to exhibit. The horse has been pushing the cart for too
long; it is time to place him in a position where he can
exert his true power, taking the cart to places un-
dreamed of in its previous relationship. Once that is
done it might even inspire the cart-builders to create
vehicles of new and unprecedented capacity.

If our identification of the villain is correct, we who have made or
endorsed this demand for acting have also assumed responsibilities that
have never been properly acknowledged. To help the young singer
achieve a true marriage of naturalistic acting life with the extended stylistic glories of the operatic form, we must give considerable thought and
attention to how such a marriage actually functions. We must know more
about the mental-emotional factors and how they interrelate to produce

an effective and healthy performance. Until we can discover and communicate this information to educators and professionals everywhere, we would do better to return to the primacy of the voice as a passport to operatic performance and let professional stage-directors deal with the acting and movement problems of the disappearing divas. And this regressive fate may be ours if we do not attend to the problem.

I have been asked by some people who have read this analysis to be even more specific about the guilty parties and about possible answers. Originally, there were no guilty parties. We were all simply responding to a sociohistorical situation in the most logical way possible and were not aware of the potential problems we were causing. We were like the burgeoning chemical industries in the fifties and sixties: new technological discoveries led to the creation of fresh and exciting materials and methods. A decade or two later, however, we have become aware of the ecological dangers connected with our exciting new insights. Improper techniques for dealing with chemicals create health problems for society in general; improper techniques for dealing with the demands of singing-acting create health problems for singer-actors. But we were not guilty when we began our exploration. Only when we become aware of the problems these new techniques have created do we also become guilty if we do nothing about it. Awareness and responsibility go hand in hand; once we are aware, we are responsible; and failing our responsibility, we are guilty.

Every voice teacher, stage director, conductor, coach, acting teacher, and movement teacher who is thus aware and who continues to encourage or tolerate an uncoordinated, unintegrated voice-body-emotion response to the acting demand is guilty of first- or second-degree voice-murder. Those who are still unaware may be justly arraigned for voice-slaughter, but they should receive a commuted sentence. Those who are aware and who do not seek out cooperative teaching with their music-theater colleagues in an effort to expand their own perceptions and capabilities in nipping incipient voice-murder in the bud are guilty of aiding and abetting, being accessories after the fact, and misprision (which are the closest terms a lawyer friend of mine could find for the sin of omission when one is aware of a crime or a danger to someone and does nothing about it). Those who actually resist attempts at cooperative interrelationships should be arraigned for criminal negligence and recklessness.

And what should be the sentence for all these crimes? If we are not willing or able to develop the competency to deal with the effects of our singing-acting demand, we should not be allowed to make that demand; all terms such as *feel it, show me, complete singing-acting, total music theater*, and the like should be banned; singers should be permitted to do what they do best without the interference of any such generalized jargon. For violators of these laws, the punishment should fit the crime: they should be sentenced to observe twelve consecutive hours of opera without hearing any sound, followed by twelve consecutive hours of opera with no "visuals" sung by especially recruited divas who have disappeared. The fact that none of this is going to happen — none of our acts will ever be judged as crimes nor will we ever be sentenced for them — does not mean that we should not take the issue as seriously as if it all were true.

"Overdramatizing it a bit, aren't you?" The voice of my wife speaking as the devil's (actor's?) advocate. She may be right. So to balance things a little, integrate points of view as it were, I note that laments for "the good old days when singers were truly great" have been sung continuously since opera began. Robert Rushmore chronicles this litany of nostalgia in his book *The Singing Voice*.[3] His account begins in 1723, when Pier Francesco Tosi, already wailing over a decline in vocal standards, suggested that singers no longer had the ability to sing long, sustained lines, the flowing legato of the bel canto. About fifty years later, the celebrated singing teacher Gianbattista Mancini said, "In Italy music is decadent, there are no more schools, nor great singers." Mancini knew as little as we do about the reason for the decline: "I do not know to what may be attributed the real cause . . . ." In 1834, at the very height of the bel canto era, Richard Wagner said concerning the vocal standards of his time: "Today one hardly ever hears a really beautiful and technically correct trill; very rarely a perfect mordent; very rarely a rounded coloratura, a genuine unaffected soul-moving portamento, a complete equalization of the registers, a steady intonation through all the varying nuances of crescendo and diminuendo. Most of our singers, as soon as they attempt the noble art of portamento, go out of tune . . . ." And he anticipated the present apologies for the vocal inadequacies of the total music-theater performer: "The public, accustomed to faulty execution, overlooks the defects of the singer, if only he is a skilled actor and knows the routines of the stage."

The lament continues. "Singing is becoming as much a lost art as the manufacture of Mandarin China or the varnish used by the old masters," said the renowned and knowledgeable singing teacher Manuel Garcia II in 1894, mourning "the disappearance of the race of great singers, who, besides originating that art, carried it to the highest point of excellence." And finally, closer to our own time, "It is plain to every careful observer that the race of beautiful singers is diminishing with every year, and that in its place there is growing up a generation of harsh, unrefined, tuneless shouters." This in 1938 by the music critic W. J. Henderson. It seems that every fifty years or so there is a fresh realization that great singing is becoming extinct. The fact that we are right on schedule with our own breast-beating might seem an invitation to dismiss all such cries of woe, our own included.

But today, as we have seen, there are new elements to be considered, new sociohistorical contexts for opera performance, new challenges to the singer, and new demands on those of us responsible for the development of the singer-actor. We must not fall into the trap of dismissing current problems because of their historically repetitive nature. The similiarity of our present cries of woe with those of the past must not blind us to the historically unique challenge with which we are confronted. It should be remembered that the boy who cried wolf too often was telling the truth the last time. And had those who were listening, who had been deceived so often, given careful attention to the sounds the boy was making on that last, fatal occasion, they might have perceived something historically unique as well: a new pressure was being placed on the lad's vocal performance, an acting-showing demand had been made, a genuine threat was present, and a new tension had entered his voice. The listeners, of course, looked at each other knowingly and said, "We've heard that song before — 'Help, help, the singer is going to die!' — but it's just another false alarm." And they went about business as usual. But had they listened more closely they would have perceived the change in the sound, responded to it, and been able to deal with what caused it. The shepherd boy would have been able to continue performing his duties instead of meeting an untimely end. It would have taken the awareness of only one of the listeners to note the difference, but it would have taken the efforts of all of them to do something about it.

The analogy is clear to a point: the threat this time is real, but unlike the jaded citizens of the parable, we are partially responsible for the presence of the threat because it was summoned by the acting demand. As a result, our young divas are disappearing; the sounds they make as they do so betray the reality of the threat, but no matter how acute our individual awarenesses may be, we can only deal with the problem collectively and cooperatively. And we can't afford to wait.

POSTSCRIPT: Years after writing the original Disappearing Diva article and during the course of writing this book, a situation occurred that demonstrated the thesis so clearly that I write it down now, only hours after it was told to me.

A young singer-actress, a member of what I consider to be the finest training program in the country, was in my class as a part of the program. On the first day of class, each singer is asked to sing an aria with no special instructions. Then it is sung again, and this time we do a tension check on the singer. Virtually every voice is richer, fuller, and more free during the tension check than it was during the first version. But the young woman in question was particularly amazed at how much easier it was to sing, as well as being pleased with how much better it sounded. This experience served as a persuasive entrée into the logic of the disappearing diva concept. She was immediately convinced of the validity of the idea, having experienced it in action, and was determined to do something about it in her performing.

A few days later, an audition was held for the staff of the training program. The young singer-actress did her best to relax her physical tension and keep her kinesthetic impulses in a ready state. I should stress that she was one of the "exciting" performers, and a great

*deal of that excitement lay in the tension of her kines-
thetic state of being. But that tension was strongly
entangled with her other modes, and it interfered with
her hearing/vocal mode in ways that had been revealed
by the tension check. (She seemed to be an obvious
kinesthetic dominant, and when I first heard her, I
mentally gave her four or five years of vocal life before
the damage became too evident to be masked by the
use of her very vital kinesthetic means.)*

*Because of her still-unpracticed attempts to get her
tension under control, the audition performance was
not as exciting as her previous auditions, as with all
skilled performers who have developed expertise in
using tension as a performance weapon. They are not
aware that they are doing damage to the voice with the
tension, nor that it is robbing them of their potential
for a truly exciting performance. Giving up that
weapon is one of the most difficult steps a performer
can take in a public situation. It means giving up the
known security of an established way of performance,
which has been praised and rewarded, for what will
inevitably be a less-effective product for the moment.
But they must take that temporary risk to gain a
healthier and more effective long-range product that
will reflect their true potential.*

*She did precisely that: her singing was better, but
her total performance did not have the same overall
excitement. I had heard about her reputation as an
exciting performer, and since I knew her only from a
single brief experience in class (only a portion of the aria
is sung for the tension check sequence), her reputation
did not seem fulfilled. I mentioned this privately to an
associate, but another member of the staff approached
the singer directly. He had seen her audition before and
told her that she was no longer as exciting. She told him
what she was doing (giving up voice-threatening tensions) and why (so that she would sing better, healthier,*

and longer). The staff member told her to forget it and go back to what she had always done.

When she told me about this advice in the next class, I was stunned. But I was also delighted, because she had decided to continue her efforts in the direction she had begun: she knew from what she had experienced that it was the only possible approach. We discussed the issue at length and began planning the reeducation of the kinesthetic skills. Once developed, they would allow her to recapture all her original excitement and far more, but in addition they would not interfere with and damage her voice and would avoid turning her into another disappearing diva.

I was very proud of her courage and told her so. But I was also deeply chagrined at the depth of the disappearing diva syndrome as practiced by staff members of such an outstanding program. I had been an unwitting part of the syndrome myself. Not having previously experienced her auditioning nor being aware of her intentions in the audition, I, too, had been concerned about her lack of excitement as a performer, although I thought she sounded wonderful. But my colleague— firmly enmeshed in the product-oriented corruption of the system, and unaware or unwilling to become aware of the disappearing diva concept—was enforcing a pattern of performance that would have led the young singer-actress to an early vocal demise had she not had the courage to follow a course that her own experience and logic told her was right. It took guts to do that, and she had them. But what about all the rest of the young singers who are asked to be "exciting" and in being so are gradually but implacably eroding their vocal potential?

Chapter 9
Beyond the
Performance Modes

In a recent singing-acting class in New York City, one of the performers said, "The modes have been great for my performance energies — the idea has opened up possibilities I would never have imagined. But even more important to me is how they have begun affecting the rest of my life in positive growing ways. I perceive and understand people and situations with a clarity which is new to me. So whatever good it does my performance is like a bonus."

The uses of the modes concept are definitely not limited to performers, anymore than are seeing, hearing, feeling, speaking, singing, moving, and communicating in general. The modes of perception and projection are the fundamental means we have of perceiving life and relating to each other. In chapter 1, I found it difficult to avoid pursuing the modes concept beyond the performance arena into general cultural considerations; but it was important at that point to focus on the essential task of untangling, developing, and integrating the modes for the singer-actor in performance. That done, let us examine implications of the modes concept in the rest of life, for they return into our performance awareness as surely as one mode affects the others. Some of the most compelling insights about the use of the modes in performance have occurred as I considered their broader cultural implications. Life and performance interact with each other in significant ways, no matter how we try to keep them separate, because the modes are part of everything we do. We can learn much about the challenge of performance on stage from a mode-oriented examination of performance in life.

Let us first look at more instances of mode behavior in performance, moving from there to the effect of mode consideration on other arts, to

305

306 BEYOND THE PERFORMANCE MODES

general cultural mode relationships, to the modes in everyday life, and finally to the implications of modal freedom of flow—beyond the modes.

The Modes in Theater and Politics

The demands of characterization interplay continually with the mode makeup of the performer. When I work with young performers who are trying to portray characters older or more experienced than themselves, it soons became evident that overuse of the kinesthetic mode lowers the seeming level of maturity or intelligence in a characterization. Clowns and children in general, and Jerry Lewis, Red Skelton, and Edith Bunker in particular, are all examples of extreme kinestheticism, whether by choice or by incapacity to do otherwise. We perceive a childlike (positive) or childish (negative) image, depending upon the character and the circumstances; it may have nothing to do with actual intelligence. Jerry Lewis, Red Skelton, and Jean Stapleton (who played Edith Bunker) are very bright individuals; but the characters they portray through the use of the kinesthetic mode are notable for their comic, clownish, childlike ineptitude, not for their intelligence. On the other hand, if the kinesthetic being is put in a state of readiness and the primary emphasis is placed on the hearing/vocal mode, we perceive the crisp, hard, mature intelligence (in effect) of British acting at its best, with Olivier, Gielgud, Hopkins, Wood, and the rest. Or even, as a contrast to Edith Bunker, her husband Archie, with his largely nonphysical hearing/vocal mode emphasis. The actual intelligence level of the clown and the king may be precisely the same, but the choice of the primary mode of communication (which is to say, the character's dominant mode) determines to a large extent how we judge that intelligence level. When the clown speaks a piece of genuine wisdom (as Edith Bunker or any Shakespearean clown often does), or when the hearing/vocal mode dominant says something stupid (as Archie or Polonius frequently does), a comic complexity enters the stereotypical impression. This complexity, which can be infinitely varied, is clearly open to artistic choice by the actor.

In keeping with Great Britain's hearing/vocal mode dominance, British actors often possess that dominance with a special skill in using

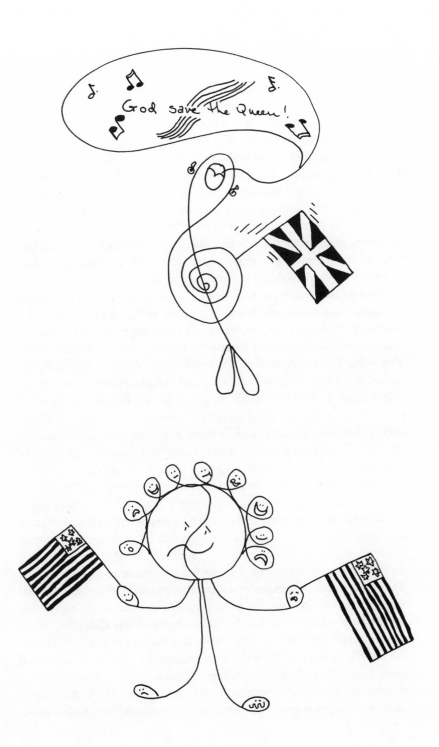

vocal energies without kinesthetic interference or entanglement. American actors have traditionally remained aloof from the British style, and British actors in turn have been bemused by the intense American concern with internal emotions. When the two strengths are integrated, however, a new level of performance is created. Sir Laurence Olivier was regarded as a realistic, method-style actor in the 1930s, the first of the British actors to begin uniting and unifying external-internal resources in performance. His long-term commitment to trimode mastery—moving between films (requiring facial/emotional mode dominance) and theater (requiring hearing/vocal mode dominance) and his insistence on making extraordinary personal kinesthetic mode statements in theater—do much to explain his international preeminence as an actor in this century.

From a theoretical point of view, it is probably easier to move from a hearing/vocal mode foundation to a skillful and artistic use of the other two modes than it is to move from, say, a facial/emotional mode foundation to a use of hearing and kinesthetic modes. British actors have been able to incorporate the best of the American facial/emotional mode tradition into their work with relative ease but American actors seldom demonstrate a similarly artistic incorporation of British hearing/vocal mode skills. American actors have even expressed contempt for British vocal technique, deriding it as artificial and pompous. That contempt must have been tinged with envy in the past decade as those phony technicians of the voice, with "no real guts," carried away acting awards from Broadway with regularity. They have demonstrated anew that live theater is more fundamentally a hearing/vocal medium than it is a facial/emotional medium, especially in the larger houses on Broadway. For those who consider cinematic acting to be the exclusive province of American facial/emotional actors, it must be disquieting to observe those same British technicians becoming a major force in the film world generally. The ability to use the hearing/vocal mode with great energy, and without entanglement or interference from the other two modes, is clearly the firmest basis on which to build a total singing-acting ability.

Although the hearing/vocal mode is dominant in the live theater, the more intimate the theater, the more important the facial/emotional mode becomes. Television is perhaps the most intimate form of filmed theater, and the facial/emotional mode often reduces the hearing/vocal mode to a minor partner. The latter mode is seldom used with real authority in television because of the incomplete modal training that has been characteristic of our acting tradition, training that leaves the performer unable to use the voice with great energy without distorting the facial/emotional mode through kinesthetic entanglement. Rather than analyze and solve the problem, coaches and directors tell the performers in question simply to eliminate the hearing/vocal demands and let the microphone do the work for the voice. As a result, they end up giving partial performances that can at least be accepted by the seeing-mode demands of television. Performers in that situation are nothing more nor less than victims of their unawareness, of their personal habits, and they are at the mercy of their untrained mode system.

The sixties and seventies saw an attempt to make the kinesthetic mode a more important part of acting technique in America. The great popularity of the musical comedy form—a double dominant medium (hearing/vocal and kinesthetic) if ever there was one—promoted this process, as did the emphasis on physical expression in experimental theater. The new physical freedom in dance and theater was paralleled by attempts to achieve new levels of psychological freedom. But although this freedom intensified interest in the kinesthetic and facial/emotional modes, the hearing/vocal mode has continued to be de-emphasized in theater except as an inarticulate expression of emotional intensity. For reasons probably connected with our heritage as a brave revolutionary colony that broke away from its fine-speaking but politically oppressive home country, the hearing/vocal mode has always tended to be connected in this country with aristocratic tradition; as such, it has not generally been honored nor trusted. We tend to prefer an inarticulate Ike (who was world renowned for the strength of his grinning facial/emotional mode) to an articulate Adlai (whose highfalutin language and thought grated against the American grain, as did his unexciting facial/emotional mode). More recently, another grinning, facial/emotional dominant (Reagan) became president. His long training as a performer in a facial/emotional mode medium (film) plus earlier training in a hearing/vocal mode medium (radio) enabled him to use those combined modes to defeat Jimmy Carter. Carter, on the other hand, had a facial/emotional mode that was so untrained, so self-conscious, that he was unable to smile genuinely in his television performances. He appeared to be a kinesthetic dominant (his interest in jogging), but

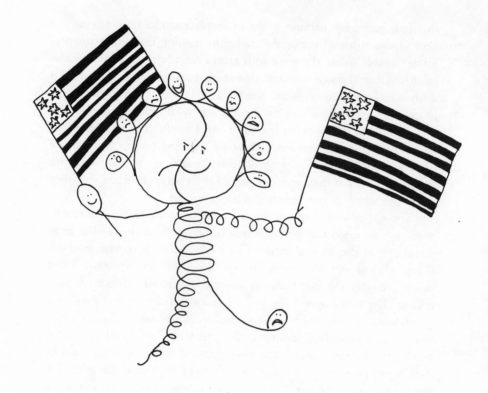

neither of his other modes—the primary ones for a contemporary presidential candidate—ever worked successfully for him. Person to person was one thing; on the tube was another. Carter's ineffective use of facial/emotional and hearing/vocal mode energies was crucial to his defeat by a man who had mastered those two modes, a man who, in his time in office, gave the most believable performance of his acting career, whatever one may have thought of the script.

Four years later another candidate, Walter Mondale, matched modes with the "great communicator" (the "great stylist" might be a more appropriate designation, because substance was less significant than the capacity to be stylistically convincing whatever the subject). In the intense Democratic primary campaign of 1984, Mondale made immense strides in activating his facial/emotional mode; he was never able, however, to match Reagan's capacity to fulfill the mode demands of television. For a brief time during their first debate, Mondale's facial/emotional and hearing/vocal tools came to life sufficiently to carry the debate by sheer contrast with his reputation for dull shrillness. But Reagan's long-term training and preparation with those two tools in radio, films, and television reasserted themselves. Voters acknowledged in polls that although they disagreed with Reagan, they were going to vote for him because he made them feel good—style rather than substance.

Psychologists studied the impact of smiles and frowns on the electorate. In one experiement that is particularly relevant to our work, three separate images of Reagan—one angry and threatening, one happy and reassuring, and one neutral—were spliced into a twenty-second news report on Central America and then shown to three separate audiences. The angry image tended to polarize the audience, making both supporters and opponents more fervent in their views; the happy image tended to unite the audience, creating synergy; whereas the neutral image *lost* interest and support for the issue, dispersing audience involvement.

The implications of this for the singer-actor and especially for the singer who has no dramatic context are significant. The neutral or passive face (a phenomenon all too common among singers) disperses audience involvement in the performance, losing interest in its meaning. Any specific positive or negative facial expression, on the other hand, involves audience members more strongly. It creates a synergistic relationship with them and thus enhances all aspects of the performance.

The general distrust of the articulate hearing/vocal mode dominant is fostered by the awareness that words used cleverly, glibly, and incongruently can and do deceive. As evidence we have a long tradition of oilcan Harrys, fast-talking shysters, patent medicine professors, and, more recently, a host of lying politicians, all of whom used the hearing/vocal mode to gain their ill-gotten ends. One is hard-pressed to think of the opposite, an American archetype who speaks articulately and well and who is also trusted and venerated. We are amused and sometimes amazed by William F. Buckley, but we probably wouldn't be comfortable with him, don't trust him completely, and certainly don't venerate him. Howard Cosell, who created his image through a pretentious choice of words and a highly stylized musicality of language, is a national figure of fun, a clown-intellectual who is most definitely neither venerated nor trusted. He is a performer, and a fake one at that. The late Everett Dirksen, a holdover from the golden days of political oratory (when it was OK to spellbind with language provided you were both a performer and a politician), might be thought of as venerable; but he also seemed a little dotty and was therefore essentially harmless, which made the golden tones and flowery language permissible. It is a wonderful irony that the hearings that did in the Nixon administration were chaired by Sam Ervin, another eccentric, oratorical political throwback.

In view of our cultural distrust of the hearing/vocal mode and our love affair with the kinesthetic mode, it is interesting that those are the two modes with the greatest potential for conflict. Emphasize one in a culture and the other tends to be distrusted. In America, the emphasis on emotion (the facial/emotional mode) and "feeling it" (with the kinesthetic mode) in both theater and the popular arts has created a two-modes-against-one situation: kinesthetic and facial/emotional against the hearing/vocal. In Britain, this situation is reversed: the hearing/vocal mode distrusts the other two and takes the communication burden on itself rather than allowing the others to play dominant roles in expression. Rock music, which features a combination of the hearing/vocal and kinesthetic modes in performance, is an exception to this modal opposition rule. The words are often inarticulate and so closely allied to the kinesthetic rhythms as to be completely dominated by them. But one should not forget that the ultimate fusion of these hearing/vocal and kinesthetic elements on a popular level — the joining of a driving, rhythmic, kinesthetic-emotional music with clear and articulate hearing/vocal mode poetry — was found in the Beatles, whose language skills made the world of rock music a culturally transcendent phenomenon.

The Modes in Opera and Music Theater

Opera, throughout its history, has been a medium almost totally dominated by the hearing/vocal mode, which may help account for its difficult and ambivalent relationship with the American public. My years of moving back and forth between theater, music-theater, and opera have taught me how much fear and defensiveness exists between representatives of opposing mode dominances, particularly between the hearing mode dominants, or the conductors, coaches, and general directors of opera; and the seeing and kinesthetic mode dominants, or the stage directors, designers, and choreographers who usually find themselves working for a hearing mode dominant.

So long as those seeing and kinesthetic types stay in their place, strictly subordinate to the hearing mode hierarchy, all is well. But if a stage director, for example, gains even partial control of a singer-actor training program in a grand opera house, the hearing mode authorities will not be able to tolerate it for long. It matters not that the results of the more balanced, integrated training thus provided are the best the program has experienced. The dogma that the training of the singer-actor must be controlled by hearing mode dominants will prevail despite the fact that their lack of perceptual balance may create unbalanced training situations that lead to demonstrable damage of the disappearing diva kind. Facts, evidence, or logic is of no use in such cases.[1] The operatic form itself, a mode-crippled affair much of the time that deserves the scorn heaped upon it by the intelligent non-opera-going public, is part of a large, vicious circle: the mode-crippled production creates mode-crippled responses, which become incapable of dealing with a healthy, mode-integrated production and demand the unfulfilled, crippled results they have come to expect.

This mode-crippling system is aided and abetted by the economic stringencies of opera, which is the most expensive performing art. Rehearsal time is money, and singing takes much less rehearsal time than singing-acting, whether for soloists or chorus. For the hearing mode dominant, singing is the only truly important thing anyway. One who suggests a therapeutic strengthening of the atrophied modes in performers (and therefore in audiences) is not only asking for more time and money but is implying that the mode makeup of the hearing dominants is not adequate to the task, which will be resented accordingly. Change modal capabilities and eventually you change production costs, in turn changing the very power structure of the form. That change, however, is a threat to the well-guarded status quo.

Theatrical do-gooders who insist upon therapeutic treatment for the increasingly mode-damaged performers in opera are not tolerated because of the amount of time it takes to do something about it. Occasionally a stage director or designer who does not tamper with the performers themselves, but simply creates strange or compelling visual spectacles within which the performer is largely left alone, achieves power and notoriety within the hearing mode dominant operatic structure (for example, Jean Pierre Ponnelle); but the innovator is accepted only as a visiting eccentric, never as an in-house controlling factor.

For the operatic performer, the degree of assistance that can be offered (or is allowed to be offered) by the other two modes depends upon the size of the opera house, the talent of the performers, the amount of rehearsal time available, and the point of view of the producer or the general director. When the three modes are truly integrated in intimate circumstances, the operatic form provides an astounding experience. Unfortunately, this is rarely the case. Opera is the most difficult and complex performing art in which to achieve genuine mode integration, and the power of the musical statement in opera is so strong that the form survives despite almost total reliance on a single mode.

ANECDOTE: A great many artistic revolutionaries seem to have been kinesthetic dominants. The same holds true for reform-oriented opera conductors. Gustave Mahler, for example, may have done more to improve production standards in opera than any other single individual in opera history, with the possible exception of Walter Felsenstein. All the descriptions of Maher's conducting, his incessant and superenergized walking, and his volatile physical energies, all point to a strong kinesthetic emphasis that was coupled, of course, with a powerful hearing mode dominance. He conducted "like a demon," and even on vacation he was always on the move: "If he was not walking, he was rowing — anything to keep from standing still.[2]

In this context, we can note his deep concern for the physical, spatial, and acting aspects of opera production when he took over the Vienna Opera in 1897. He got rid of singers who refused to act with sufficient energy; he hired a scene designer, Alfred Roller, whose slogan was "Space, not pictures"; he had the pit from which he conducted lowered so that the orchestra lights would not intrude upon the stage space; and he treated the drama and staging "as having equal importance with the singing in order to achieve unified, well-balanced performances." He did all this in the context of an operatic tradition in which such ideas were unheard of.

At the other end of the music-theater spectrum, musical comedy demands skill in all three modes as well as a high degree of integration between them. This need for integration may explain why musical comedy seldom attains a peak in any one mode, depending for its greatest impact upon the power of trimode cooperation. The singing in the best musical comedy is good, and so is the music; but neither attains the scale, depth, or impact of the best opera. The acting is also good, but it seldom attains the power or integrity of acting in straight theater. The dancing is good, but it falls short of the impact of pure dance, whether ballet or modern. This is not a criticism but simply a definition of the musical comedy form in mode terms. If any of the separate modes were to dominate as, for example, singing does in opera, the very form itself would be altered, no longer being musical comedy.

If history tells us anything, it is that the gap between musical comedy and opera is not easy to bridge. The greatest impediment to the bridge lies in the area of the hearing mode. The vocal demands of opera are such that they virtually exclude the amount of dancing and movement necessary to musical comedy. These vocal demands are accompanied by a depth of musical thought that also seems antithetical to the musical comedy tradition. Opera is long-winded, in the best and worst meanings of that phrase; musical comedy speaks to the common person, in the best and worst meanings of *that* phrase. Both forms relate to the hearing mode from either end of the spectrum and seem largely irreconcilable. This is no misfortune unless one is bent upon uniting the forms, a pointless enterprise except for opera producers who are trying to expand their minority audience or for musical comedy producers who aspire to Higher Art.

The Modes in Other Performing Arts

Ballet and dance are clear cases of kinesthetic dominance, with no demand upon the performers for hearing/vocal mode skills except as they hear the music and relate to it with their kinesthetic skills. An interesting aspect of dance training in general is that the facial/emotional mode of the performer is generally trained to be capable of a total passivity or blandness of expression, regardless of what the body may be doing. In our terms, the kinesthetic and the facial/emotional modes are isolated from one another. In recent years, a certain amount of dancer-acting has been called for in both ballet and modern dance, and the facial/emotional mode has been called back into play. But the form stresses a high-energy output in the kinesthetic mode, none in the hearing/vocal mode (except on rare occasions with choreographers such as Alvin Nikolais, Meredith Monk, or Margie Beals.), and a controlled and carefully modulated neutrality in the facial/emotional mode.

Movies and television are predominantly seeing or facial/emotional mode media. The expression of pure personality through the facial/

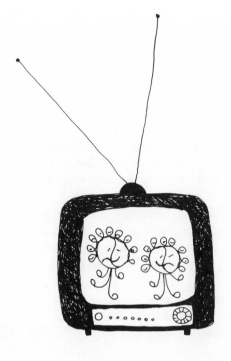

theater

opera

dance

emotional communicators is the most important aspect of film acting. Genuine acting, in the sense of playing characters unlike themselves, is rarely seen in films because this would involve a kinesthetic and hearing/ vocal mode alteration of the "real" personality as perceived through the facial/emotional mode. It is interesting to consider the impersonator in light of these ideas. The good impersonator is a clear-cut double dominant: able to alter the hearing/vocal mode to sound like another person and also be able to alter the face and body masks so that they resemble those of another person. But the impersonator must repress completely the personal quality of the facial/emotional mode, or at least allow it to lie dormant. If not, if that personal quality emerges, it automatically alters if not destroys the facial, physical, and vocal masks so carefully created by the skills of the kinesthetic and hearing/vocal modes. For this reason, the good impersonator is rarely a good actor. The facial/emotional mode has been schooled into performance dormancy; when performance demands change, the impersonator finds it difficult to allow personal emotional energies to flow through the facial/emotional channels.

ANECDOTE: A friend who is a very good impersonator, with several years experience of uninterrupted impersonation performance, was attempting to expand his career into the so-called legitimate theater. He got an excellent role in a straight play and was a moderate success, except . . . .Although no critic or audience member with whom I spoke connected their feelings about his performance with the concept of the modes, there was an almost unanimous sense that the performance, while it was very skilled and gave the performer many opportunities to exercise his talent as an impersonator, somehow lacked "feeling." From our new perspective, it seems clear that any impersonator who wants to make the switch to straight acting could very profitably spend time exercising the facial/emotional mode in isolation. Methods of doing this have been discussed in detail in chapter 5, but the perspective here is a bit different. The skilled impersonator has brought the facial/emo-

tional mode under conscious control, but the habit of
repression is such that it takes equally conscious exercise
to release it.

Like impersonators, conductors (as suggested in the Mahler anecdote) must also be double dominants. Their hearing/vocal mode must be dominant and acutely sensitive (although their voice may be whatever God has given them), but they must somehow communicate these mode sensitivities by the use of kinesthetic skills. If they are highly skilled kinesthetically, they are likely to be criticized for flamboyance or theatricality by hearing mode dominants. Leonard Bernstein springs to mind as a conductor of great kinesthetic power (who also has a remarkably expressive facial/emotional mode), as does Gustave Mahler. Kinesthetically skilled conductors seem to be the rule rather than the exception today. If they are not skilled kinesthetically but have the urge to express more kinesthetically than their skill allows, they may have physical tension problems, as with Sir Georg Solti and his overstressed trapezius and shoulder area.

The same reasoning applies to almost all instrumentalists. All must begin as hearing mode dominants, but they must develop their kinesthetic skills to a high degree. If they are kinesthetically dominant to begin with, it is possible that the urge to express themselves physically will interfere with the necessary isolation of the means to do so.

ANECDOTE: The accompanist who played for my university
classes also performed in the class on occasion as an
actress. As a result she became very involved in the
mode dominance concept. She came to realize that she
was a kinesthetic dominant, which explained one of her
continuing problems as a pianist (particularly as far as
her teachers were concerned). She moved too much, she
did too much physically while she was playing, and this
interfered with the necessary isolation of finger-arm
activity that is vital to good piano playing.

Once she became aware of her dominance, she was

able to quiet her kinesthetic demands almost imme-diately. This was something that years of nagging by her teachers (and herself) had been unable to accom-plish. The change for the better in her playing was also immediate, and it was noticed by everyone familiar with her work.

One wonders how many instrumentalists suffer from a similar kines-thetic problem in their efforts to make music, and how many might be as easily assisted in eliminating that interference. This is a different tack from the idea of release through physical expression, but in either case one must release the kinesthetic need in one instance by allowing it to express itself freely, in the other by relieving it of the responsibility to do so.

An area for further exploration is the relationship of the three modes to the left- and right-hemisphere functions in the brain, particularly as it relates to an artist's career choices. Just as with the modes, individuals tend to have a favored hemisphere. In general terms, the left-brain dominant falls into the corporate, control-oriented, product-making world of discipline, predictability, and logic; whereas the right-brain dominant gravitates to the artistic, lilies-of-the-field, process world of freedom, variability, and emotion. Combine this two-way division with mode dominance choices, and a variety of artistic career possibilities emerge. A kinesthetic dominant with left-hemisphere, control-oriented needs might gravitate to classical ballet. A predilection for right-hemisphere fantasizing and improvisatory play might send the same kinesthetic dominant to modern dance or contact improvisation.

Examples can be multiplied at will, but the important point is the possibility—and for the performing artist, the necessity—of expanding one's capabilities in the direction of their opposites by conscious analysis and exercise. The analytic, control-oriented artist, for example, can profit from the exercise of improvisatory, free-play potentialities; and this exer-cise can be facilitated and made palatable by an intellectual understand-ing of the values involved. A little intellectual motivation is useful in overcoming individual defense mechanisms, which tend to be conserva-tive and can protest mightily against any change in behavior patterns, especially when the point of view is already based in the left brain. The imaginative, improvisatory artist, in turn, can profit from analysis and discipline exercises. Resistance is likely to be even greater because the right-brain, nonverbal orientation has no reasons for its habits, only feelings that are less responsive to intellectual argument.

Conflicts in mode suitability occur not only between artists and their media but also between artists and architecture, between directors and theaters.

ANECDOTE: When Sir Tyrone Guthrie conceived of his well-known theaters in Stratford, Ontario, and Minneapolis, Minnesota, they clearly sprang from a hearing/vocal dominant with a strong liking for sculptural, kinesthetic pageantry. Both theaters required strong hearing/ vocal dominants as performers, reducing the impact of the pure seeing mode contribution of the scene designer while heightening the intimate, kinesthetic presence of the actor as a human being. So long as these requirements were observed, both theaters tended to thrive. Michael Langham, a true hearing/vocal dominant director who followed in Guthrie's path in both theaters, had much to do with their continuing success. Then Alvin Epstein was hired as the artistic director of the Guthrie Theater in Minneapolis. He is a wonderful performer himself, and he hired a great many facial/ emotional dominant actors for the company. He also selected a repertory to match. The performer's lack of hearing/vocal capacities and the repertory's lack of suitability to the theater (along with other factors irrelevant to our point) created widespread audience dissatisfaction. Epstein was replaced by Liviu Ciulei, a seeing mode dominant (an architect by training) who, being an East European, seemed to have little interest in the hearing/vocal mode as it related to the speaking of English. But there sat the theater, with its hearing/ vocal demands, restricting the pure vision of the seeing mode design by its thrust stage and audience surround. Ciulei needed a proscenium theater to express his vision adequately, and thus the theater underwent a change of structure painful to those who admired and respected its needs. It has become an inadequate proscenium theater with an ungainly thrust stage, a monument to a mode clash between an artist and a theater.

The Modes in Life Performance

We now approach the area where psychotherapy and theater sometimes overlap. The modes concept, of course, comes originally from the field of psychology and psychotherapy, my specific source being the work of Richard Bandler and John Grinder in neurolinguistic programming. One of their principal working mottoes is, "If your behavior pattern isn't working, change it." Although that is easier said than done, their concepts provide specific tools and methods for creating behavioral change in life. Our work is focused on the behavior of the performer in performance, but in-depth work on the problems of music-theater performance are also reflected in life. Integral work on music theater raises all the issues of life itself: expressing emotion, releasing the tensions that block that expression, allowing greater communicating energies to flow in all areas, and dealing with the relationship of the internal and external expressive systems. If one exercises these interrelationships in detail, they resonate in life as well. Many performers with whom I work find their personal behavior positively affected as they develop their performance capabilities. The intense life of music theater, experienced freely and fully with awareness of its relationship to life, cannot help but affect the life of which it is a selectively intense version.

From the audience perspective, one of the primary values in observing a great performance of any kind is the expanded sense of human potential that it conveys. We receive a glimpse of what each of us could be as human beings apart from the actual characters portrayed. The art itself is important, but in many cases we already know the piece of art being performed. It is the collision of the human being as artist with the demands of the art that reveals to us what that human being can be and could become, and that is what is truly significant. When the art—like music theater—involves the imitation of a human action lifted onto a new and higher plane of being, the perception of human potential is increased for the audience. If it is increased for the audience, it can be doubly so for the performer. Awareness of human potential in performance is an important link in realizing that potential in life itself.

The modes concept intensifies this interaction of performance with life. We are all fascinated by anything that offers us insight into what we are, and how and why we function as we do. When I discuss the modes with a group of people, they are inevitably fascinated and immediately begin wondering about their own dominance. Unlike most acting theories (with the exception of Cohen's *Acting Power*), the modes concept relates as specifically to life as it does to performance. For instance, a performer who wishes to strengthen her facial/emotional mode in performance has no alternative but to exercise that mode in life as well, to communicate more freely with her facial/emotional resources in all circumstances. In so doing, she changes her life behavior and her relationship to those with whom she communicates. She does not, of course, lose the capacity to conceal or inhibit such communication; she merely gains the new capacity to choose to communicate or not to communicate with that means. In my experience, this new capacity is always a positive addition to the person's life; the new flow of energy through the previously inhibited mode is exhilarating for the person and gratifying for friends and family. It has often literally changed the person's life.

The awareness generated by working with the modes concept is a positive aid to personal relationships. It can be enlightening to learn that interpersonal miscommunications are often the result of mode dominance mismatches. Stories from the therapeutic context about mode misunderstandings are matched by those that performers tell. "I finally understand why my husband and I can't communicate sometimes: I'm a kinesthetic dominant and he's a hearing/vocal dominant. But now that I know that, I find that I *listen* to him with more awareness, and I also try to say more clearly with my *voice* what I need to tell him. I told him about the modes idea and he was fascinated—he's even started to hug me more!" Such reactions are common, simply pointing to the universal applicability of the modes concept. The unique power to change performance behavior, which is the chief merit of the modes concept, is also its most useful application to life: it has the power to change behavior there as well. The same logic that says, "Become a master of your energies—make the communication choices *you* wish to make at any given moment," relates as well to life as to art. Mastery of one's mode energies means being aware of the messages we are communicating with all three modes and being able to make any other choices or combination of choices we desire. The projective modes *are* our communicating selves. They are the only means given to us to communicate with our fellow human beings (beyond extramodal projection and perception). Mode mastery can only enhance our capacity to live completely.

As I work with performers, I stress the fact that my concern can only be with their stage performance behavior and not their life behavior. At the same time I tell them that one of the best ways to change performance behavior is to exercise that behavior in life—beyond the performance modes. The basic behavior pattern underlying all growth is a freedom of energy flow in all three modes, a freedom that can best be attained by practicing it at all times, not merely in performance. Stories keep coming back from performers who practice what they perform: the lessons learned in changing performance behavior with the modes concept has the potential for changing life behavior precisely because *it is not the behavioral choice that is being changed but simply the behavioral capability*. Attack the behavior directly and it becomes the "don't think about elephants" challenge; but exercise as many different behavioral potentials as possible, create new expressive potentiality, and the nature of expression changes of its own accord.

Mode Transcendence

In the foreword to *The Complete Singer-Actor*, I commented on the depth of emotional experience attained in our summer institutes at the Minnesota Opera Company. I speculated that the reason these experiences happened was because we didn't try to make them happen. We didn't focus on baring our souls and becoming better people through emotional release. Instead we concentrated on the act of singing-acting, and in trying to fulfill the unique and extraordinary demands of music theater we attained the very things that would have escaped us had we aimed at them.

Having just completed another such institute experience (July 1983), I would like to speculate further about the relationship of that experience to performer growth. In this case, however, the modes concept has been added to the institute for the first time, and it has further stimulated thought about the meaning of the modes beyond the performance arena.

This institute was the most compelling demonstration to date that if you surround performers with a nonjudgmental environment and give them specific techniques with which to channel their singer-actor energies, they will give performances that astonish themselves, the observers, and their teachers-coaches-directors. One would think that those of us who had already worked within that context would have been prepared for what human beings can do if released from judgment and provided with appropriate performance tools. Yet it never ceases to amaze us because we too spend most of our time in the world outside, where such circumstances are found only too rarely and usually by accident. But those circumstances are being created more often, and they continue to increase in frequency. Once that kind of situation has been experienced, the participants find ways to help it happen again. As one performer in the last institute said to me, "It's as though we were creating a little universe where things were done the way they ought to be."

But lest it be thought that we were simply enclosing ourselves in a process-womb with no contact with actual performance, doing "fun" exercises that had nothing to do with the real world, let me explain. The institute is three weeks long. During that time, each participant rehearses and performs two scenes (eight to fifteen minutes long), one on the second Wednesday and one on the final Friday. On the days preceding and following these performances, a regular daily sequence of classes is offered as well as rehearsals: singing-acting classes, coachings, movement classes, and Alexander Technique sessions. The singers are not auditioned for the program—anyone who can afford it may attend. Very few of the participants are on the level of the various opera apprentice programs with which I have worked (such as Merola, Wolf Trap, Central City, and Aspen). Yet those final Friday performances—after a total of eight to twelve hours of total preparation, from learning the score to performance—were of a caliber that surpassed most of the scene work one would see at those more advanced programs after weeks of rehearsal. Several of the coaches in this recent institute, who had also worked with me in more selective and prestigious situations, were incredulous at what was happening. Performances of astonishing power were being given by people who, based on previous experience and objective appraisal of their talent, should not have been able to do so. "It's beyond belief," said one coach, and the others agreed. One of the participant directors said, "If anyone had told me in advance that we'd be directing scenes with only three to four hours of rehearsal, I wouldn't even be here. But the fact that we all did just that and these incredible performances are happening, just blows me away!"

I tell about this experience for two reasons: it *did* happen, and it happened as a result of putting into practice the two dominant themes of this book—the removal of judgmental fear from the performance process and the acquisition of specific techniques to release the energies of that process. Allowing that experience to occur did not depend upon clever motivational schemes, new and dazzling interpretations, or special personal charisma on the part of the staff. One participant said, "Now I know I can keep growing without a teacher following me around because I have the tools to work with."

On a more important level, however, making those two themes part of a tangible performing experience revealed to everyone the deeper meaning of what it is to be human. New levels of experience and potential experience came into awareness. And the applicability of those two philosophic themes to the art of singing-acting opened up channels for other experiences outside the performing circle, experiences that were even less verbal but even more significant. It is this idea that I would like to develop in conclusion.

We have seen the law of holism in action: no part of any true system can be touched without affecting all the other parts. The modes form such a system, and if one aspect of that system is blocked, the others are also blocked to some degree; free a blocked part of the modes system, and energy flows more freely in the other parts. But let us focus again on the relationship between the projective and perceptual systems. Earlier we stressed the importance of developing the performer's perceptual capacities to assist the development of projective capacities. Similarly, opening the flow of projective energies also opens the perceptual capacities. If we open up one part of any system, we begin to open all parts of that system. Thus as we allow the modes to project a greater flow of energy, we also increase the perceptual capacity to receive a wider range of energies.

With that projective and perceptual interplay in mind, let us place the modes in the larger context of the total human experience. Perceptually there are layers of that experience that transcend the ability of our everyday vocabulary to describe them. Sometimes they are called "cosmic," sometimes "spiritual," sometimes "transcendent," sometimes "far out," and sometimes a cry of "Wow!" has to suffice. Unless one has unusual verbal gifts, it is often best to leave them unverbalized. They originate beyond the verbal to begin with, and the exclamations of "Wow!" and "Incredible!" are not only meaningless to those who have not had the experience themselves, but they are often associated by those who hear them with a kind of simpleminded naiveté. This allows them to reject the possibility that the experiences behind those expressions of awe may be the most important things that ever happen to us, and their resistance to articulation in language is integral to their power.

If they are that potentially important, it is worth making the attempt to explore them from our new perspective, difficult as it may be to verbalize about them. We need not describe the experiences themselves, but simply place them in a different context by drawing upon a fundamental concept concerning systems in general.

The Modes and Other Energy Levels

Thanks to contemporary physics, quantum mechanics, and Einstein's famous formula $E = mc^2$, we now know that everything is energy in different vibratory states. A granite slab and a sunbeam are part of the same energy continuum, as are a cry of joy, a waving hand, and a smiling face. In exploring the spectrum of human energies, let us place the physical being at one end of that spectrum and the highest, most refined energies we can conceive of at the other. These include energies beyond the mental even though we may not be able to measure them at present (and even with mental energies, although we know they exist, measurement has not become a precise science). One way of visualizing that spectrum is shown in the accompanying representation.

Projective Energy	Energy Level	Perceptual Energy
	UNIVERSAL-TRANSCENDENT	
	HIGHER CONSCIOUSNESS	
	(Beyond Verbal)	
— — — — —	MENTAL INTUITIVE	— — — —
	(Verbal Access)	
(Judgmental Level)	MENTAL INTELLECTUAL	(Language Level)
	(Verbal Access)	
— Hearing / Vocal Mode —	— HUMAN SOUND —	— Hearing Mode —
	(Nonverbal)	
Facial / Emotional Mode	EMOTIONAL	Seeing Mode
Kinesthetic Mode	PHYSICAL	Kinesthetic Mode

There are seven levels of energy ranging upward from the solid, slow-moving, and clearly perceived physical plane to the increasingly subtle and refined energies that may be responsible for our transcendent experiences. These higher frequencies of energy are not perceived in agreed-upon ways at this stage in our evolution; they are beyond the verbal and are difficult if not impossible to define and discuss with words. Nonetheless, despite their subtlety, they are intensely real and powerful in proportion to their subtlety.

There is a relationship between the energy planes that touches one of our recurring themes: the greater the solidity or density of the lower plane energies, the less perceptually responsive they tend to be to higher plane energies. Our granite slab is less perceptually responsive to the sunbeam than is a human being or a plant. The greater the density on any plane, the less responsive to higher energies that portion of the plane will be. In the context of the projective modes, let us call this the density-blocking principle. For example, a muscle (or an emotion) that is in a state of tension is more dense than if it were in a state of readiness or flow, and that condition of greater density is less receptive to higher energies. Conversely, the state of readiness is more receptive to higher energies. But physical tension not only creates greater density in the kinesthetic system; it also blocks the flow of energy in the total modes system. Interference of one mode with another also increases density and blocks the energy flow in the total modes system.

Looking at the larger system of projective and perceptual energies, we see that any increase in the density of the projective modes system reduces the sensitivity of the perceptual system. Conversely, the reduction of projective mode density through the release of tension and mode interference not only increases the energy flow in the projective modes system but also heightens the perceptual responsiveness.

In chapter 1 we saw how difficult it is to change our perceptual capacities because we seem to be "doing" so little in order to perceive. The best way to change these capacities, therefore, is by altering our projective capacities. We do something when we project and we can therefore change that doing. Because a means of projecting energy on higher planes is not widely available at this point in our evolution, the only area with which we can work freely and effectively in making change seems to be with the lower plane projective energies—the modes. A primary tool for opening our perceptions to higher plane energies thus seems to lie in a gradual *lightening* of the modes of projection by freeing, developing, and interrelating the modes while simultaneously lowering the judgmental barrier. If that is accomplished, all parts of the total energy system will open up. By learning to give energy more freely, we begin to receive energy more freely.

Unlocking the Total Energy System

Examining the energy chart from another point of view, we find the mental-intellectual plane standing midway between higher and lower energy planes and acting as a potential barrier between them. The verbal outreach of the mental-intellectual plane extends into the sound plane below and the intuitive plane above. The gray area overlapping these three planes represents the actualization of the barrier by the intellectual creation of verbal densities. If the mental-intellectual plane attempts to dictate to and control the upper and lower nonverbal areas, it restricts the flow of energy from those areas in both directions by the limitations of its language-based understandings.

Practically speaking, this is the situation for most of us. We are all victims of our verbal gifts to some extent. Ideally, there should be a free, unimpeded interchange of energy between upper and lower energy planes. But the density-blocking principle comes into play: language can either facilitate the flow of energy between planes or it can block the flow with verbal-density patterns. This potential for verbal-intellectual interference with the modes system includes the perceptual system as well as the projective one. A principal factor in creating this verbal-density blocking is judgment; language is, in turn, judgment's principal tool. Thus judgment belongs almost exclusively to the mental-intellectual plane.

From this perspective, there are two kinds of density that block the flow of energies between the upper and lower planes: projective mode density created by internal tension and interference patterns; and mental-intellectual, language-created density. If we are able to activate and develop a free flow of energy on the lower nonverbal planes (the modes) and let down the language barriers of judgment and overcontrol that are erected by the mental-intellectual plane, those lower planes will make contact with the upper energy planes. When this happens, human consciousness experiences an expansion, an opening of potential, a sense of wholeness and new understanding from a larger and more inclusive perspective. There are no words to adequately describe this new level of awareness. If there were, it could be achieved through the use of language itself. But the energies that create the experience lie beyond the language barrier.

Words are not denied by such an experience; *nothing* is denied. The experience transcends duality and is inclusive of all of life, but the language tools that are created by and then create what we call the mind can only lead to the borders of this transcending experience. At that point, their dominant role must be given up as they become one synergistic aspect of a larger whole. It is not a denial but an opening of the entire energy system, an experience without parallel. Throughout history there has been an enduring human search for a means, a vehicle, a technique, or an art that can allow such experiences to happen.

In *The Awakening Earth*, Peter Russell discusses this search and its increasing importance today as we "see the development of higher states of consciousness to be an essential part of the evolutionary process itself."[3] Evolution for humans is no longer a matter of physical change, although those changes will continue to occur over extended periods of time. But as the speed of technological change has increased and we have become aware for the first time of our own evolution and have become potential participants in that evolution, the evolutionary process has shifted to the mind-brain. The process of becoming consciously one with a larger whole, of attaining a greater receptivity to higher energies, of letting down all barriers (language and otherwise) to an inclusive experience of life is one way of viewing the new (and ancient) inner evolutionary process. The need to accelerate this process today is urgent. As Russell puts it, "The question now facing humanity is how we can facilitate this inner evolution, and, even more important, can we do it in time?"[4]

The search for a means of aiding the inner evolutionary process, of increasing the interchange of energies on all levels of our being, has developed many new disciplines in this century. On the physical plane these include (in addition to the ancient technique of Hatha Yoga) the Alexander Technique, Feldenkrais Technique, Bio-Energetics, Rolfing, the Trager Method, and many others; on the emotional plane, a multitude of therapies includes, at the extreme end, primal scream therapy; and on the vocal plane, the use of mantras that attempt to lower the mind-language barrier by intellectually meaningless repetition or by voice training that removes density from the sound-producing system. Techniques such as Arica and EST use combinations of energy-release techniques, including exercise on the mental plane. Mental-intellectual analysis, as in some psychological therapies, adds some clarification to the lower planes but tends to increase the strength of the language barriers because that is the tool they must use. (It is the paradox of lifting one's self up by one's bootstraps.) On the mental-intuitive level, the path of visualization is also related to the seeing mode plane. Object meditation or clear-mind meditation are still other means of lowering the language barrier.

The more energies called into play by the technique being used, the more the total system is opened by the release of those energies. By choosing singing-acting as our vehicle, we have engaged a maximum output of human communication energies on the lower planes, specifically the three projective modes. We also try to release the judgmental interference of the mental-intellectual plane as well as calling intuitive energies into play. In working on the many planes necessary to the art of total singing-acting, we are establishing, inadvertently, a synergistic relationship with higher plane energies.[5] This may explain why revelatory, life-changing experiences can happen in a brief period of intense singing-acting training. And it may be why performers keep working at an art in which there are already twenty times (and more) the number of performers to fill every available job: getting a job is not the primary purpose (albeit a very useful bonus); the real goal is to explore, however unconsciously, human possibilities that are beyond words and jobs, to open up the total system to experiences that are beyond price.

To complement this work with the lower plane projective energies, let us hypothesize a technique that would allow us to relate directly to the higher planes without having to deny the lower plane necessities of our performing art. The techniques we have already mentioned do not do this. For example, it is difficult to do yoga and to perform *Tosca* at the same time. This is not to slight yoga (or any other technique), nor to suggest that yoga might not be a very useful practice for the performer outside of actual performance; the same limitation applies to the other lower plane disciplines with respect to singing-acting. But our hypothetical technique would surmount the language barrier without the use of language itself (as in prayer or chanting) and without the use of other means that are incompatible with performance demands (as with physical or emotional techniques).

Russell poses the same hypothetical need in *The Awakening Earth*: "In order for the shift to a higher state of consciousness to become widespread, society will need to develop techniques or processes that are simple to practise, can be incorporated into most people's day-to-day life, are easily disseminated throughout society, and produce the required shifts in consciousness fairly rapidly." Unfortunately, as he points out, "most of the techniques available today do not appear to achieve these ideals . . . ."[6]

A Technique for Total Energy Integration

It will probably come as no surprise that the hypothetical technique just described actually exists. It is called *Reiki*, a Japanese word meaning universal (*Rei*) life energy (*ki*), and it was not publicly introduced into the United States until 1975. Without mental-intellectual effort, without language involvement, without physical or emotional effort, the Reiki technique permits direct access between lower and higher plane energy. Reiki is the art and science of activating, drawing upon, and directing a greater flow of higher plane energies in the human system. It is a synergistic technique, which allows it to interrelate holistically with all other systems whether they are therapies; physical, mental, or emotional techniques; performing arts; or simply life itself in any of its manifestations. The Reiki technique enhances the energies and interrelationships of any human activity it accompanies. It brings a greater quantity of universal energy to the human system, and this energy is then utilized by that system in whatever way is most appropriate. If there is a physical problem—for example, a sore throat or tight vocal musculature—the energy promotes the healing process or helps release the tension creating the problem. If there is emotional or mental tension of some kind—for example, stage fright or performance anxieties—the energy is utilized in calming and releasing those tensions and facilitating the mental flow. Whatever the human system needs, the additional energy made available by the Reiki technique aids the process.

Reiki is a nonexclusive technique that allows each person to develop his potential on all levels to the fullest. It requires no change in one's belief system, no specific religious orientation, and no mental or physical exercises of any kind. It helps the singer-actor become one with the energies of the music, the character, and the situation; it allows an alignment of the performer's energies with the flow of the total performance energies. In relating to that larger context of energy, the performer and his personal energies are expanded and enhanced. As the singer-actor increases his capacity to receive energy, his capacity to give energy also increases.

Although Reiki is an ancient technique (possibly the oldest energy science available today), it was lost and not rediscovered until the nineteenth century. Because it was not introduced publicly in the United States until the late 1970s, it is also one of the youngest sciences in the modern Western world. And a science is precisely what it is: an objective technology of energy that uses the human body-mind system as a part of the technology without subjective or emotional involvement being able to interfere with the process. Because the Reiki technique is so new to our experience, its potential interrelationship with the life activities it can serve is still being explored and developed. Some singer-actors have reported profound experiences in integrating the technique with their art; although there are many other methods and therapies that relate to the art of singing-acting, the science of Reiki has special significance with respect to this book and to the modes concept. We can only suggest here the possibilities of the Reiki technique for the performer, and those possibilities in turn are limited only by the imagination and creativity of the performer exploring them. A growing network of performers use the Reiki technique, and their experiences and specific applications of the technology in rehearsal, private practice, and performance are becoming part of a substantial body of integrative information. This information is being shared with other performers who have learned the Reiki technique and it is the subject of a future book.[7]

The potential of the Reiki technique is directly related to the theme of this final chapter: the implications, beyond performance, of freeing, developing, and integrating the modes. Let us recapitulate that theme as a concluding coda.

When the factors of freedom, development, and integration are applied to the lower planes of energy in a singing-acting performance, experiences occur that transcend the meaning of the performance itself. Why those significant experiences do not happen more often in music-theater performances is an important question. What prevents us from bringing together the two crucial conditions that nurture those experiences: a technique with which to approach the art and a nonjudgmental environment in which to exercise the technique and fulfill the art?

Many factors surround this issue of judgment; but in music theater and particularly opera, the form itself is strongly product-oriented and intensely judgmental. The problem of creating a climate that is as non-judgmental as possible (even while striving for a flexibly controlled discipline) falls on those of us responsible for that climate. Whatever we do

to lighten judgmental density, we must also deal with the second issue, which has been the subject of this book: the clarification of the technique of singing-acting. The lack of a clear, technical understanding of the art creates density in the performance itself, but it also gives rise to the imprecise, generalized, and negative descriptions of that performance that further increase the judgment potential.

To help the performer achieve that state of oneness with the flow of performing energies on the lower planes and receptivity to the inflow of higher plane energies is the challenge for all of us working with the

music-theater form. And if the singer-actor can achieve it, so can we all.
The image of human potential, which is nowhere more powerfully revealed than in music-theater and singing-acting at its best, dares each of
us to fulfill that potential. The modes concept clarifies a technique for
achieving the necessary energy flow on the projective planes. We only
need to establish environments in which the language barriers can be
lowered to allow contact between all energy planes. That depends upon
each of us, upon our willingness to challenge ourselves even as we challenge the performers, to allow the same freedom of energy flow and liberation from judgment in our performances as teachers-directors-coaches
that we want to experience in the performances of the singer-actors with
whom we work.

Appendixes

Appendix A
A Continuing Parable

*My book The Complete Singer-Actor began with a little
parable about opera and theater. It concerned the
neighboring countries of Theatrylvania and Musiconia
and the disputed territory between them known to its
inhabitants as Operania. The parable served to clarify
general issues in a light-hearted way and to set the tone
for the main theme of that book, which was the artistic
necessity of integrating opposites for the maximum
vitality of the operatic form. For those readers of the
previous book who are curious about the continuing
saga of Theatrylvania, Musiconia, and Operania, I
record here some of the changes that have taken place
in these mythic countries.*

A great deal has happened since we last visited these volatile territories. When we departed, the disputed territory of Operania was torn with strife, with both Theatrylvania and Musiconia trying to assert dominance over the Operanian inhabitants. The OLF (Operanian Liberation Front) was struggling to create an independent principality with its own laws, but its efforts were being increasingly diverted by a growing interest in technology. We concluded our last visit just as the technological diversion was beginning to be felt.

Since that time, however, a new party has arisen that has united the countries of Musiconia and Theatrylvania with a radical, but simple and ultimately peaceful, solution. The new party, called the Modeocratic Party, has created a new division of the land in which *all* of its citizens are to be treated according to their nature (their *modality*, as the party slogans call it) regardless of accidents of birth or situation. The country is to serve the people, not the people the country.

The party's proposal, which is still being put into effect, is for Musiconia (the land of hearers and sounders) and Theatrylvania (the land of viewers and emoters) to contribute a portion of their land to form a new state to be known as Kinesthetica. The Kinesthetanians (the feelers and movers) had previously formed a splinter party in both Musiconia and Theatrylvania, but they were not adequately represented by the previous boundaries in the land. Because they represent about one-third of the total population, they were overjoyed by the Modeocratic proposal.

The next part of the proposal helped ease tensions in Operania as well. The previously informal boundaries were to be acknowledged and formalized, and Operania was to be treated as a separate territory that allowed each of the three states to have custody of a zone within it. Operanian citizens may move freely from one zone to another and may begin creating their own Operanian laws.

The name of Operania, however, is to be changed to Musitheatica, which recognizes the territory's relationship to all three parent states. This decision was controversial, especially with Musiconians who insist that Operania is still, fundamentally, a Musiconian territory. They were mollified to some extent by the fact that the new name begins with the word Music (other names proposed for Operania included Theamusetica and Kinestheatonia) and by the fact that Musiconia received a larger portion of land than the other two countries (Kinesthetica received the smallest portion). A faction in the Musiconian legislature wants to erect a wall separating their zone from the others, but it seems unlikely that such a threat will be carried out. Peace reigns for the moment, with only a few traditionalist grumblers in each of the state legislatures.

The new country as a whole is now called the United Modalities of Humania. Citizens are encouraged to spend vacation time in other modalities, which has led to a boom in tourism in all three states and the enactment of one of the Modeocratic Party's most unusual proposals: although citizenship is determined by the testing of mode dominance and mode makeup, the multiple modality clause in the Humanian Constitution makes it possible to be a citizen of more than one modality. Under the clause, citizens may take appropriate tests and become certified dominants (or *doms*, the popular term for modality citizenship) in any modality. The eventual goal is to have all citizens in all modalities become *Tridoms* (triple dominants). Cultural exchange programs have been initiated to help achieve this long-term goal. At present, there are an increasing number of *Dudoms* (double dominants) but only a few Tridoms, who are among the most honored Humanians in the land.

Slogans have been created to help cement relationships between the new states. Some of these are "All Good Things Come in Thirds"; "A One-Mode Man Is a One-Mood Man"; "From Each Mode According to Its Projections, To Each Mode According to Its Perceptions"; and "Honor Your Dominance."

There is great interest in modal-exchange programs between states, and each state has training centers in the other two modalities. Musitheatica has a new and rewarding function as cultural negotiator between the states, and it offers special cultural transition programs that include Dudom and Tridom training as well as individual preparatory courses in the customs and cuisine of each of the states. These programs have helped to ease interstate tension, as past diplomatic problems have occasionally been caused by ignorance of cultural customs. Musiconia, for example, has an old statute prohibiting unnecessary movement through space, whereas in Kinesthetica it is a minor misdemeanor to stand still for more than thirty seconds. Theatrylvania, as we noted on our previous visit, takes a more indulgent view of life, and its laws are less restrictive. The only law that creates an occasional diplomatic flap is the "feel it or forget it" ordinance, which bans movement, speech, or song without prior motivation. But this statute has proved hard to interpret: "What if the motivation is not communicated?" cry critics of the law. As a result it is rarely enforced, even among its own citizens, many of whom swear by the statute without being able to define its meaning.

Humanian artists are largely supportive of the Modeocratic platform. Many cultural events have been created to encourage its acceptance by the country as a whole. For example, the longest running play in Theatrylvanian history, *A Man for All Modes*, has been the basis for a ballet in Kinesthetica, a symphonic poem in Musiconia, and (of course) both an opera and a musical comedy in Musitheatica.

We could continue recounting the recent history of the United Modalities of Humania; but, happy in the knowledge that new understandings have emerged and are working their way to a satisfactory and ultimately integrated conclusion, let us say farewell and return to the business of the modes in our own land.

Appendix B
The Modes and the
Audition Process

Although the audition process is not the subject of this book, the concept of the modes clearly applies there as well as to performance itself. For that reason, I've included this appendix to suggest special applications of the modes concept to auditioning.

People who talk about how to audition are talking about how the process works best for *them*. If their special audition needs relate to the needs of auditioners in general or to the acting process itself, their comments are useful. Michael Shurtleff's book *Audition* is an excellent resource in both respects.[1] The comments that follow are not intended as a prescription for auditioning for me, but rather as a way of viewing the audition process from the modes perspective.

Performers sometimes point out negative aspects of the modes concept. As with all power, mode mastery is available for negative uses, as when it is manipulative, insincere, or phony. In performance, insincerity and phoniness are simply mode incompetency in action, whereas manipulation is precisely the performer's challenge: to manipulate or guide the energies of the audience without their knowing it. But the issue becomes more complex when we apply the same ideas to life. Beyond the negative implications of insincerity and phoniness, many pejorative connotations are associated with the idea of "performing" in life, including "role-playing," "putting on airs," and "not being yourself."

In the audition situation, as nowhere else in the performer's experience, that no-man's-land between self and character is crossed repeatedly. The first view of the performer in an audition is as a person, the role of the auditionee. Then, before one's very eyes, that person becomes (or fails to become) the character. This change lasts for the duration of the first audition piece, whereupon the character again becomes the person.

If another selection is called for, the whole process is repeated. The audition may be the single greatest psychological challenge faced by the young performer who is trying to create a career. There is no lighting, no costume, no set, no props (unless the performer brings them, which can be risky), and no orchestra—in short, none of the things that we imply are necessary for an audience to enjoy theater, music theater, or opera. Yet we expect the performer to be able to create a viable performance without any of these helps. And to their undying credit, performers do it again and again.[2]

The audition situation brings into play all the worst judgmental fears, along with the overcontrol syndrome that accompanies them. The auditioner is there specifically to render judgment, to analyze the performer's capabilities and decide whether to cast that person or not. Because auditioners seldom share with a performer a detailed analysis of their reaction, the decision is often interpreted as a judgment of the performer's absolute worth. It is seldom that, however, for a rejection can be based on inappropriate height, weight, character quality, vocal timbre (however beautiful it may be), or any number of other nonjudgmental categories including the idiosyncrasies of the auditioner's hearing mode preferences. But the performer does not know this, and judgmental feelings are almost inevitable.

Not only are the performers expected to create compelling performances under such daunting circumstances; they are also asked to be themselves and then make the transition from themselves into the character in plain view, something a performer rarely has to do in a performance situation. While passing back and forth from themselves as themselves to themselves as characters, the question of what state of being is really appropriate to the character under such circumstances is part of the performer's awareness. If the character is to appear "natural," which state is the natural one in an audition? Is the *character* state-of-being to be differentiated from that of the *person* by physical changes, emotional changes, both or neither; and if so, how? All these questions, whether consciously asked or not, must be answered in some way or other. They create the unique and problematic circumstances of the audition situation.

Whatever the performer's attitude about the rest of life, the audition is clearly something that must be dealt with. To do so, the performer must gain control over the messages sent to the auditioners. The modes are the message senders, and it follows that the performer must gain specific control over their functioning and interrelationship *in the audition context* in order to succeed.

In working with a young singer on the audition challenge, I told her that I was receiving the following messages from her: her physical being felt unready, not vital, back on its heels, unenergized, nervous, and out of control; her facial/emotional system was sending me messages of hostility and fear. The singer was surprised, for she had had no intention of sending any of those messages, nor was she aware that they were being sent. We discussed the fact that even in life there is often little relationship between what we are thinking and feeling and what other people think we are thinking and feeling. In this case, her fear and hostility messages were probably true on some level (it is easy to dislike those judging us), but they were the last messages she wanted to send to auditioners. I reiterated the fact that in performance or audition situations, there should never be a one-to-one relationship between what is going on in our mind and what we want the audience to perceive from our modes system. Even if the fear and hostility messages are true, the performer must develop the capacity to send other messages. In life it is a person's prerogative to send any messages they wish (even though they may be unaware of them); for performers and auditionees, however, it is vital to be able to send whatever messages they choose at any time, which means that they must develop an awareness of all the messages they send.

No auditioner, I continued, is likely to hire a performer who looks frightened, hostile, and unenergized. All other things being equal, they will hire the performer who looks confident, open, pleasant, and vital. Both sets of messages are the responsibility of the mode systems *regardless* of what the inner feelings may be. Most auditionees, I pointed out, are in a state of anxiety on some level, but they do *not* want to transmit that message. If she *does*, the auditioner is likely to think, "If she can't handle it here, what will happen in performance?" And the performer certainly doesn't want to convert personal anxiety into messages of fear or anger. Yet it happens constantly.

The young woman with whom I was working objected: "I don't want to come off phony, cutesy, or insincere." I suggested that there is often a confusion between what it is to be real or yourself and what it is to make communicating choices in performance. Cutesy messages are not the only alternative to fear, hostility, and nonvitality: the real issue is the ability to choose the messages you wish to send rather than having them chosen for you, outside your awareness, by the combination of a difficult psychological situation and a faulty message-sending system. The young woman accepted that answer, and we went to work.

Feedback is vital in developing an awareness of the kinds of messages one is sending, but that feedback is seldom given except to reinforce what is already positive. We tell a person how nice they look: "What a happy smile, what an excited, eager expression"; or, "I love the way you stand with such confidence." But seldom do we discuss the negative messages that are sent. How rarely do we ask a person who appears to be hostile whether they are actually angry about something. We are fearful of finding out that they are angry, or of becoming the object of their anger, or of arousing even more negativity. And yet these unmentioned areas of negative message-sending are often destructive in our relationships with other people precisely because they are not mentioned. The irony is that the messages can also be totally unintentional, but we never find it out. We act as though they *are* intended, are "real," and we create a negative feedback loop (sometimes called a vicious circle) based on illusion.

It is the same for the performer in audition as it is for the performer in life. If the young performer wants to make positive changes in her auditioning or in performance behavior, she must seek out honest feedback. To receive such feedback, she must give signals that encourage it: she must begin her behavioral change by exercising it even as she asks for that feedback. She must pretend, act the role of a character who *likes* being told the truth about herself, and continue to act that role as she is actually given that information. Defensiveness, withdrawal, hostility, pain, or hurt shut off the flow of that information from any sensitive person. Not all critics are sensitive, of course, but their knowledge is useful to the performer regardless of their sensitivity. One can prime the critic's pumps, increasing the flow of that knowledge (*especially* from the insensitive ones) by seeming to enjoy the criticism.

As the young woman accepted all this information and began working with it, it was remarkable to see her facial/emotional mode soften and grow more positive, sending new and more useful messages even as we discussed the need for it to do so. (I have seen this feedback process in action virtually every time I discuss a person's facial/emotional mode with them. Whether consciously or not, they begin making facial/emotional modifications that respond to the discussion and that are always a welcome and believable change.) Within an hour we had established a basis for the continued development and cooperation of her kinesthetic and facial/emotional modes, both as a performer and as a person before and after an audition. Once she had accepted the idea intellectually, she was able to make a remarkable amount of positive change in a short time. Having overcome inhibitions about not being true to herself, mugging, and being phony and artificial, many new energies were allowed to flow through the facial/emotional mode.

I also recommended that she practice face-brushing every day (see chap. 5), the basic self-help technique for habitually inactive or deadpan facial/emotional modes. Three days later, I received a long-distance call from her. She had been practicing her facial exercises on her job, which involved wholesale selling at random intervals with bookkeeping work in between. She had always hated the selling part, the facially-relating-to-people part. But after practicing loosening and projecting exercises for her facial/emotional mode, she found for the first time in her experience that she not only enjoyed relating to the first client, she didn't want her to leave. She was enjoying the process of pretending to enjoy the process of interrelating with the other person with her facial/emotional mode. By releasing those modal energies on a conscious and technical level, the expressive energies within her found a pathway to expression and she felt differently about the total situation. Because permission was available from her external means, it changed the very quality of the inner feelings.[3]

This is a piece of ancient wisdom that every person can only learn by experiencing it personally: we change the way we *feel* by the way we behave, and we change our capacity to feel by changing our behavioral capacity. Increase the range of behavioral capability, and the range of potential feeling increases as well. The problem in the past has always been, how do you change your behavioral capacity—what do you *do* specifically? The modes concept offers a clearly defined way to approach this challenge by clarifying the nature of the message-sending systems. Another way of expressing the inner and outer relationship might be as follows: Increase the capacity of the modes to receive energy from the inner feelings, and you increase the capacity of those inner feelings to give.

Notes

Notes

Notes

Introduction: A Report from the Laboratory

1. See Tom Wolfe, *The Painted Word* (New York: Bantam, 1976) and *From Bauhaus to Our House* (New York: Farrar, Strauss, Cudahy, 1981); and Henry Pleasants, *The Agony of Modern Music* (New York: Simon & Schuster, 1955).

2. See Charles Hampden-Turner, *Maps of the Mind* (New York: Collier-Macmillan, 1982).

3. Mahler, the man who virtually created the contemporary concept of the conductor, was principally an opera conductor who was also very concerned with the total impact of opera—scenery, costuming, lighting, movement, and acting. See chapter 9 for more information on this topic.

4. Eugene Herrigel, *Zen and the Art of Archery* (New York: McGraw-Hill, 1964); W. Timothy Gallwey, *The Inner Game of Tennis* (New York: Random House, 1974); Robert Pirsig, *Zen and the Art of Motorcycle Maintenance* (New York: William Morrow, 1974); and Eloise Ristad, *A Soprano on Her Head* (Moab, Utah: Real People Press, 1982).

5. I am aware that life itself is a technique and that Zen as a concept is applicable to any and all aspects of a person's life. Our concern is with an approach to an art—singing-acting—in which technique is primary and yet has not been defined or recognized as such. The techniques of acting and thus of singing-acting are very muddled in the minds of many performers (as is the technique of life for many people), and this is an effort to begin untangling them.

6. From Toby Cole and Helen Krich Chinoy, eds., *Actors on Acting*, rev. ed. (New York: Crown Publishers, 1970), 423.

7. Uta Hagen and Haskel Frankl, *Respect for Acting* (New York: Macmillan, 1973).

8. The principal inspiration came from Richard Bandler and John Grinder in their books *The Structure of Magic*, vols. I and II (Palo Alto, Calif.: Science and Behavior Books, 1975–76) and *Frogs into Princes* (Moab, Utah: Real People Press, 1979).

Chapter 1. Exploring a New Description

1. By *method* I mean method as such but also the generic American versions of the Stanislavski Method.

2. For our purposes, taste and smell can be classified as part of the kinesthetic system, thus allowing us to refer to the intellect as the fourth mode. See chapter 9 for discussion of the modes distinctions as they relate to Jung's classification of personalities by their preferred mode of functioning.

3. Richard Bandler and John Grinder, *The Structure of Magic*, vols. I and II (Palo Alto, Calif.: Science and Behavior Books, 1975-76) and *Frogs into Princes* (Moab, Utah: Real People Press, 1979).

4. For the theatergoer who is seeing mode dominant, the interrelationship of the seeing and hearing modes is also an issue. Hearing and understanding the language—knowing what is going on—is as important as the seeing mode for most theatergoers. The hearing mode involves the words that are spoken or sung, the understanding of which relates to the intellect, and the music with which they are spoken or sung, which relates to the nonverbal, nonintellectual resources. Theater can thus swing in several directions and still be theater: it can be strongly visual, strongly kinesthetic, or strongly auditory. Opera, on the other hand, is definitely hearing mode dominant, but because the words are much harder to understand because of the increasing complexity of the music, a problem is created for the theater-loving operagoer. Wanting to know what is going on, the operagoer is often prevented from doing so by the difficulty of understanding the words because of musical complexity, orchestral interference or bad diction, and the lack of clear acting communication to go along with the words. (Not to mention that a great deal of opera—contrary to the stated wishes of Verdi, Puccini, and Richard Strauss, among others—is sung in a language foreign to that of its audience.) That problem is solved by the theater-loving opera *buff*, who has virtually memorized the meaning of the words and doesn't need (and sometimes doesn't care) to understand them from moment to moment.

The recent addition of surtitles to some performances of operas sung in languages not understood by the audience raises comprehension at a cost to other factors in the performance. Surtitles are projected on a screen *above* the stage picture (as opposed to subtitles at the bottom of a movie screen). Thus reading them places the seeing mode in a bind. If you read about what is happening, you sacrifice seeing it for the moment. There is constant distraction from attention to the messages of the facial/emotional mode and the kinesthetic mode, and there are resultant timing incongruities. For example, one might read the punch line to an action sequence before or after it occurs on stage. Whatever this does for verbal understanding, it disintegrates what was intended to be an organic statement. And it does so to preserve a standard of artistic integrity to which the composers themselves were opposed—that is, to produce opera in the original language regardless of the language of the audience.

5. Anecdotal evidence has been so important to the development of the concept that I will insert anecdotes wherever appropriate.

6. Stanislavski's contributions and shortcomings are brilliantly analyzed in *Script into*

Performance by Richard Hornby (Austin: University of Texas Press, 1982). Hornby rightly calls Stanislavski's concepts of the objective, of communion, of adaptation, and of relaxation as being truly significant contributions to an art that might better by called "holistic acting." But the villain concept is that emotion memory which, although not central to Stanislavski's system, is "the one that has created the popular image of the 'Method' actor, as a kind of autohypnotic. . . . But unlike the other Stanislavskian techniques . . . it does not draw upon the performance itself or the playtext but upon something totally external to them. It may even be destructive to other techniques like communion, since it takes the actor's attention off his immediate surroundings and into a private world of his own. Actors who are addicted to emotion memory often appear on stage to be in a dazed trance, oblivious to what is actually happening around them. The result is as 'mechanical' as the performance of the most old-fashioned, bellowing, ham actor, because in both cases the performance is not part of the continuous process that exists in a good production" (46–47). By focusing the actor's attention on his or her own emotional system, the concept ends up distorting that system and often creating tension and interference in the projective modes system. With its guiding motif—"I do what I *feel* like doing"—it has also led to an undue emphasis on individual personality and from there to the star system, an ironic conclusion for a teaching that stresses ensemble as a primary value.

Chapter 2. Determining Mode Makeup

1. Frederick Mathias Alexander, *The Resurrection of the Body*, ed. E. Maisel (New York: Dell, 1971). See also Wilfred Barlow, *The Alexander Technique* (New York: Random House, 1973) and Frank P. Jones, *Body Awareness in Action: A Study of the Alexander Technique* (New York: Schocken Books, 1976).

2. Desmond Morris's works are *The Naked Ape* (London: Cape, 1967), *The Human Zoo* (London: Cape, 1969), *Intimate Behavior* (London: Cape, 1971), and *Manwatching* (New York: Harry N. Abrams, 1977).

3. A scene on stage, of course, cannot exist without the presence of the kinesthetic mode (except when the performer is hidden from view) and the facial/emotional mode (except when the face is obscured or hidden). A statement from these two modes is always being made on stage, even when it is a statement of neutrality or negativity. In beginning with the hearing/vocal mode, I am simply focusing on the conscious passage of energy through that mode and not on the energy uses of the other two except as they are entangled or interfere with it.

Chapter 3. Implications of the Hearing/Vocal Mode

1. Kinesthetic meaning, which is more complicated, will be dealt with at greater length in chapter 6. The verbal meaning of a shaking fist, for example, beyond the statement "This

fist is being shaken," depends upon both the hearing/vocal mode message ("Hooray" or "You bastard!") and the facial/emotional mode message (a smile or a snarl) that accompany it.

2. Chapter 8 chronicles this problem and its effect on a whole generation of American singers.

3. Dr. Roger Sperry, the scientist who is most responsible for the widespread interest in right and left brain research and who received the Nobel Prize for his work in that area, avoided specific physical localization of function; that is, the left and right brain worked together and shared functions more than the dichotomy suggests. However, as with many scientists today, he took an almost mystical approach suggesting the presence of two minds, two spirits, even two souls who handled the differing functioning. Timothy Gallwey may have picked up this idea in the self 1 and self 2 concepts in his tennis and golf books. The image seems to be of two differing kinds of mind within the brain, each of which uses the brain computer for differing functions. Self 1 (the control, discipline, logic-oriented self) happens to use the left-brain computer more often, and self 2 (the flowing, holistic, imaginative, improvising self) uses the right-brain computer more often. Whatever the metaphor, it seems clear on both scientific and experiential grounds that there are two systems at work in the mind-body-voice energy grid and that it can be useful for the performer to use this metaphor as a way of understanding and dealing with the two systems effectively. I am using the concept of three minds (the body mind, the voice mind, and the emotional mind), one for each mode of projection and all operating on an intuitive, nonverbal, non-intellectual basis; to operate with maximum effectiveness, all must be free of the overcontrol of the verbal-intellectual resources. We tend not to trust what we cannot monitor with our verbal-intellectual mind, but developing that trust in our mode minds is an essential purpose of this work.

4. The concept of dominance has become part of the right-brain/left-brain concept. An instrument called the Hermann Brain Dominance Instrument, developed in the past five years, is currently being put through an extensive series of validation studies. From this work has arisen the Applied Creative Thinking Institute, which bases its efforts on the idea that dominance (of one hemisphere over the other in making life decisions) is the human condition and that for most of us one of the two hemispheres is dominant as a preferred mode of processing. This concept of dominance, however, should not be thought of as a dichotomy, but rather in the nature of a continuum in which the dominance is distributed between the two hemispheres, typically on the basis of a primary and secondary relationship. Therefore, for the great majority of individuals in this culture, brain dominance means two hemispheres working together with one taking the lead, a concept that relates strongly to modes theory.

5. Some research has indicated that when music becomes a professional study, its functioning is transferred to the control of the left brain, the source of logic, order, and discipline. It would be interesting to know whether emotion, the professional study of the actor, is not also transferred to left-brain jurisdictions when so studied.

6. Because the United States is a seeing mode nation, it must deal with all the ambiguities of the seeing mode dominant spectator; since both the kinesthetic and facial/emotional

modes are perceived with the eyes, the dominance issue is not as clear-cut. Our shifting allegiance between the two modes attests to this.

7. From Toby Cole and Helen Krich Chinoy, eds., *Actors on Acting*, rev. ed. (New York: Crown Publishers, 1970), 397.

8. At least one book on acting has excellent advice built into its title—*No Acting, Please*, by Eric Morris and Joan Hodgkins (New York: Putnam, 1979).

9. During the writing of this chapter, I had an actress in a singing-acting class who had just graduated from a professional acting school in New York City. She was a performer of great and ingratiating energy; but, as she put it, the training had taken all the play out of acting for her, and she was trying to find her way back to the joy of performing. Only rarely is a school in any art able to strike the necessary balance between the artistic opposites of freedom and discipline, control and release, intellect and intuition.

10. From Cole and Chinoy, *Actors on Acting*, 339.

11. Ibid., 340.

12. From Alfred Rossi, *Astonish Us in the Morning* (London: Hutchinson, 1977), 41, 42.

13. From Logan Gourlay, ed., *Olivier* (London: Weidenfield and Nicholson, 1973), 97.

Chapter 4. Exercising the Hearing/Vocal Mode

1. Sergius Kagen, *On Studying Singing* (New York: Dover, 1960).

2. Toby Cole and Helen Krich Chinoy, *Actors on Acting*, rev. ed. (New York: Crown Publishers, 1970), 424.

3. Marilyn Ferguson, *The Aquarian Conspiracy* (Los Angeles: J. P. Tarcher, 1980), 118.

4. I borrow the term from the excellent book *Focussing*, by Eugene T. Gendlin (rev. ed.; New York: Bantam, 1981). It refers to a body knowingness that is preverbal but that is used as a guide to learning something that will eventually be translated into verbal terms.

5. Eric Bentley quotes this remark by Hegel in *Life of the Drama* (New York: Peter Smith, 1984), 167.

6. In the 1960s, Harold Pinter virtually created the long, pregnant and paranoic pause that came to be known as the Pinter pause. His plays are a compendium of super-significant but nontraditional pauses. They can only exist with the power that they do, however, because of the words that surround them with such tangled complexity of intention.

7. We must search for ways of rehearsing and practicing that do not create ruts but that take a slightly different route each time so that the road remains accessible to as many choices as possible.

8. I do not intend to suggest that music theater or opera coachings are free from judgmental tensions. On the contrary, the overcontrol and judgmental fear in young singers is more common than not—a theme touched in my previous book, *The Complete Singer-Actor*.

Chapter 5. The Facial/Emotional Mode

1. It is not an overgeneralization to refer to American acting as a one-mode system, however much the kinesthetic mode has attempted to become a partner with the facial/emotional mode. American acting gravitated to the emotional, internal aspects of the Stanislavski Method and largely ignored the technical, external aspects in which Stanislavski was equally interested. America became the film capital of the world as much because of the facial/emotional dominance of its acting system, which coincided with the seeing mode dominance of films, as for technological reasons.

The American political philosophy of implied egalitarianism may have encouraged this tendency toward the emotional as a touchstone. Human beings may look different and sound different, but they all feel the same emotions. I may be unequal physically, I may not talk as brilliantly as others, but I feel as deeply as anyone and on that basis am equal to all men and women.

2. Robert Cohen, *Acting Power* (Palo Alto, Calif.: Mayfield Publishing, 1978).

3. The same singer sent me an article later that summer that announced the results of recent psychological research done at the University of California at San Francisco about the relationship between external expression and internal effect. It validated in a striking way the experience of the singer. In the study, professional actors were asked to make masks according to instructions: "Raise your eyebrows and pull them together; now raise your upper eyelids; now also stretch your lips horizontally back toward your ears." And so on. The actors were not told what the contortions of the face were meant to mimic—in this instance, fear. Variables controlled by the autonomic nervous system were measured continuously. In this case, heart rate went up and skin temperature went down, effects that are known to accompany real fear. The actors could produce the same nervous system effects by deliberately acting out fear, but the research results showed that the changes were more pronounced when the actors simply followed orders and mechanically moved their facial muscles. An extraordinary laboratory affirmation of the power of external choice on our emotional life!

Chapter 6. The Kinesthetic Mode

1. The same is true of many related therapies that are valuable in themselves. The Alexander Technique, for example (see chap. 2, no. 1), a method of psychophysical reeducation of the body-mind, is an outstanding means of improving singer-actor performance, but only if it is carefully integrated into that performance with an in-process approach. Otherwise a performer can take years of Alexander Technique with little impact on performance.

2. I fear this picture of the potent teacher has been severely damaged by the authority that has been taken away from teachers in recent decades. If the rules prevent action despite

the ability to act, the teacher is rendered impotent by situation. But the point remains the same: one teacher has personal power, the other does not.

3. Everything we do has a reason, whether or not the reason is conscious or verbal. We do whatever we do because some part of us believes that is what we should be doing. That belief may be grounded in faulty logic, erroneous cultural conditioning, or imitation of bad models; but we are convinced on some level of the usefulness of the belief. That is what makes it so difficult to change harmful behavior: to do so we must act wrongly (according to our nonintellectual understanding) to satisfy our conscious intellectual understanding. And if the intellect tries to make the behavioral change, it simply interferes with the greater and necessary flow of the total process, just as it often interferes with the performance process in trying to alter individual problems. Neurolinguistic programming—best known through the work of Richard Bandler and John Grinder, whose books first made me aware of the perceptual modes concept—uses direct communication with the part of the mind that creates the behavior in question. (See *The Structure of Magic*, vols. I and II [Palo Alto, Calif.: Science and Behavior Books, 1975–76] and *Frogs into Princes* [Moab, Utah: Real People Press, 1979]). That part of the mind—always an unconscious part—is asked to create other behavioral options (in cooperation with the rest of the mind) that will also satisfy the needs satisfied by the undesirable behavior.

Many of the exercises in this book attempt to find alternative performance behavior options through free play and improvisation with the body-mind, the voice-mind, and the emotional-mind. Once these new options and understandings are experienced in actual behavior, the original basis for the unacceptable performance behavior is also weakened and can often be discarded at once. By proving to the three nonverbal minds that they need not behave in restricted ways, their reason for doing so will often be understood as the false tyrant it is and will be overthrown or ignored. This external-to-internal path parallels the internal-to-external route of Bandler and Grinder. Both sides of the "freeway" can be used at the same time, of course, and we do. But in working with performance behavior, we can only be concerned with the alteration of that behavior, and not with altering the internal workings of the mind through psychotherapeutic dabbling—which is what it would be for most of us in the field of singer-actor training.

4. In obedience to the process imperative behind the book, I must state that since August 1983 I no longer begin with memorized material for such things as the tension check. I have found that beginning with improvisation and remaining there until improvisation is the norm is a far more useful way to approach performer growth. For example, in a recent six-class sequence totaling 18 hours we improvised for 14 of those hours. The singers, who began by expressing their culturally conditioned need to work on "products," agreed unanimously that they grew far more than they would have if we had used memorized material.

This approach depends on having coaches who are willing to improvise. All coaches are capable of doing so; they have the vocabulary and the skills in their kinesthetic and hearing mode minds. All that remains is to free those minds to "play tennis," to free them from the inhibitions and judgments of the intellectual-verbal mind. I have yet to encounter a coach who could not, only an occasional coach who would not.

5. The approach to gesture outlined in *The Complete Singer-Actor* is useful in stimulating thought as to *what* gestures can do; it is not as helpful in clarifying *how* they can do it. The how process dealt with in this book can be applied to any gestural statement.

6. Kinesthetic dominants among us have a greater measure of that power initially. But we are all trimodal beings, and we can allow the less developed modes to attain their full strength.

7. There are many other ways of examining the communicating function of the kinesthetic mode. Desmond Morris's *Manwatching* (New York: Harry N. Abrams, 1977) is recommended as the best comprehensive and nontechnical compendium of kinesthetic means of communication. Among possible categorizations is the division into functional and abstract, or gestures that are related to a specific physical function—scratching, rubbing, adjusting a piece of clothing, picking up something, throwing something—and those that accompany, clarify, enforce, or modify the verbal or emotional meaning of a verbal statement but that are basically abstract without the words or situation to accompany them—a waving hand, a pointing finger, a fist held in the air, or even two hands clapping.

Chapter 7. Mode Combinations

1. The 136th Annual Meeting of the American Psychiatric Association (May 1983) included a paper that detailed cases of mental illness in opera, concluding: "To know opera in all of its manifestations is to understand clinical psychiatry."

2. The score referred to is the G. Schirmer edition of the vocal score for both arias. To understand the relationship of music and meaning better, however, I have made the English translation more literal and less singable. We need not join the endless debate of original language vs. translation, except to note that the singer-actor must take the responsibility for knowing the original language as specifically as possible so that he or she can understand the reasons for the composer's original musical choices and adapt to the new blend of music and meaning created by a translation.

3. Del Sarte, the man who catalogued and illustrated physical gestures from and for nineteenth-century theater, has been much maligned—and unfairly so. Because his illustrations were static pictures, contemporary actors who wish to make farce out of melodrama strike these postures and sustain them with held tension. They appear unnatural and ridiculous. Yet the actors from whom Del Sarte derived his illustrations may have been (and, more important, *could* have been) stunningly alive, emotionally powerful, and utterly convincing as they moved, swiftly and softly, from gesture to gesture, sustaining them when appropriate without held tension, and remaining in a poised state of readiness at all times. Great performing has always been an exciting, thrilling flow of energy, and the misinterpretation of a stop-action illustration does not invalidate a given gestural statement any more than Stanislavski's profound process-approach to acting is discredited by isolating and rigidifying one part of that process as a final product.

Chapter 8. The Annotated Disappearing Diva

1. Much of this material appeared in two articles published in *The Opera Journal*, a publication of the National Opera Association, vol. 14, no. 3 (Fall 1981), 14–29, and no. 4 (Winter 1982), 17–32. Many of my colleagues thought at the time that I had abandoned my efforts in training the complete singer-actor. I had not. I simply expressed my belief that we cannot guide young performers through a complex process that we do not understand in depth and detail. We must accept the responsibility of protecting the performers in our charge from the many pitfalls that will occur as we develop the process.

2. *Miami Herald*, 14 December 1979.

3. Robert Rushmore, *The Singing Voice* (New York: Dodd, Mead, 1971), 21–23.

Chapter 9. Beyond the Performance Modes

1. The ironic tone in these comments may suggest that this course of events was personally experienced. It was. It was also a remarkable demonstration of the deep-seated and irrational mode animosities that hover beneath the surface of the opera world.

2. Both quotes are from Egon Gartenberg's excellent *Mahler: The Man and His Music* (New York: Schirmer Books, 1978), 118, 72.

3. Peter Russell, *The Awakening Earth* (London: ARK Paperbacks, 1984), 143.

4. Ibid.

5. There seems little doubt that if we had worked with the idea of establishing a relationship with higher plane energies, it would not have happened — at least not to the same degree.

6. Russell, *Awakening Earth*, 151–52.

7. There is an excellent book on the Reiki technique, the only one now available, called *The Reiki Factor* by Barbara Ray (New York: Exposition Press, 1983). The author is founder and president of the American International Reiki Association and the world's leading authority on the subject.

Appendix B. The Modes and the Audition Process

1. Michael Shurtleff, *Audition* (New York: Bantam Books, 1980).

2. This raises the question of the relative value of performers and their technical backup. Planks and a passion, it has been argued for centuries, are often enough; in fact, they may create a stronger experience than when technology is added. That question is a subject for another book, but it allows us here to acknowledge the singer-actor's courage

and talent.

3. The San Francisco experiments (chap. 5, n. 3) showing that external masks affect us more than the effort to summon up internal feelings are a useful reference in working with such situations.

Bibliography

Bibliography

Alexander, Frederick Mathias. *The Resurrection of the Body*. Edited by E. Maisel. New York: Dell, 1971.

Balk, H. Wesley. *The Complete Singer-Actor: Training for Music Theater*. 2nd ed. Minneapolis: University of Minnesota Press, 1985.

Bandler, Richard, and John Grinder. *The Structure of Magic*. 2 vols. Palo Alto, Calif.: Science and Behavior Books, 1975–76.

——. *Frogs into Princes*. Moab, Utah: Real People Press, 1979.

Barbe, Walter B., and Raymond H. Swassing. *Teaching through Modality Strengths: Concepts and Practices*. Columbus, Ohio: Zaner-Bloser, 1979.

Barlow, Wilfred. *The Alexander Technique*. New York: Random House, 1973.

Bentley, Eric. *Life of the Drama*. New York: Peter Smith, 1984.

Bunch, Meribeth. *Dynamics of the Singing Voice*. New York: Springer-Verlag, 1982.

Cohen, Robert. *Acting Power*. Palo Alto, Calif.: Mayfield Publishing, 1978.

Cole, Roby, and Helen Krich Chinoy, eds. *Actors on Acting*. New York: Crown, 1970.

Craig, David. *On Singing Onstage*. New York: Schirmer; Macmillan, 1978.

Edwards, Betty. *Drawing on the Right Side of the Brain*. Los Angeles: J. P. Tarcher, 1978.

Ferguson, Marilyn. *The Aquarian Conspiracy*. Los Angeles: J. P. Tarcher, 1980.

Fuchs, Peter Paul. *The Music Theater of Walter Felsenstein*. New York: W. W. Norton, 1975.

Gallwey, W. Timothy. *The Inner Game of Tennis*. New York: Random House, 1974.

Gartenburg, Egon. *Mahler: The Man and His Music*. New York: Schirmer Books, 1978.

Gendlin, Eugene T. *Focussing*. New York: Bantam Books, 1981.

Gourlay, Logan, ed. *Olivier*. London: Weidenfield and Nicholson, 1973.

Hagen, Uta, and Haskel Frankl. *Respect for Acting*. New York: Macmillan, 1973.

Hampden-Turner, Charles. *Maps of the Mind*. New York: Collier-Macmillan, 1982.

Herrigel, Eugene. *Zen and the Art of Archery*. New York: McGraw-Hill, 1964.

Hornby, Richard. *Script into Performance*. Austin: University of Texas Press, 1982.

Jones, Frank P. *Body Awareness in Action: A Study of the Alexander Technique*. New York: Schocken Books, 1976.

Kagen, Sergius. *On Studying Singing*. New York: Dover, 1960.

Morris, Desmond. *The Naked Ape*. London: Cape, 1967.

——. *The Human Zoo*. London: Cape, 1969.

——. *Intimate Behavior*. London: Cape, 1971.

——. *Manwatching*. New York: Harry N. Abrams, 1977.

Morris, Eric, and Joan Hodgkins. *No Acting, Please*. New York: J. P. Putnam, 1979.

Pirsig, Robert. *Zen and the Art of Motorcycle Maintenance*. New York: William Morrow, 1974.

Pleasants, Henry. *The Agony of Modern Music*.

Ray, Barbara. *The Reiki Factor*. New York: Exposition Press, 1983.

Ristad, Eloise. *A Soprano on Her Head*. Moab, Utah: Real People Press, 1982.

Rossi, Alfred. *Astonish Us in the Morning*. London: Hutchinson, 1977.

Rushmore, Robert. *The Singing Voice*. New York: Dodd, Mead, 1971.

Rusell, Peter. *The Awakening Earth*. London: ARK Paperbacks, 1984.

Shurtleff, Michael. *Audition*. New York: Bantam Books, 1980.

Wolfe, Tom. *The Painted Word*. New York: Bantam Books, 1976.

——. *From Bauhaus to Our House*. New York: Farrar, Strauss, Cudahy, 1981.

Index

Index

Acting: theories, 7, 323; process, 8, 15–16; in academia, 75–76; and overintellectualization, 91; history of, 93; and sports, 99–100; and music of character, 100; defining good, 285–86; in sixties and seventies, 310. *See also* Actors; Performance; Performers; Singer-actors; Singing-acting
— systems, 7, 22: as reductions of behavior, 13; Brook on, 15; traditional, 35; American, 54, 55, 71, 75–76, 78
Acting Power, 145, 149, 323
Actor Prepares, An, 54
Actors: and judgment, 6–7, 18–19; growth of, 8; compared with musicians, 9; internal process of, 16, 17; influenced by Grotowski, 20; as projectors, 40; and directors, 40–41, 62; as perceivers, 41; and modes, 42–43, 44, 78, 109; naturalism of, 74; vocal energies of, 84; musicality of, 97; authenticity of, 100; styles of, 308. *See also* Acting; Performance; Performers; Singer-actors; Singing-acting
Actor's Studio, 19, 55, 181

Adler, Kurt Herbert, 268
Agee, James, 147
Alexander, F. Mathias, 57
Alexander Technique, 57, 325, 331
Allen, Steve, 77
Applied Creative Thinking Institute, 354n4
Aquarian Conspiracy, The, 128
Arica, 331
Artaud, Antonin, 21
Aspen Music Festival, 3, 325
Audience: and mind reading, 16, 23; modes and, 29, 31, 40, 155, 257; integrative capacities of, 30; and critics disagree, 31; response to music theater, 32; perception of, 40, 138; release of energy to, 130; understanding of quality, 285
Audition, 343
Auditions, 343, 344, 346
Awakening Earth, The, 331, 332

"Baby modes, " defined, 137
Ballet, 316
Baltimore Opera, 268
Bandler, Richard, 29, 322, 357n3
Bateson, Gregory, double-bind concept of, 82–83

INDEX 369

Gestures: kinesthetic, 199–200,
234–35; phases of, 200–201, 202,
205; successful, 201–3, 213; arbitrary, 203, 208, 232–33; exercising, 205–8, 211–13;
facial/emotional, 208–9, 213; Zen
of, 210; classified, 215; as energy
statements, 234; rejection of, 261;
illustrated by Del Sarte, 358n3
Gielgud, Sir John, 89, 306
Gluck, C. W., ix
Great Britain, mode dominance in,
96, 146, 306–8, 312
Grinder, John, 29, 322, 357n3
Grotowski, Jerzy, 20, 21, 182
Guthrie, Sir Tyrone, 96, 224, 321
Guthrie Theater, 31, 321

Hagen, Uta, 19
Harrison, Rex, 87
Hearing/vocal mode: dominance, 31,
96, 146, 256, 306–8, 312; in
singing-acting, 33; checklist,
69–70; specificity of, 75; as essential, 78; in U.S., 81, 95, 109,
158, 312; and judgment, 83–84,
277–78; and kinesthetic, 85, 121,
230–31, 232–33, 289, 294; and
brain functions, 88, 91, 282;
struggle within, 90–91, 240; and
readiness, 106–7, 153; free-flowing, 112; exercising, 126–28,
137–38; and tension, 129, 229,
238–39; and overcontrol, 138;
and facial/emotional, 155, 229,
230, 235–37; and trigger effect,
159; stylistic demands of, 281; in
television, 308–10; in opera, 313;
of instrumentalists, 319–20
Hegel, G. W. F., 132

Henderson, W. J., 301
Hermann Brain Dominance Instru-
ment, 354n4
Herrigel, Eugene, 9–10
Hill, Arthur, 96
Holon, mode as, 229

I, Claudius, 76
Impersonation, 19–20, 318–19
Incongruency: defined, 222; intellectual-intuitive, 227–28; freedom
from, 239–40; contradictions of,
240–41; exercising, 242–43
Indicating, 288–89, 292, 297: (gesture) defined, 215
Inner Game of Tennis, The, 9,
95–96
Instrumentalists, 319–20
Intellect, 6, 24, 94, 138: and intuition, 25, 226–28; and language,
112–13; overcontrol of, 131, 195,
238–39; repressing, 194; and
energy decisions, 209; and modes,
225–26
Interference: among modes, 53, 77,
85, 129–30, 175; and intellect,
131; and incongruency, 222; and
readiness, 228; learned, 244;
kinesthetic, 308
Internal-external relationships, 134,
145, 150–51, 227
Intuition, 24, 25, 117, 226–28

Judgment: effect on performer, 5,
11, 12–13, 18–19, 238, 344; comparative, 5–6; and life processes,
9; internal, 12; of hearing/vocal
mode, 277–78; density of, 334–35
Jung, Carl, classification of personalities, 352n2

A graduate of the Yale University School of Drama, H. Wesley Balk has been a professor of theatre arts at the University of Minnesota since 1967 and, from 1965 through 1984, served as artistic director of the Minnesota Opera Company; he is now the company's director of artistic development. Balk has also directed for the New York City Opera, Santa Fe Opera, Houston Grand Opera, Washington Opera Society, San Francisco Opera, and other music and theater groups. He founded and continues to direct the Minnesota Opera Institute, a summer training program for singers, directors, and coaches, and has worked with similar training programs elsewhere, including those at Wolf Trap Farm and the Aspen Music Festival. Balk is the author of *The Complete Singer—Actor: Training for Music Theater* (1977; second edition, 1985) and *The Dramatization of "365 Days"* (1972), a chamber play based on Dr. Ronald Glasser's book about the experiences of American soldiers in Vietnam.